ENERGYCITY

AN EXPERIMENTAL PROCESS OF NEW ENERGY SCENARIOS: PESCARA, ARCHITECTURE AND PUBLIC SPACE

BY

ALBERTO ULISSE

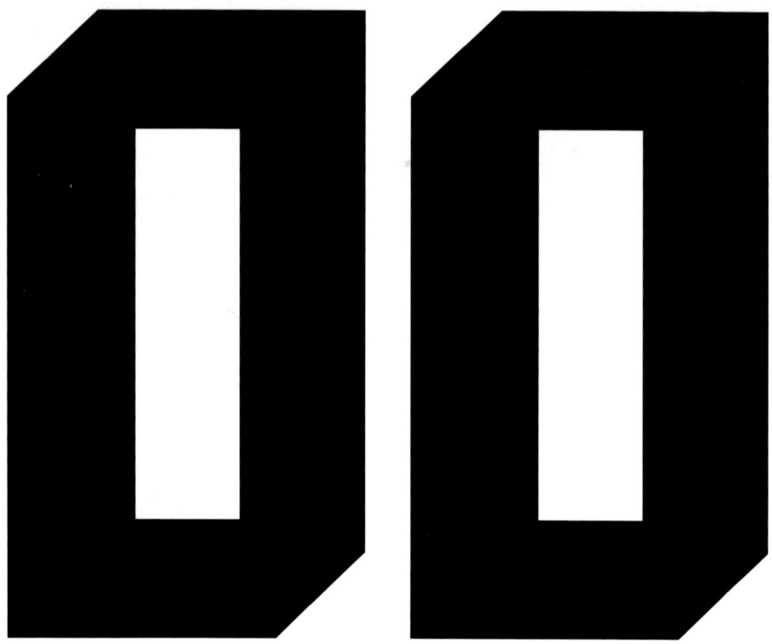

TERRITORIES OF ENERGY
by **Pepe Barbieri**

University "G. d'Annunzio" faculty of Architecture, Pescara

ENERGY LANDSCAPES AND URBAN TRANSFORMATIONS
by **Nicolas Tixier**

Architect, Dr. Researcher of Cresson Laboratory (Centre de recherche sur l'espace sonore et l'environnement urbain – UMR CNRS no 1563)
Lecturer at the Ecole Nationale Supérieure d'Architecture of Grenoble

TERRITORIES OF ENERGY

This text is meant to answer a central question - in the pressing need to observe, from the standpoint of architectural design, the various themes of the relationship between new ways of producing energy and the shape of the territory and the city -: **in what way does the system of "decentralized" energy production give rise to new organizations and spatial configurations, particularly in areas of the Mediterranean?**
It 's a fundamental issue if we assume the knowledge that vital strategic relationship between the project of "energy system" (production and distribution) and project area can be one of the main factors that can lead to new opportunities and "quality" in the transformation of contemporary landscapes. In the thesus of Ulisse, presented here, you find a guiding vision focused on overcoming the concept of a centralized hub to service large territorial extensions. It envisages a scenario of distributed energy production, divided and consumed locally (auto-prodotta/consumata). Thus forming a consistent "archipelago city", even in terms of energy, with that reading amending the consolidated image of the large linear conurbations - as the medioadriatica city - according to a juxtaposition of bands, replacing it with a more porous and structured organization . Organized through territorial space devices (or cluster platforms) designed as islands of energy of variable size and configuration. In this way the interpretation of the shape of the area is enhanced by a "transversal" and articulate dimension where the strip along a coast of undifferentiated thickens to differing contexts, in which various devices (including those related to energy production) may become the multicentral foci of an alternative organization.
The energy design of the territory must also be able to express several symbolic and configurational potentials, extracted from these identities, which they call into question, with unusual aesthetic values, the different components of natural and artificial - from the sea, countryside, hills, junctions - generating a new landscape of sustainability and energy. In this perspective, the major infrastructure networks - especially with the use of "road-border" - can contribute, with different devices, to the production and distribution of renewable energy.

One of the main case studies - the mid-Adriatic context - an example for the many similarities with other Mediterranean areas, suggesting a new point of view, the intersection with other visions of a possible future (or already unconsciously present?) idea of other cities. There are many towns that are transformed into another shape by overlapping materials: one in which the same hyper-fit (extensions of hundreds of kilometers) becomes a resource. A figure drawn in the case mid-Adriatic, from an article, but the constant relationship between the dynamics of coastal settlements and projections to the inside. This today is the possible Adriatic geo_city. A complex urban organization, because it can be open to a wider framework of relationships and connections where, as its new size, may allow to play successfully in competition, a role denied today by the fragmentation and overlapping of the different administrative areas. A way to "shape" the domesticity in the Adriatic city of automation of a production of houses that is being uniformly stretched over the coastal areas, valleys and folds of hills, opposed to the idea of public works - and of these, in an innovative way, consider those related to energy production - the engine, this time conscious of a transformation capable of recognizing and mobilizing contexts, giving value to differences. Contexts made to live in a dynamic open system of relations and flows, that without contradicting the identity, generate new "figures of meaning", capable of representing not only opportunities for new devices of form, but to provide, also the different economic and social contexts, the opportunity to influence the national and international competition. For this reason it becomes necessary to use some ideas in a strategic instrument in the service of creating large urban and regional devices: from the National Strategic Framework (NSF, 2007-2013), which developed in Italy a vision for the future, multi-layered, which is an expression of the changing mix of strategic platforms, joint territories, infrastructure corridors, areas of identity and territory's competitiveness, in a balanced way to ensure adequate infrastructure including energy. It is a view consistent with the commitments taken to reduce World pollution (Copenhagen conference, the Kyoto Protocol; Leipzig Charter) and that may be, from the standpoint of the method, extended to other similar realities. In the research presented here is offered a methodology based on a novel reading of the territories - in terms of architecture in relation to the energy potential of different contexts to identify the means (e-tools) - **tools of architectural design** - capable of activating the process and building the energy community in the network. A method that is just a different reality, with varying degrees of built density, where to use strategies, with an appropriate weight and role, the various e-tools to build, in a manner consistent with many identifying characteristics of the contexts, **the new architecture of energy.**

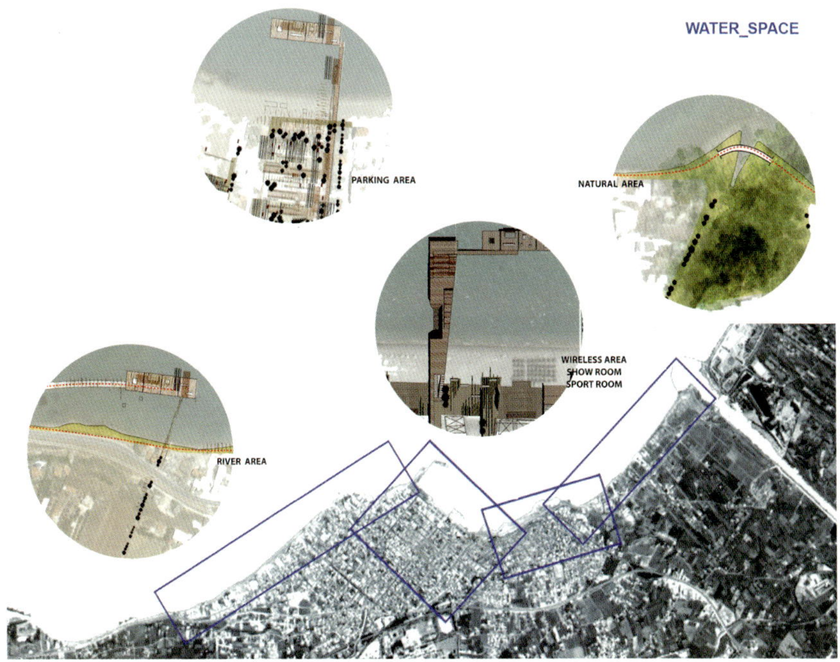

ENERGY LANDSCAPES AND URBAN TRANSFORMATIONS

The current issues of energy management require us to rethink our design practices. Given the scale of architecture of such a territory, it is no longer possible to design a space to live in without looking for energy optimization. If this need is to be taken seriously, it should be accompanied by three developments:

- First, a fundamental change in design tools for the project must fall into place - methodological challenge.
- Then a renewed architectural design which does not necessarily overcome the logic of living - an interdisciplinary challenge.
- Finally, a crucial and critical historical thinking must be at practice - theoretical issue.

Thinking of architecture flows, energy landscapes and urban change, requires one to supply other design tools (dynamic models, parametric design, relational architectures, ...) which are not only a change of tools, but also involve a real paradigm shift for the project. New types appear with a corollary, the need to provide additional tools for representation taking into account energy efficiency and the direct relationship of a project with its environment. How then to pass from static to a dynamic, interactive and networking?

This rehabilitation of streams in the architectural design is not only considered from a physical point of view. It is also looking from a social and sensitive point of view, for the establishment of a design by the atmosphere, which would cover not only the energy industry because it would not forget that there are practical ways to live and that it maintains a sensible relation to the world. How then does one pass from standardized comfort to sensitive comfort? From a sense of neutralization to a sense of excitement? If discomfort is undesirable in general, the homogenization of the situations and feelings is probably even less. How can users in these new designs be found energetically efficient to adapt the environment to its way of living? The thermal environment is also a landscape, which is assessed and found with his variations and decisions that we have made with it. We have sound designers and lighting designers, why do we not have thermal landscapers?

If energy efficiency is becoming a major criterion for evaluating a project, and that, whatever its scale, one can also consider this as an opportunity for input that anything designed for it can be used for other things than just the purpose it serves. This is the price of inventing challenging, varied and livable energy landscapes.

Let us then make the assumption that architecture, a territory will be sustainable only two conditions:

- firstly, urban transformations, scenic or cultural, should be based largely on existing qualities and potential , it is necessary to identify and mobilize in order to develop,

- Secondly, the townspeople should be involved in the formulation process and ownership of these transformations.

The work of Alberto Ulisse with success shows that it is possible to combine design and research, provide parametric design principles, so far without being rigid but responsive to local situations, from energy issues without neglecting the social and sensitive sides, and connect the scales without forgetting the user.

01

INTRO

The new models of urban society are constantly looking for proposals aimed at **the rehabilitation of the archetypal image of the existing spaces** (*public and otherwise*), actions to **revitalize its parts** (*tissues and figures*), to propose instruments of **urban regeneration** capable to enable growth (*or decline/implosion*) related to changes in response to which the contemporary world presents us and that set the conditions for a *modern recycling*. The reorganization of this must first take control of the relationship between *the locations* (defined as contexts) and their *different parts*, through questioning the interpretation of *the formative theory of Pareyson* as an instrument capable of addressing the critical design action. The future goal is linked to two fundamental aspects: one is the *limitation of the use of land*

in cities, the other, *the balanced budget between energy expenditure and production*, all this is inherent in the concept of **recycling** as urban change of the existing: a *reminder to the future.* Today there is no longer the need for adjectives or prefixes: such as *bio, eco,* and they do not add anything new to a *discipline* that can only arise in an integral, unitary and ethical response to problems that concern it since its origin. ...
How to regain possession of *designing a look in the vulnerable areas of the city?*
EnergyCity expresses, through a case application, the development of a set of operational tools trying to redefine the new relationships (energy) between the contexts through new project templates for the architecture of the twenty-first century. EnergyCity is part of a range of innovative experiments, investigating the relationship between architectural design and new variations of "sustainability" as part of a new mode of production and exchange of energy, in relation to the different local contexts.
EnergyCity becomes a possible vehicle for the application of these waste devices (e-tools) capable of becoming real elements (systems) that make up the city. With this critical spirit was built the research process that applies within a well-defined territory of the city of Pescara: a sample slide "geo-referenced between the parallels [42 ° 26'49, 11" N - 42 ° 26 '15, 05 "N] in which you re-read the different parts of the urban space, the existing energy networks, the potential energy of some urban areas (towards the specialization of community energy) for the construction of architectural experiments, through the introduction of new materials for the urban contemporary maps, diagrams and actions. EnergyCity verifies and applies, on an experimental basis, what is expressed in the "guiding concept" in research: the construction of a device (and its parts) that can build a new city model based on new energy relations, towards the construction of a city-energy archipelago. All this opens up to new urban and architectural devices: e-tools are able to build new energy relations.

02

ELECTROPOLIS

48 51 30,07 N - 30 03 05,67 N

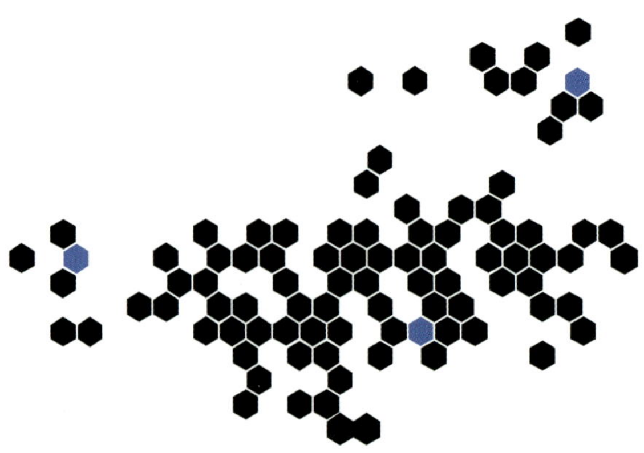

Electropolis is a reflection on the development of urban communities due to changes related to energy development of more and more territories, and outlines a different variation of the polycentric urban systems, in which one has the greatest concentration of activity and human presence. *Electropolis*, starting from devices that have always characterized the sites of production, accumulation and consumption of energy in the city, tends to define a possible vision of the Mediterranean territories by identifying, in the areas of consumption, more opportunities and potential for the production energy.

ELECTROPOLIS: OPEN QUESTIONS AND FUTURE OBJECTIVES

The project for the city and the territory is in transition toward new energy and sustainable devices, with reference to new developments, research, applications, and developments in legislation on the matter. This research is part of the contemporary debate in reference to the conference on climate change (not least *the conference in Copenhagen*, **COP 15**), as a consequence of the choices and commitments taken to reduce global pollution (**Kyoto Protocol**) in relation to the ethical responsibilities of engineers working actively on the ground (**paper architecture Rifkin**), in relation to a regulatory and proactive role that European cities considered *"pillars of sustainable development"* can play (as set out in the **Leipzig Charter**). Today the energy crisis and climate change issues appear crucial to our future. In the current energy situation, the relationship between cause and effect with the ever-increasing environmental upheavals, climate shocks and possible geo-political conflicts, dependent on a rising cost of nonrenewable energy (oil, gas, coal and uranium) and the progressive exhaustion of fossil fuels are recognized. Whereas the city of the future will be an "energy city": a city capable of self-produced energy needed for its operation, the *Energy Cities* of the XXI century will indeed be those cities that can compete in local and international scene for an 'attention to the sensitive issues that affect the climate and world peace.

The new century opens a large window (the challenge of the century) which is the discovery (or awareness, a sense of awareness, a common recognition) *of the Earth's fragility, the vulnerability of cities,* architecture is increasingly called for a "reasoning power". Historically, the city is the place of concentration of energy demand. *In the succession of forms of social organization that have marked the course of history, power consumption has been accumulating in different ways and amounts in time and space, in particular those places which are cities. The city has always been, therefore, the specific place, physically small and also clearly marked out for a long period of humanized territory in which they variously deployed energy uses and their effects on the economy, the environment, culture and society in general.*

In the past, power systems have evolved through the construction of large power plants, which become increasingly larger (and a source of pollution) were moved to more distant locations from urban areas / inhabited. The distance between the centers of energy production and the *energy-user* has determined the need for transmission lines, long distance and high capacity. This has produced and still produces a loss of energy in transport across the network. This mode of production and supply of cities and settlements have a model for development of the territories to-branched network ("branch" while the matter).

The network of energy transport compared to other devices and networks that have over time innervated our territories, is the most centralized and hierarchical network. The cities of the XXI century will be those cities and territories able to trigger self-energy systems, especially due to the value of the unique characteristics of different contexts, seen as assets to be reactivated in key energy and sustainable development. Currently there is a change in the areas related to new forms of production-use-transport-release (*energy sharing*) of energy. Can one venture a hypothesis, where territories and cities are transformed in the near future from **power_house** in true "*sinks*" (such as the Kyoto Protocol defines the green areas, public spaces and the *future fossils*) through the introduction of infrastructure for the production of energy from renewable sources? These "***pioneer territories***" of the energy, create a new mechanism for sustainable urban landscape, which will be built on the renewable cities: new devices capable of self-produce where-how much/when need energy. The harness of energy determines the beginning of a new era of electrification of cities and territories (*Charter for the architecture of the next millennium*, J. Rifkin), where buildings (primarily urban objects) will be called a process restyling under the guise of energy: both for the reduction of fuel consumption and energy loss (*passive house*), and for the adoption of active energy production systems (on site). We are moving towards the *building's energy self-implantation* (**power_houses)** and the concept of territory as a *platform of energy* (for popular urban marketing).

"How can architecture reveal, own and tame those systems, mostly technological in nature and do so in a way that makes us feel at home in the modern world"?

That is the question that Bertsky Aaron, director of the XI International Architecture Exhibition of Venice (2008), places at the base of research and experiments in architectural exhibited at the Biennale, which go *beyond building*. The buildings (public and private) that inhabit the neighborhoods that we live in, the public spaces we occupy, the town which will soon be called (more than they are) to be the substructure of the sensors of renewable energy. They will welcome all the elements of energy, separate and overlapping, photovoltaic panels, in their various market solutions, but always inclined and south-facing; they will be covered with solar thermal systems, poorly integrated (... a problem of integration or energetic hybridization?); they will be dotted with wind or mini-wind farm production systems, not to mention all the possible co-generation energy systems (and where possible trigeneration). The transformation from territory to "dense city" can be implemented through a possible expansion of the materials of urban design and architecture, instrumentation available, the reference frames (of rules, standards and best practices), so that projects are able to belong to different scales, to understand and to take over the global nature of the energy issue and trigger new urban figures and are able to investigate new energy devices / envisage / check for possible changes induced in the geography of the areas of coastline. This is an opportunity to redeem their territories and to "reinvent the city (The city Renewable Peter Droege).

Some, including Rifkyn, suggest the city as real power plants that produce renewable energy. The "city as a powerhouse is one of the key points of the" Charter for the architecture of the next millennium," comment made at the 11th International Architecture Exhibition of the Venice Biennale.

"...**We** also recognize that recent technological advances make possible for the first time the renovation of existing buildings and the design and construction of new one generating all the necessary energy from renewable and locally available sources, allowing us to retrain them as "energy centres"...**We** also recognize that the same design principles and smart technologies that made possible the Internet and large networks" distributed "global communication, is only now beginning to be used to reconfigure the mesh of world power, that would through its buildings and people produce renewable energy to share equally across regions and continents, as it now produces and shares information to create a new, decentralized form of energy use; ...**We** also recognize that redefining the buildings as power plants and converting the meshes of world power in networks of smart utilities to deploy that power will open the door to the Third Industrial Revolution, which in the twenty-first century, should have an economic multiplier effect equal to those of the First and Second Industrial Revolution ' 800 and 900; ...**be it resolved** that such buildings should be collected locally and generate energy from the sun, wind, waste, waste from agricultural and forestry, water sources and geothermal, waves and tides: enough energy to meet their needs, but also to create surplus energy to share ... "(in Living n.486 - 10/2008). These are just some of the points (I believe the main) of the proclamation to address the global energy crisis and climate change. Questioning the area, can one think it can generate energy and produce new urban forms? New conceptions of space morfoEnergetic (**power_city**)?

The **Mediterranean** is the range (and application) of this research..

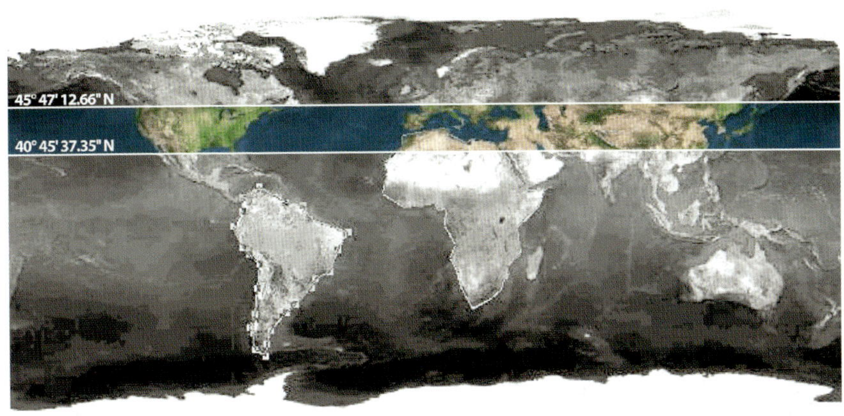

ISSUE

How does the system of decentralized energy production, widespread and discontinuous give rise to new paradigms, or even new urban spatial configurations in the territories of the Mediterranean?

The current energy situation calls for a reflection on the (self-) production, accumulation and consumption of energy on site, redefining *new localization formulas* for a **short chain of energy**. The *efficiency of energy self-sufficiency* requires the introduction of *new paradigms and new spatial configurations* capable of building *scenarios* and urban landscapes. Taking advantage of the ongoing transformation, we define *new devices in key urban energy* (**e-tools**), capable of building *alternative models of cities*, based on *new relations* between the various distributed energy systems (*Electricity Transforming* / Walt Patterson).

HYPOTHESIS

The research is part *Electropolis* as fundamental building block within a path of study that has in recent years investigated the changing of the *polycentricism (spread)* of the contemporary city becoming increasingly place the potential for energy production (and not just consumption). The experience of *Chaleurs Urbaines* (at the Ecole Nationale Supérieure d'Architecture de Grenoble - 2008), Project Velocity (X Architecture Biennale in Venice - 2006), some bankruptcy experience, have led to set the research not only as logical construction of key passages, but mainly to use a *case study* (taken within the territory of Pescara) as a *probe* to test the proposed use. The points made in the research fit, albeit with nuances and different purposes, *in two university research and design explorations of some insolvency.*

The first is a research called PRIN_OP "Public Works and the Adriatic city" (University "G. d'Annunzio" School of Architecture, Department DART-research coordinator prof. Barbara Pepper), the second regards the research (and work in Aterliers) that have led to present at the Biennale de l'*Habitat Durable* Grenoble (2008) the results of "Urbaines Chaleurs" (Ecole Nationale Supérieure d'Architecture de Grenoble, Dept. Cresson, coordinator prof. Nicolas Tixier). The energy issues, research OP (*Electropolis Adriatic; 3azioni/5indirizzi (+1) for regions more and more energy*) become one of the keys to read the *mid-Adriatic area*. In recognition of the foundational characteristics of various systems of the Adriatic landscape, one tries to define those characters for a *rhizomatic* Adriatic city-cost line, both dynamic and energetic. It outlines a new metaphor for the organization, operation and configuration of the Adriatic city: the

City Cell-Adriatic understood as a *metabolic labyrinth*, a model of spatial structure like a bowl of energy space of the city.
Chaleurs Urbaines however, researches applications and forms to define energy devices that experience a different way of applying photovoltaic technology (*solaire*, well imagine that concept for the *roses*) systems within the urban areas of the city of Grenoble. The temperature increase in the hot summer, influenced by the abundant production of pollution from cars, heat released from air conditioners in summer heat engines, record a change of lifestyles in cities. This feature is properly called the *urban heat island effect*, an official from another physical characteristic: the *albedo*, depending on the texture, color and texture of urban surfaces. Overheating of roads (asphalt), has a direct impact on the quality of urban space, which enhances and promotes the use of artificial air-conditioning systems, affecting a growing demand for energy. The theme of the open spaces, public spaces, roofs, streets, squares, shells of living, become places for the application of the 5 workshops *Urbaines of Chaleurs*.

01 DECENTRALIZATION AND ATOMIZATION ENERGY (SPRAWL-ENERGY)

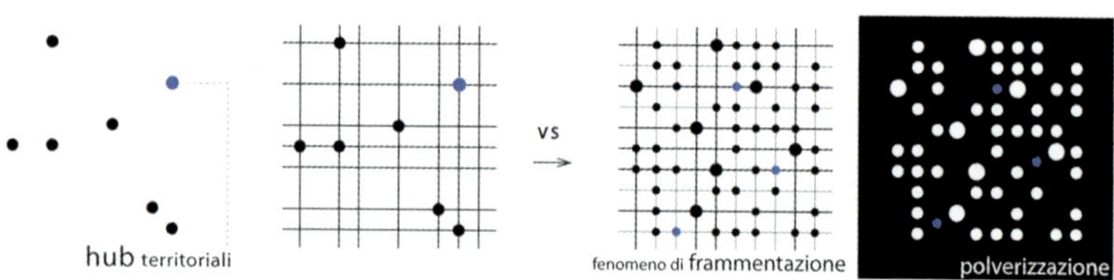

the former is linked to contemporary research on the decentralization of production of renewable energy, according to the theories of the leaders in the current theoretical and cultural landscape (*Jeremy Rifkin, Peter Droege, Walt Patterson*). The spreading and spraying systems of renewable energy production attributed to the city see the actual place (role) of energy production (*the Worldwide Energy Web*), then the city (designed as a separate residence) will be called to a new role (place), the import of the "city" is not only intended as a source of energy but rather as new production equipment in order to enable devices that can generate energy on site (power_houses) the cancellation of the distribution networks of Traditional city founded fossil energy.

02 FOCUS THE "DENSE CITY" OF THE COAST (IN THE MEDITERRANEAN AREA)

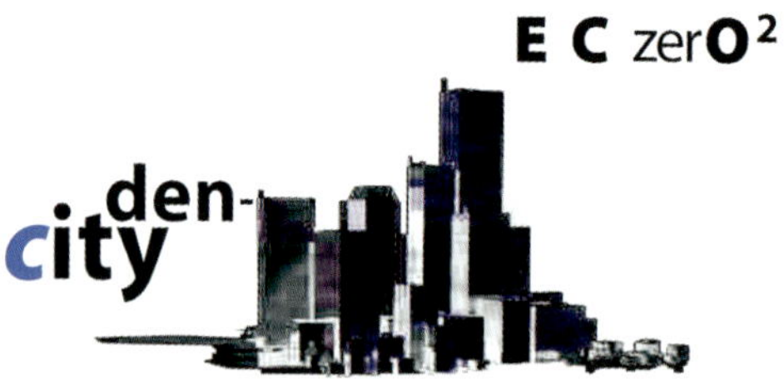

2007 is a historic moment: the year in which for the first time more than half the world's population lives in urban centers (*Jacques Véron, demographer all'Ined - Institut National d'Etudes Démographiques*) and, according to the UN-HABITAT report (*State of the Cities World 2008/09*) the levels of global urbanization will continue to grow dramatically over the next forty years, from almost 60% in 2030 to 70% of the population in 2050; according to data from the *Trends and Future Challenges for U.S. National Ocean and Coastal Policy (Washington DC, 1999)* imagines the increase in population will be mainly in the areas of the coast (in 2010 20 will be the "coastal megacities" exceeding 8 million inhabitants). The modern cities as well as being the greatest structures ever built, also use most of the world's resources. About 2% of the earth's surface, and with half the world population, cities consume over 75% of resources (*Developing Sustainable Cities*).

03 RENEWABLE GEOGRAPHIES
(48 ° 51'30 .07 "N - 30 ° 03'05, 67" N PARALLEL)

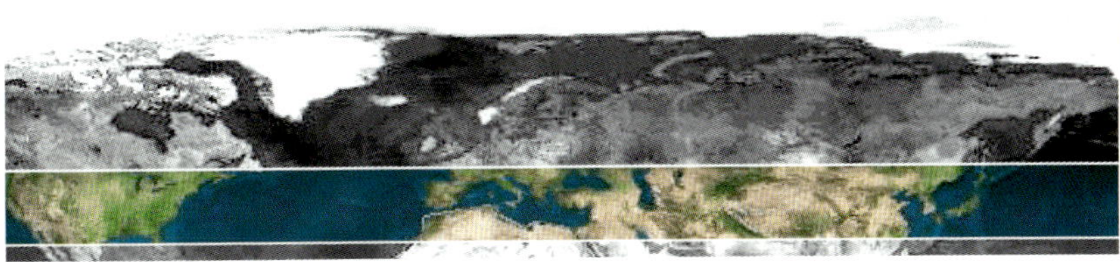

one defines a window between the parallel 48 ° 51 '30.07 "N and the parallel 30 ° 03' 05.67" N to define visions for the geo-city of different parallels. Of course not accidentally the two parallels frame the Mediterranean Sea, intended as a *square in Europe*. The *Mediterranean* has never been simply a sea that separates Europe from Africa and the Near East or, *to use Braudel, a simple crack in the earth's crust that stretches from Gibraltar to the Isthmus of Suez and Red Sea*. The Mediterranean is a sea which is overlooked by so many different lands, town and desert, nomadic and sedentary, ways of life far away from them, prepared in a certain way by dualisms and congenital hostility; *on the Mediterranean have been developed modern civilizations and traditional cultures, city and modern metropolis hinged on a past that remained immobile and those who are frequently antagonistic hatred and enmity (La Maison de la Méditerranée)*. That *crack in the earth's crust* is mainly represented by the shoreline in its continuous *evolution*. Thus the scope of the research does shed light on new energy devices (sampling) in a large area (the Mediterranean), but in a geographic context of peculiar characters, where conditions are common to the places of living and of life, and elements of absolute difference, denial and indifference. The territories that belong to a single context (the Mediterranean) will be even more different because they will be *geo-referenced*, as belonging to the place before, its geographical references that determine the climate, the exposure, the solar efficiency. These new *ecotonal* characters will be representative of the Climate Zones (*Danish pavilion, ecotopedia exhibition, Venice Biennale 2008*)

04 LATE MOMENT/
CELL-CITY

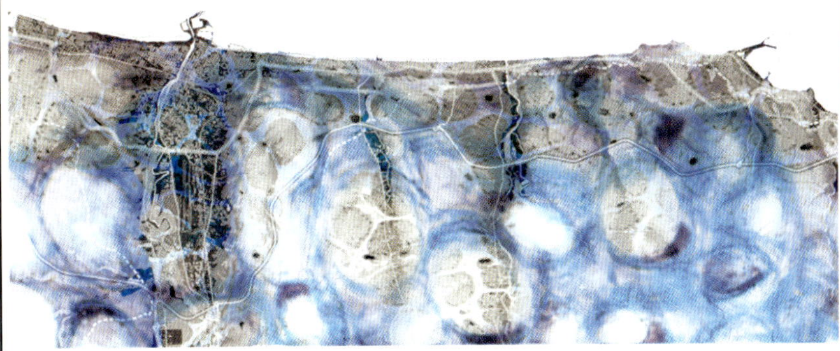

the energy issue outlines a new metaphor for the organization, operation and configuration of the contemporary city: the Cell-city, designed like a maze capable of metabolic energy independence (Hermann Scheer). It is recognized that to live fully the contemporary, Peter Eisenman calls *"Late moment"* (quoting Edward W. Said, author of *On Late Style*), understood as a *historical phase in which there are no new paradigms; ... where style describes a late time, evolution of culture, before moving to a new paradigm, but inherent in it a possibility for innovation and transformation.* The energy cabling is the beginning of a new electrification (the third Industrial Revolution, *Jeremy Rifkin*) of the city-region. The transition from a model of energy supply in the branched network to a *rhizomatous device*, consisting of energy districts (*Cell-city: cellule produttive*) leads to a configurational metamorphosis that will bring the city to be more and more *No Oil cities* (*Fabio Orecchini, Vincenzo Naso*) converting the existing device, now *subsidiary of the oil age.*

A new style of living is rising and the substantial transformation to be seized is in changing the network access. The *cellular vision* of territorial devices is delineated by the capacity of *autopoiesis* of a city (ie the self-generated energy) through the *development of a system (distributed network)* of the different parts that compose it (*e-tools*), a new spatial configuration that can build the city: the model of the *Cell-city* (made from a device of the *islands*, for the construction of an *archipelago system*, in analogy with the biological metaphor of *cellular automata*) that is capable of producing energy from renewable sources. The research applies models of reading and organizing the city's lay back in the seventies (or even before), not considering the devices and equipment for energy systems as isolated points, but considering the *territories* in order to build an *energy vision* of the city.

05   ENERGETIC SCENARIOS

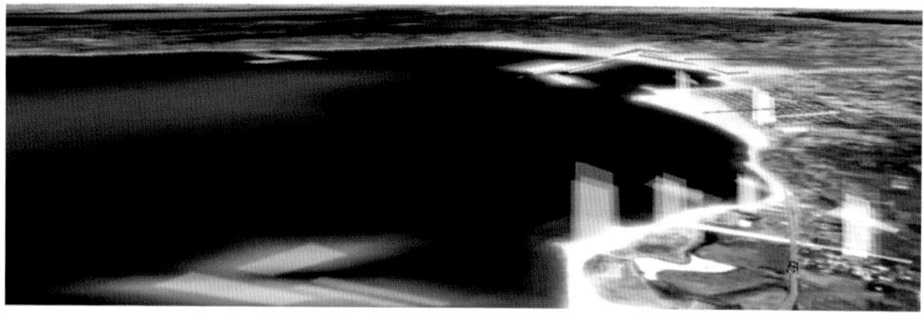

"what would happen if............" This is a scenario! (Bernardo Secchi).

OBJECTIVES AND RESULTS

To answer the question posed in *Issue*, the research builds a "guiding vision" able to configure a *cellular device* to operate as an *island* of the different parts of the city in order to activate a **polycentric lattice** of / in the city (to the *city archipelago*). This *energy vision of territories*, capable of *self-production* and **mutual energy aid** *(sharing)*, defines codes and repeatable processes within different areas of the Adriatic. Through the application of *case-studies*, one outlines the actions, methods and devices capable of becoming urban tools (*e-tools*) for the definition of a **short chain of energy**. *Sprawl-energy* is a phenomenon that affects all of the territories inhabited our *small planet* (Rogers), where:

$$\text{wellbeing=growth}, \; > \text{pollution}, < \text{sustainability;}$$
$$\text{vs}$$
$$\text{wellbeing=development}, \; < \text{pollution}, \; > \text{sustainability}$$

The wider implementation of energy collection systems has resulted in radical trans-formations and changes in some fields (aerospace research, car design, urban-design, fashion and art), but not inside cities and territories.

The main objective is to define, in *future scenarios*, exploration projects that pre-figure the development of energy in *Climate Zones* (recognizing, in the territories of the Mediterranean, the field of research: *geo-territories* between 48 ° 51 '30 , 07 "N and 30 ° 03 '05.67" N parallel) constructing the devices (**e-tools**) to the **TOOL-KIT (TOOLBOX) for the renewable Mediterranean city**. The expected results of the research have defined the possible application tools and equipment (e-tools) capable of activating the construction of a **weak energy fabric** (branziana theory), capable of building the network and enabling new relationships to develop and exchange (**energy sharing**), starting with those that have the potential of the territories for the activation of a common energy production (*toward a* **sprawl-energy**).

01

evoluzione dell'archetipo

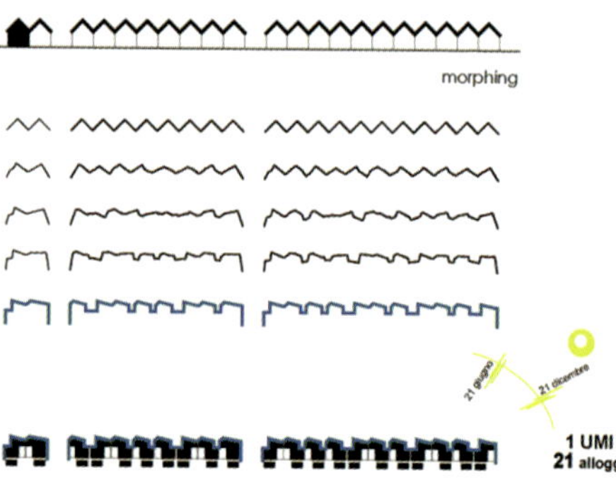

02

sguardo alla tradizione

...la corte

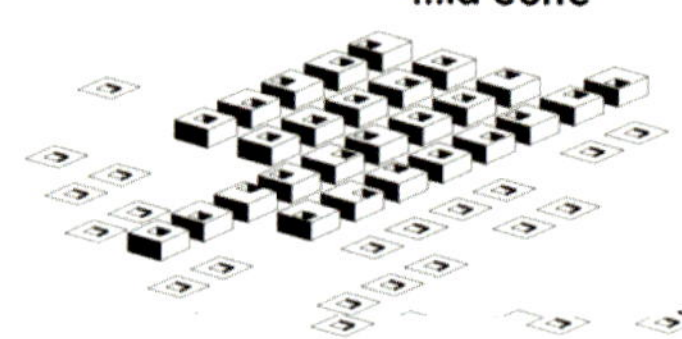

03

S.E.A.A. + S.E.A.P.
SistemiEnergeticiAlternativiAttivi + SistemiEnergeticiAlternativiPassivi

STRATEGIES (OR METHODS)

The research in an initial analysis has identified three key steps in the evolution of energy devices: *power_house, power_houses, power_city.* The **methodology** used is one that recognizes in the **experimental process** an application for the construction of new energy scenarios. In order to define *energy paradigms and new spatial configurations*, devices and materials have sought to define the character of **e-tools**. The *experimental process* is described and applied in the *RESEARCH-ACTION/***tool-kit.** The main strategy of the research consists in DIAGRAMMATIC elaboration of georeferenced information (MAPS) according to an experimental approach.
The objective is to identify a number of possible SCENARIOS achievable through AC-TIONS defined **for the construction and renewable-tools for the city**.
The *Mediterranean* is the *field of action* (and *application*) of this research.
The *methodology* recognizes in the application of *case-study (a project as a probe)* the survey instrument capable of questioning the territories, to anticipate and build scenarios. **The applicative-inductive approach** to of the *case-study* on the Pescara area (between 42 ° 26 '49.11 "N and 42 ° 26' 15.05" N parallel) declares three key assumptions:
- recognize within portions of the territories or parts of it are capable of expressing the different memberships and to define the *family* of **"standard elements"** (*the e-tools*) by identifying characteristics and similar potential
- declare an **analogy between urban systems and biological systems**, not linked simply to *formal similarities (or of shape)*, but identified in correspondence with some *key concept*s, such as: *organization, linkages and dependencies,*
- The various parts of the system, not as elements (or parts) in isolation but as a **autopoietic communities** capable of activating the construction of a *cellular vision* of the areas linked to *self-organization* and *reticular functioning* of the metropolitan areas.
In the first instance the research acknowledges the differences in the territories, the degrees of similarity, the climate conditions (*climate zones*), thus declaring the characteristics and *potential energy* of the place, in a second step, through the *ideograms and abstraction* of community defined as the *generalized action*, capable of building *new paradigms and urban devices*, through the *repetition of codes and processes*. These principles have always guided and verified the steps in *theory and application* of research.

SET UP OF THE RESEARCH

The research was divided into THREE parts (+ 1):

In the first part of the research: 01.YESTERDAY / **power_house** one tries to define the path through the eras change and energy invariant structure of cities as innovation networks.

In the second section: 02.TODAY / **power_houses** based on the concept of Worldwide Web Energy trying to define and redefine what possible devices, shapes and patterns the contemporary city can seek and make their own (Cell-city), in the era of the Third Revolution Industrial.

In the third part: 03.TOMORROW / **power_city** structures the conditions for a NON-STOP ENERGY CITY redefining new forms of location and moving the idea of a new economy: the Energy sharing.

The last section (**City Vision: PEscara**), through a *process of experimentation-application (case study)* identifies and defines new energy tools for the Mediterranean city: the **e-tools**.

Eletropolis describes the processes of change and transformation of land use by virtue of the evolution of energy transitions. Until the pre-industrial era the *limitation of "physical proximity"* between the places of production and energy consumption has always influenced the use of territories and settlements, and this has led them to conceive urban structures less related to *morphological-configuration-environmental* aspects (YESTERDAY /**power_house**), often resulting in the growth of organisms indifferent to their contexts. The electrification of cities has led to the breaking of the *localization bonds* between the sites of production and consumption of those facilitating the growth of highly dependent on *(non)places* of energy: the central hub of production. Today there is a redistribution of resources and energy opportunities in the territories (as Mitchell acknowledges in the *evolution of new types of networks*) through a system that determines that decentralization and atomization energy theorized Rifkin, Droege, Petterson (TODAY / **power_houses**).

What will the future scenarios develop if we imagine that we live in metropolitan areas that are more comparable to most dedicated mechanisms for energy efficiency and to its production?

It is defined as a *case study*: **"City Vision: Pescara [42 ° 26'49, 11" N - 42 ° 26'15, 05 "N]"** that determines the configuration of a **vision-guide** able to define the character and processes of a city increasingly linked to systems, devices and the logic of power generation from renewable process of construction of the devices determines the City "making the network" of community energy degrees to redistribute power, resources and opportunities in the territories (through development models related to trade in services, such as *energy sharing*). After reading the territories and the potential energy of the different contexts, we define the principles, actions and tools (**e-tools**) able to build *relationships* between different *energy communities*. These *energy relationships* come from **three evolved scenarios** (*centralized, de-centralized, distributed network*) capable of building a *network* between the various strategic areas. All this tends to define a scenario for future development capable of recognizing, in the community of network sources, the ability to define more and more devices similar to *No-Stop City Energy*, bringing to an effective constraint loca-tional bonds existing between the areas of production, accumulation and consump-tion (TOMORROW / **power_city**).

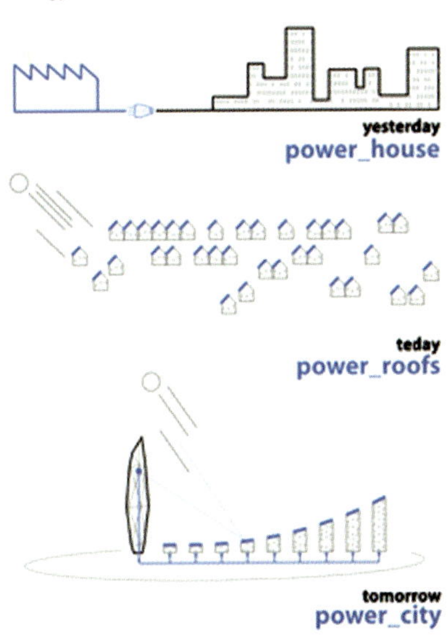

03
TOOL-KIT

TOOL-KIT: EXPERIMENTAL PROCESS FOR DEFINING NEW ENERGY SCENARIOS

The Research-Action section defines *new scenarios*: **new energy paradigms and spatial patterns in the Mediterranean**, for the determination of several tools: the **e-tools**, through the development of *new materials* for the urban *maps*, *charts*, *act* to define urban *energy scenarios*. A *process* is a logical sequence of *steps ordered linearly* through *external actions* that build and *define the system*, in computer science, process means an *instance of a program running in a sequential manner*. The word *experimental* can have different meanings, but is always associated with a scope that encloses and directly uses the observations of the phenomena, with the aim of obtaining data and information. An *experimental process* can be understood from the moment it tends to be specified in a given context (a both logical and spatial context), defining a logical sequence of ordered steps (which does not necessarily have to run in a linear fashion, but through processes that are more circular) through the construction of patterns and actions to view and process data and information. The process that will be put in place is an **experimental process**, which intends to use (at different scales of analysis and application) results, applications, projects, as a *probe*, as a *means of method*. The instruments put in motion by the research are: maps, charts, stocks, **e-tools**, in order to define the *tool-kit* for new energy paradigms in the territories of the Mediterranean.

SCENARIO: MEDITERRANEO/MEDITERRANEI

is the scenario of reference, which will be considered for this research. The territory of the Mediterranean embodies all the characteristics of different territories which belong to it. The Mediterranean is not just a sea, but it is a *thousand things together* (to synthesize Braudel). The Mediterranean has been traversed for centuries, lived, sailed, and is now setting the stage for wars, conflicts, victories, defeats, massacres, defence, has created and distributed wealth, has been an itinerary and map (*cost to cost*). Today, it seems, it is called *to give a new meaning*. These reflections are inserted in reflections on different contexts, different tissues, city counterparts, similar situations, parallel evolutions, different morphologies, changing geographies through the introduction of a unique point of view: the diffusion of new energy production systems.

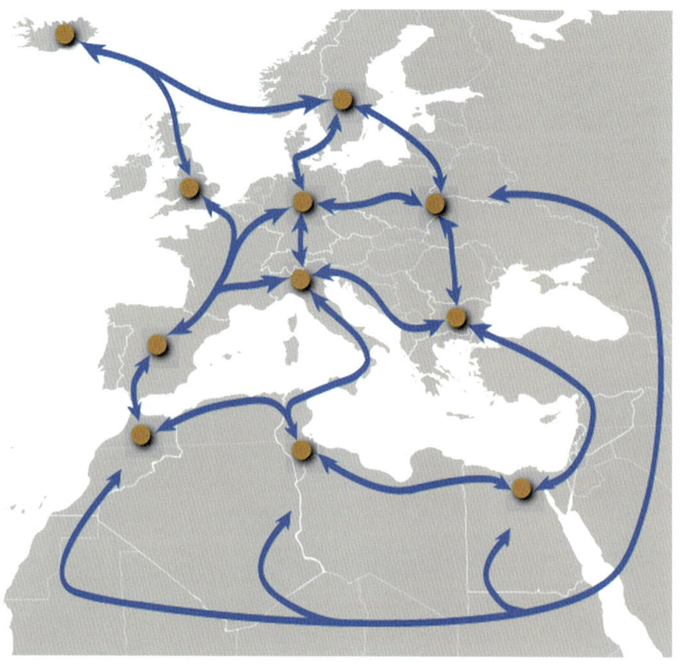

Against this background, the Mediterranean is once again seen as the square area of the report, within the **corridors of the Mediterranean** as a *new armor for productive, commercial and creative capital flows, able to reshape new Mediterranean cultures that work together* (source: *Dicoter, 2007*) for the construction of shared paradigms of a single Mediterranean city of the XXI century.

In the very near future the Mediterranean area with its territories will be called to a new definition in the light of the **SSG** - *Super Smart Grid.*

MAPS

we can define the map as a superposition of *two layers*: area and information (data). The information (data) represents the intellectual knowledge, the linguistic convention, the territory's physical and sensory experience. The interaction between information and the area is like that between knowledge and experience.

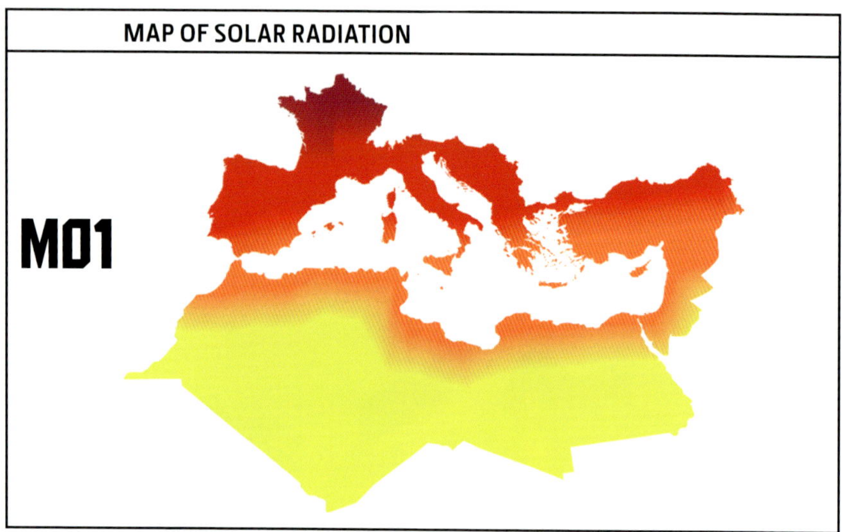

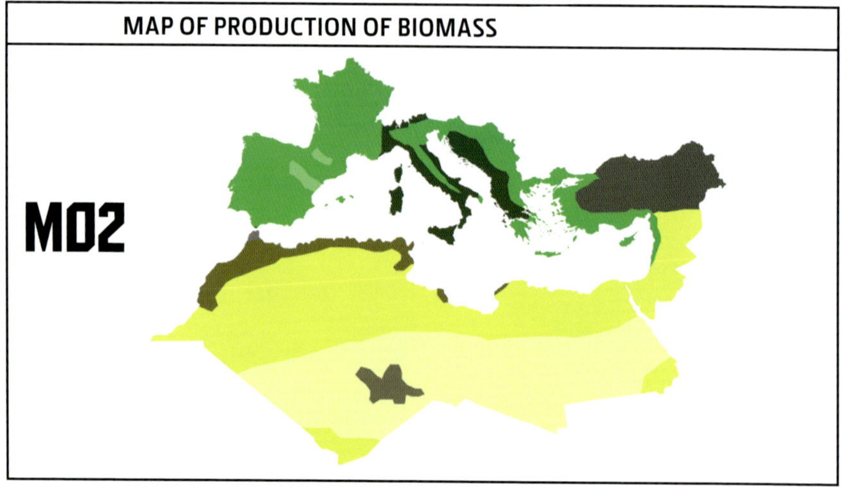

The figure is an abstract code and at the same time a precise limit (a number) that needs to gain a geo-measure.

(Maps/to map, [FS]-[MG] The metapolis dictionary of advanced architecture, Actar).

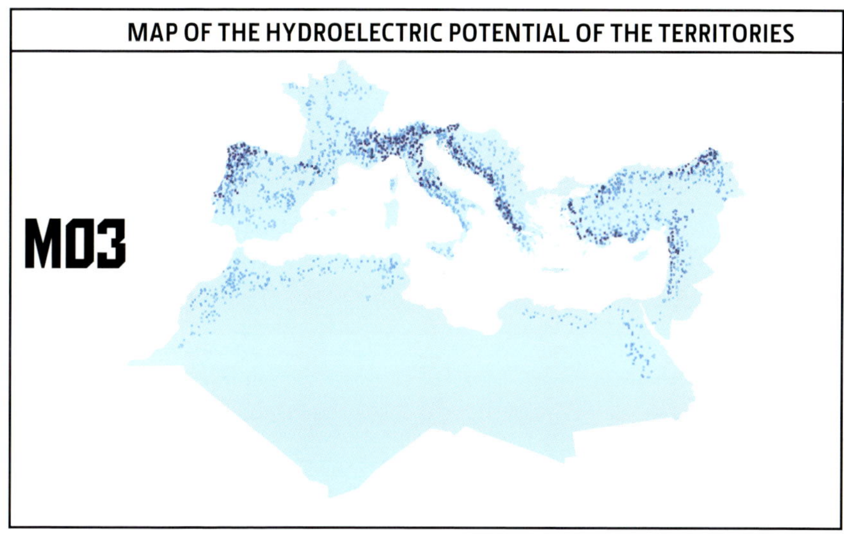

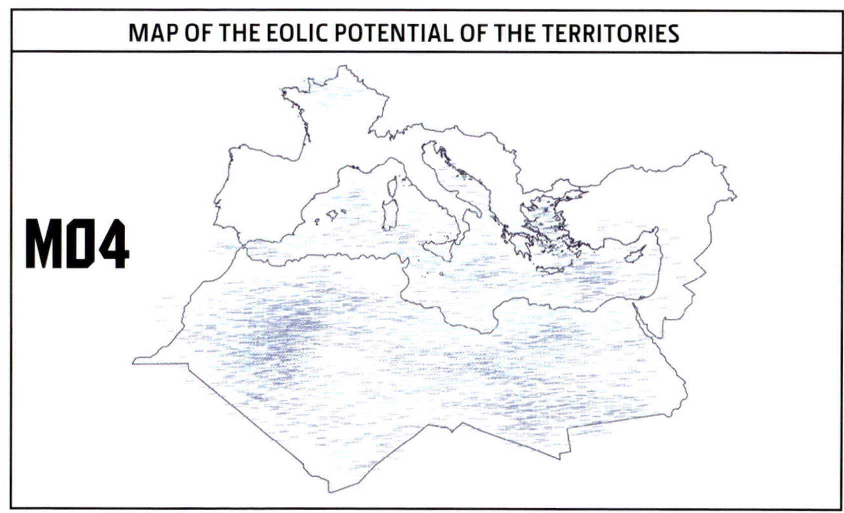

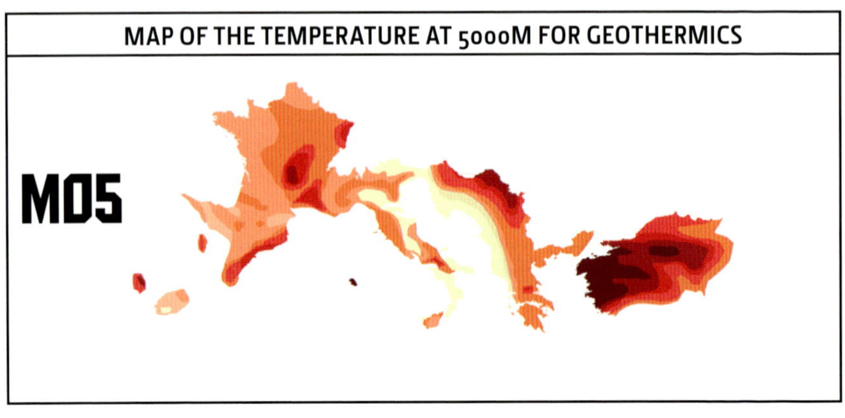

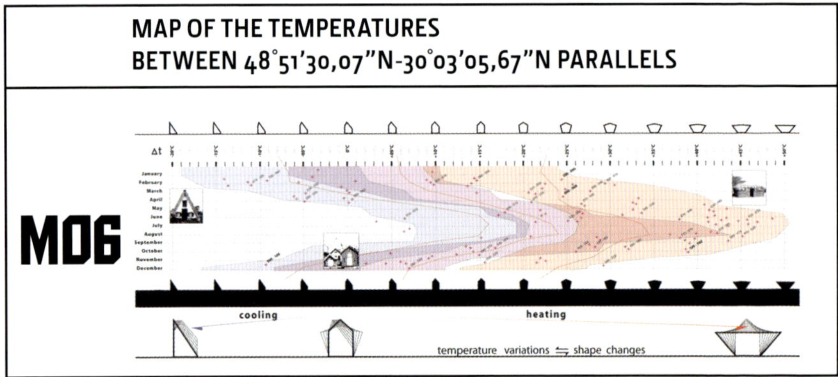

M07- MAP OF THE POPULATION AND DENSITY

M08- MAP OF THE METROPOLITAN AREAS

M09- MAP OF THE DEMOGRAPHIC PROJECTION (AL 2025 – CNR-ISSM)

M10- MAP OF PRODUCED ENERGY (DA RINNOVABILE)

M11- MAP OF ENERGY USE (ENERGY USE)

M12- MAP OF ENERGY CONSUMPTION (ENERGY CONSUMPTION)

M13- MAP OF ICT DATA

M14- MAP OF THE SUPER SMART GRID – SSG

DIAGRAMS

Assembly diagrams consider the graphs in the report combined with data of various kinds and with data on different spatial axes, overlapping relationships and intersecting information. The plot "does not map" a situation that already exists, but ***anticipates new organizations and specific actions yet to be realized.***

(Diagram, [CO]-[MG] The metapolis dictionary of advanced architecture, Actar).

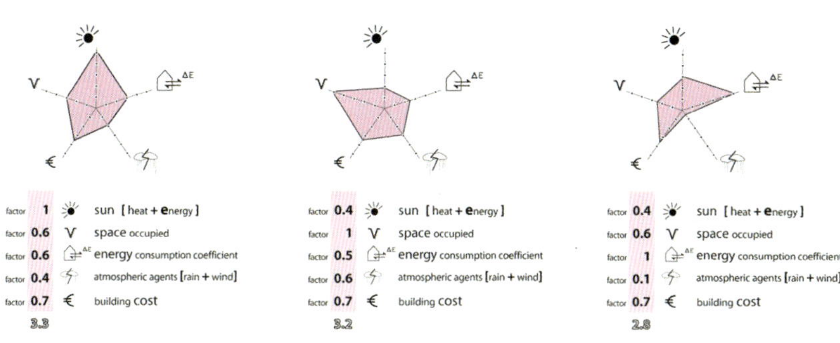

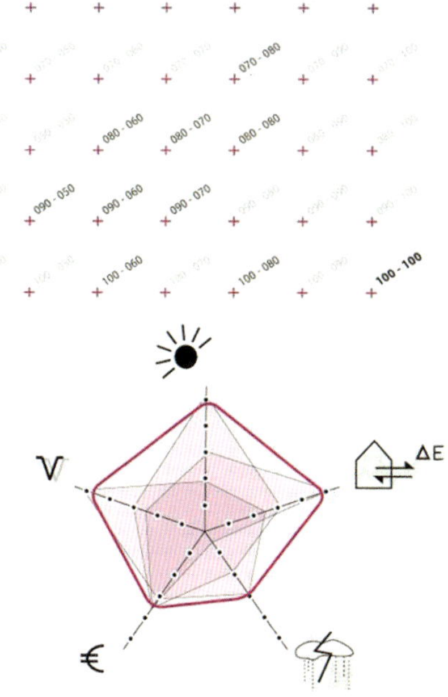

The data (*variables*) developed and correlated in the diagrams are divided into *three orders*:

1ST ORDER VARIABLES

GEOREFERENTIABLE
Latitude
Longitude
Azimut
Shade factore #1°
Equisolar Axis
Eliothermic Axis

2ND ORDER VARIABLES

GEOMETRIC	
Shade factore #2°	
Base geometry	
Surfaces	
Height	
Volume	
Inside surface	
Outside surface	
Form ratio S/V	>1
	=1
	<1

3RD ORDER VARIABLES

EXOGENOUS	
Thermal variation -▲t	
Orientation ratio	
Windows	
Materials	
Costs	
Main functions	
Property (public/private)	
Integration factore	
Typology of integration	*annex*
	superstructure
	parasite
	implant

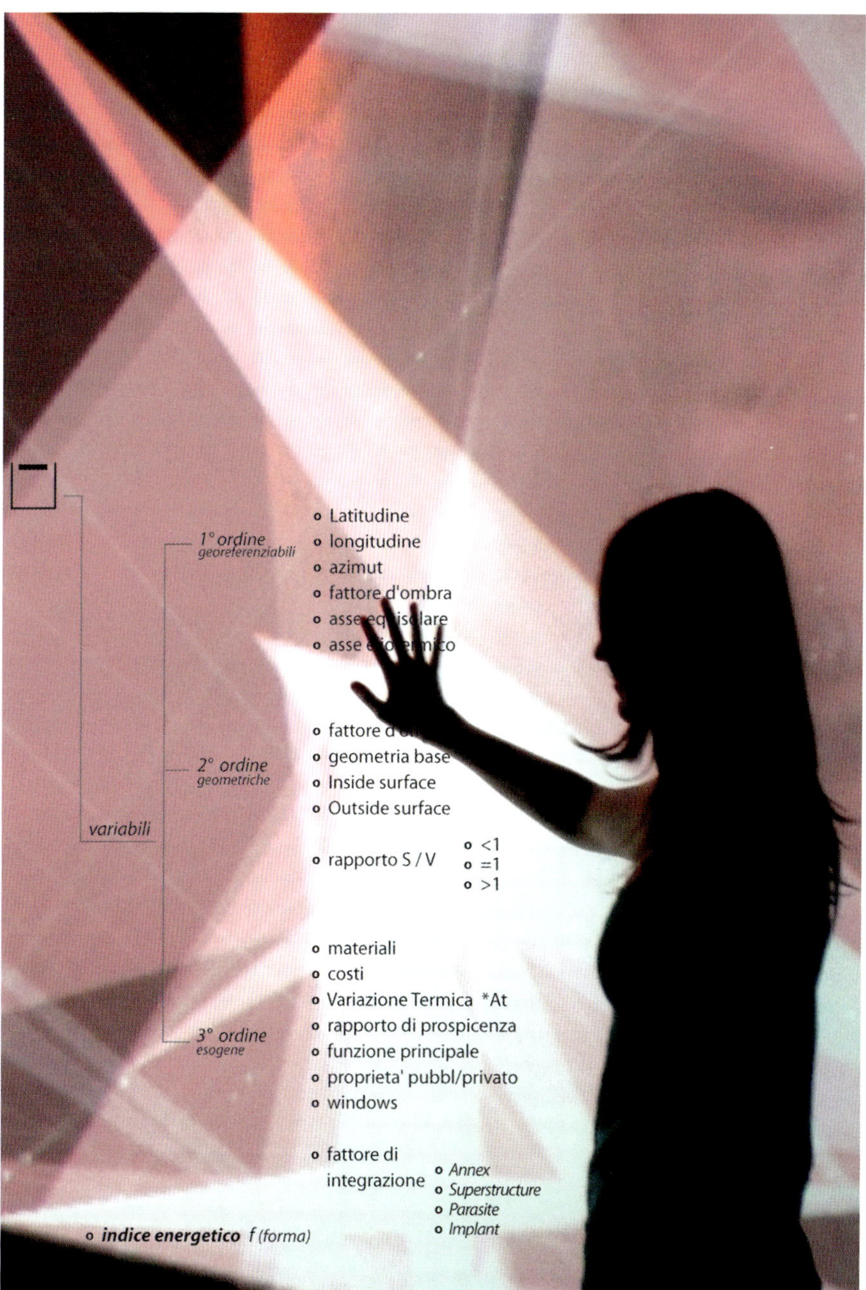
variabili

1° ordine
georeferenziabili

o Latitudine
o longitudine
o azimut
o fattore d'ombra
o asse equisolare
o asse eliotermico

2° ordine
geometriche

o fattore d'o...
o geometria base
o Inside surface
o Outside surface

o rapporto S / V
o <1
o =1
o >1

3° ordine
esogene

o materiali
o costi
o Variazione Termica *At
o rapporto di prospicenza
o funzione principale
o proprieta' pubbl/privato
o windows

o fattore di
integrazione
o Annex
o Superstructure
o Parasite
o Implant

o indice energetico f (forma)

ACTIONS

action generates the mechanisms that have developed and prefigured charts. We define, within the *Climate Zones*, three main actions for contemporary urban design:

A1- e-fit
A2- e-fill
A3- e-pull

A1 E-FIT
ADAPT

The redevelopment of the city, heritage buildings, improving the energy efficiency of buildings and the expansion of the availability of housing and services are priority issues common to all Mediterranean countries. The action, in this sense, cannot be limited to the exploitation of the remaining availability of land but will be aimed at *testing innovative strategies*, especially regenerating and reactivating the existing.
E-fit is designed as an action on the existing, re-definition, transformation, in some cases spatial adaptation of identity to a new lifestyle in order to make Mediterranean cities suitably energy self-sufficiency.

A2 E-FILL
FILL, SATURATE, OCCUPY

It is not always possible to act on the existing sufficiently. In this case the action is tense and fills *to colonize empty areas, engage new systems*, according to various approaches. The grafts are still closely connected to the existing pavement. The networking here is not only physical but also intellectual. In fact, the new settlements, such as new buildings will be *energy self-sufficiency* but also in close energy ties with the established settlements, and will develop along the lines of *energy cells*.

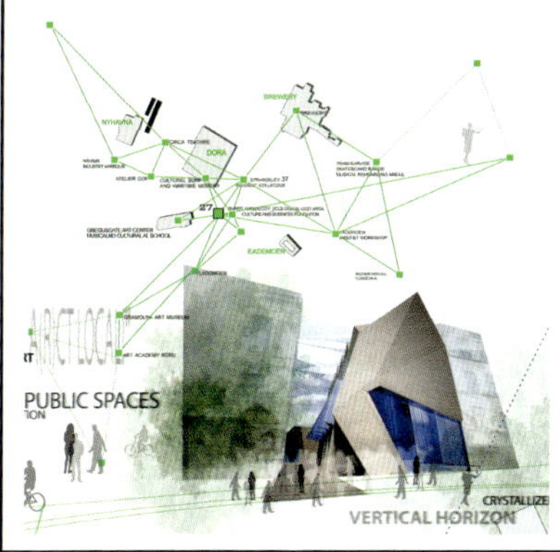

A3 E-PULL
PRESS, DEMOLISH, PULL OUT

Sometimes it is important to remove the excess. *E-pull* action is understood as the desire to eliminate the energy waste, indiscriminate pockets of those no longer useful when viewed in the logic of the *new energy network model assumed*. The disconnection does not only consider the appearance of the *"demolishing"* but also the optimizer of areas of cities, factories, or portions of the *behavioral patterns (depending on the scale that is being dealt with from time to time)*, the *network* of the city.

Logica Abierta

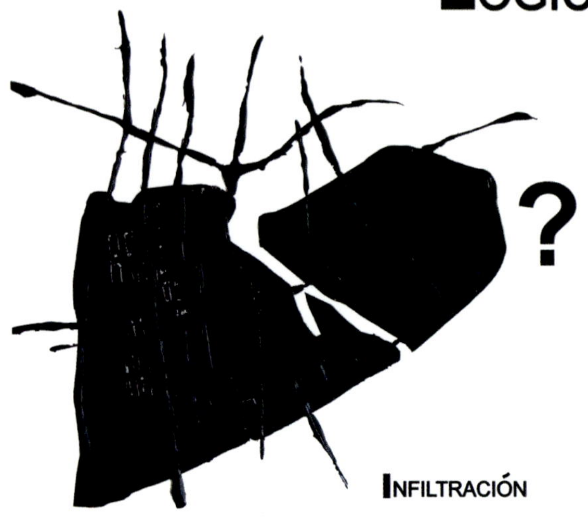

INFILTRACIÓN

ECO ISOLATO
manzana ecològica

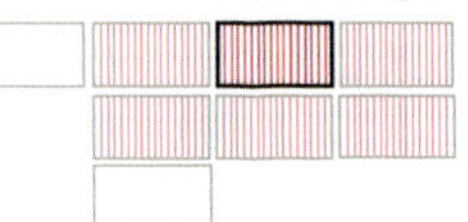

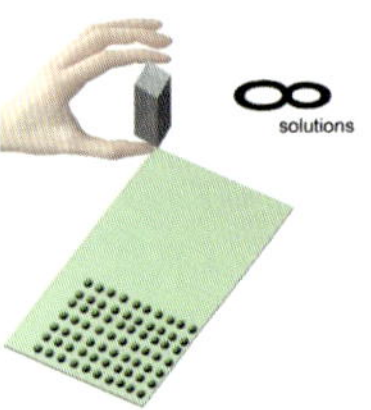

ECO ISOLATO_**A**		**ECO** ISOLATO_**B**		**ECO** ISOLATO_**C**		**ECO** ISOLATO_**D**	
ecology _Mobility	15 %	ecology _Mobility	5 %	ecology _Mobility	8 %	ecology _Mobility	15 %
ecology _Green park	10 %	ecology _Green park	22 %	ecology _Green park	23 %	ecology _Green park	15 %
ecology _WAter park	5 %	ecology _WAter park	2 %	ecology _WAter park	23 %	ecology _WAter park	2 %
ecology _Built	40 %	ecology _Built	20 %	ecology _Built	23 %	ecology _Built	45 %
ecology _Energy park	35 %	ecology _Energy park	51 %	ecology _Energy park	23 %	ecology _Energy park	23 %

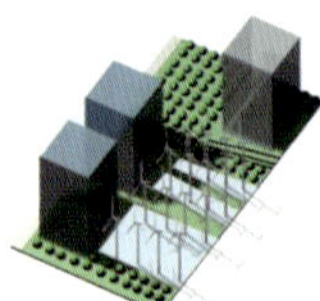

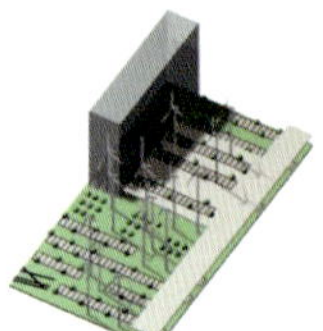

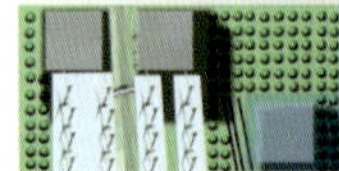

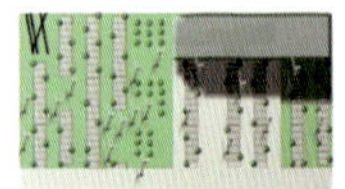

E-TOOLS FOR THE PROJECTION THE MEDITERRANEAN CITY INTO THE XXI CENTURY

The tool-kit is meant to be an instrument applied to a strategy of building, through what are known as **operational tools**, useful to the action of the architectural design for the operation of **more and more energy of the territories**. The term *tool-kit* (which in Italian is only used in computing) refers to a set of *tools (software)* used to facilitate and standardize the development of more complex derivatives. The *tool-kit* of the devices refers to **three different scales**:

- the **urban** scale, which examines and configures devices in the territories of metropolitan areas and cities:
- *micro energy nodes;*
- *energy infraSPACES;*
- *e-border energy;*
- *e-plugs;*
- *cluster Energy;*
- *energy park;*

- the **building**, which looks at the urban scale of the object or a series of urban objects defining the possible strategies and possible energy devices:
- *e-surfaces 2d e;*
- *e-overstructure;*
- *e-parassites;*
- *e-infill;*
-*e-box;*

- the scale of **1:1**, that is, the scale of individual mobile-life of the city: the cars and people:
- *e-shop;*
- *e-markets;*
- *personal e-makers;*
- *public share-car.*

URBAN SCALE (cuty/district/region):

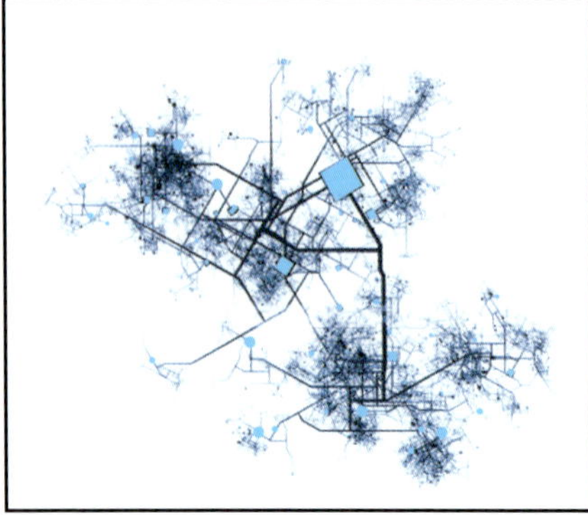

MICRO ENERGY NODES

urban energy acupuncture: acupuncture deals with different issues through re-intervention on some specific points that interact with the global system. In an urban sense, it defines the means by which some sites, much more extensive in their actual size, are enabled to act as a micro energy nodes produced on time in order to form urban effects at territorial level.

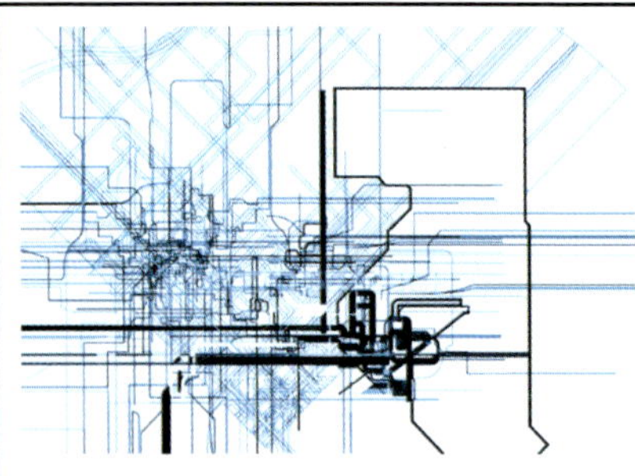

ENERGY INFRA-SPACES

some linear spaces can play a strong role in the structure of established urban areas, roads, lines of communication and infrastructure that are converted into places of energy production, thanks to traffic, linking their development to their context, strengthening their role as public spaces and communications.

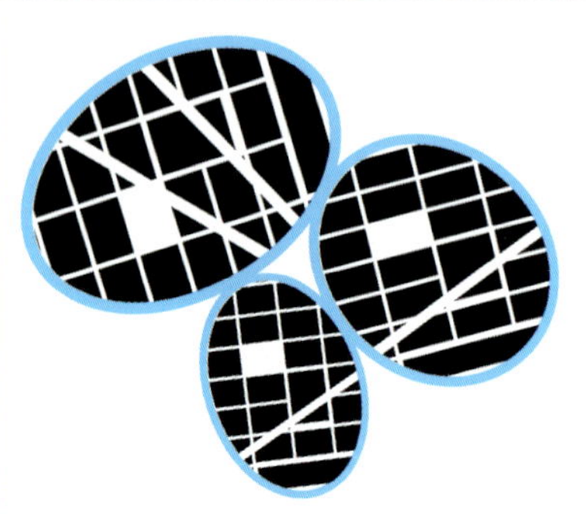

E-BORDER ENERGY

the policy that establishes the city as a series of *energy self-sufficient districts* is of strategic importance. These *border* regions may be used for their design, *as dense linear elements able to trigger devices for energy production and the supply of all inter-district services* contained within it.

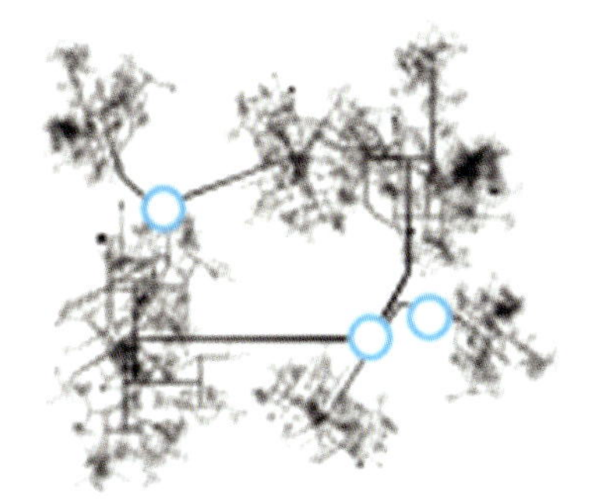

E-PLUG

Right in the contact zone between several districts **are placed those devices that act as a** LINK, **and** *connection between* **them. This is the** PLUG, **while energy producers and exchangers double output. They are** useful devices to exchange the surplus energy from one district and turn it over to the bordering, and vice versa *(for implementation energy sharing between district adjacent islands).*

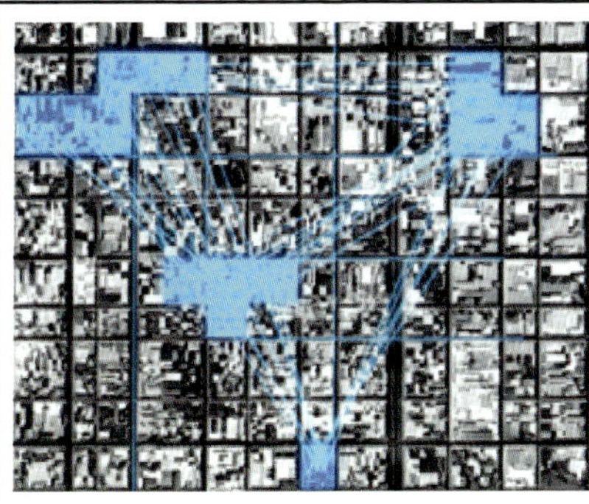

CLUSTER ENERGY

sensitive platforms, *islands within islands*, the clusters represent all areas within the city, which for various reasons have not yet acquired a vocation, or have been lost over the years. These spaces are delineated in direct contact with the established areas of the city, as of great strategic importance as potential energy poles. These may be *empty spaces* (A1), from industrial wasteland to be *reactivated* (A2), to *relocated* portions of the city, which will then be subject *to revision* (A3). However, these areas will be tested on *energy, and form new central government* able to regenerate around, to influence and sew. At the same time they will provide the space for aggregation and social interchange.

ENERGY PARK

areas of natural energy: the green areas, the sea, the lakes. These areas will, however, be featured in the energy network. These places, where activities will take place for leisure, *will also be the sites of experimentation in the field of energy* production of hydrogen, the collection of rainwater and its wetlands, crops for the production of biodiesel, for the placement of photovoltaic plants and offshore wind. In addition, you can create new habitats where *suburban housing develops innovative nature*. The existing natural areas will then be *regenerated* (A1), while in the case of cities with high density housing, will be created the natural / artificial way or by connecting the green roofs of buildings (A2), and relocating existing building mass, in order to cut inner-city green areas needed to restore a proper eco-environment balance (A3).

BUILDING SCALE (lived urban device)

E-SURFACES 2D E:

are those interventions on existing buildings that are realized through the use of two-dimensional surfaces, designed to accommodate devices of various kinds of energy production, **or *overlapping surface devices*, such as green roofs or double walls. You can use the free surfaces of the existing building (A1) or add *layers energy* along the front of the buildings, creating *double skin energy* (A2), or replace entire walls with *new active surfaces* (A3).**

E-OVERSTRUCTURE

architectural solutions that provide for retraining with the elevation of building types, along with increasing the volume of energy efficiency and overall functionality. **Although affected by many technical, regulatory and business is certainly a great opportunity when assessed in the context of wider strategies for urban regeneration. (A1) The expansion in coverage helps to create new housing or space and services for the community, to improve the appearance and overall performance of the building, but without new urbanized areas.**

E-PARASSITES

architectural *"non-integrated"* mechanisms *separate from the existing building*, **almost in conflict with it,** added **with the aim of extending the surface and improve energy performance. They "hold on" like *hackers* and may, for example, take the form of greenhouse climate, energy availability, etc. ...**

E-INFILL

instruments which provide for the overlapping of existing buildings and devices in volume production of energy interpenetrating architecture **that can replace parts of it.**

E-BOX

new devices are designed and implemented in full as *energy machines*, **defining its shape as a result of *morfoenergetici* parameters that affect the different variables (first, second and third order) of the system. It is their shape and positioning which determine all the opportunities to host energy devices,** *taking shape as new opportunities for complex urban energy networked with other points that make up the city,* ***at the scale of the building and district level.***

SCALE 1:1 (car/person)

E-SHOP

Energy-Shops will offer the products and equipment for alternative energy from renewable sources and energy conservation, a working action *to educate and inform the public about new lifestyles related to energy*, providing complete packages and easy to install, to allow each user to have the devices needed for daily production.

E-MARKETS

will be real *energy markets*. Assuming that all activities of daily life will help to produce energy, and that some of this *do-it-yourself* energy will not be consumed, it can be used as a bargaining chip to obtain goods and services. Also being able to exchange energy will provide a stimulus to increase energy production staff.

PERSONAL E-MAKERS

as personal computers, the *tools of "self made" energy production* will spread. Every daily activity has a corresponding tool producing the energy needed to accomplish that or other activities. *The energy produced in excess can be traded in the Energy markets.*

PUBLIC SHARE-CAR

is a tool to change the lifestyles associated with the use of cars within the city. A dedicated public transport for personal use will be provided in picnic areas. These are *micro-electric cars capable of self-catering in the parking space and on the go.* These vehicles will, in turn, be shared to maximize space, reduce the need for parking and traffic restrictions.

ENERGY PARADIGMS
AND NEW SPATIAL CONFIGURATIONS: SCENARIOS

"What if ... ..." This is a scenario! When we reason about the future we are dominated by uncertainty and unpredictability. In reality we are only thinking about the future. Maybe we can start thinking about possible scenarios as an intended outcome, or even as a possible escape of the policies that have centered on the confrontation between different cultures and people which is a very important point today. Removing this aspect I think is a shame. I say this not so much and not only as an urban planner, but from a broader perspective.
(Bernardo Secchi, *New Territories*).

The construction of scenarios will use a *design* process:
- This process involves the definition of devices, writing scores for urban elements such as **weak energy elements** and parts, *character-energy production* that can be defined as a **new array of a weak urban re-write** (starting from the *urban theories* of Andrea Branzi);
- the application of different families of devices, will be resolved by each party (designed devices such as *systemic, generalized, repeated and adaptive*) to offer various joint and intersecting possibilities, and meetings so as to facilitate the interaction (or conversely, determine their mutual indifference).
This process could be likened to the operation of decomposition and recomposition of the different parts of a system in the trials of the **"planned deconstruction"** applications and Bernard Tschumi. The principles involved in targeting energy devices for the city have also been addressed within the work in the **International Workshop __SSUD "Sustainable Sensitive Urban Design"**, held at the Faculty of Architecture, University "G. d'Annunzio "of Pescara **(01:02:03 XII 2009)**.
One of the issues faced by the different work groups was **the energy improvement of the residences with assistance of the massing and arrangement of open spaces** (*work group coordinated by Edward Zanchini*). Within the project a considerable part of the project involved the exploration of the redevelopment of **affordable housing and Ater Pescara** (near the Tiburtina): strategic area for its location and sensitive to its social character. In fact, the work carried out by *Frederick Bilo (with Alberto Ulysses, Mario Pugliese, Alessandro Chiola, Carlo De Gregorio, and the collaboration of Fabrizio Tucci and Anna Laura Petrucci)* has affected aspects of sustainability principles related to **sustainable energy, urban sustainability and social sustainability.**

The *design concept* was to first explore the *possible spatial configurations* for the relocation of the *performance reserve volume* (set at **20%** - as stated in Art. 4 - n.16/2009 LR) and to *envisage future scenarios* that define images that were shared: **cube-city, roof-city, south-city, pixel-city. 10 targets** have been identified **(+1)** able to identify the needs of system space design. In this way, actions defined in the project can define different approaches capable of being repeated in the existing buildings in the neighborhood. Also, a study was carried out on one of the buildings (**"building standard"**), which recognized the ability to generate general principles of the proposed intervention.

Following are some images of the work;
project coordinators: Edoardo Zanchini, Federico Bilò, Paola Misino e Fabrizio Tucci;
tutor: Alberto Ulisse;
students: Mariangela Pugliese, Alessandro Chiola, Carlo Di Gregorio

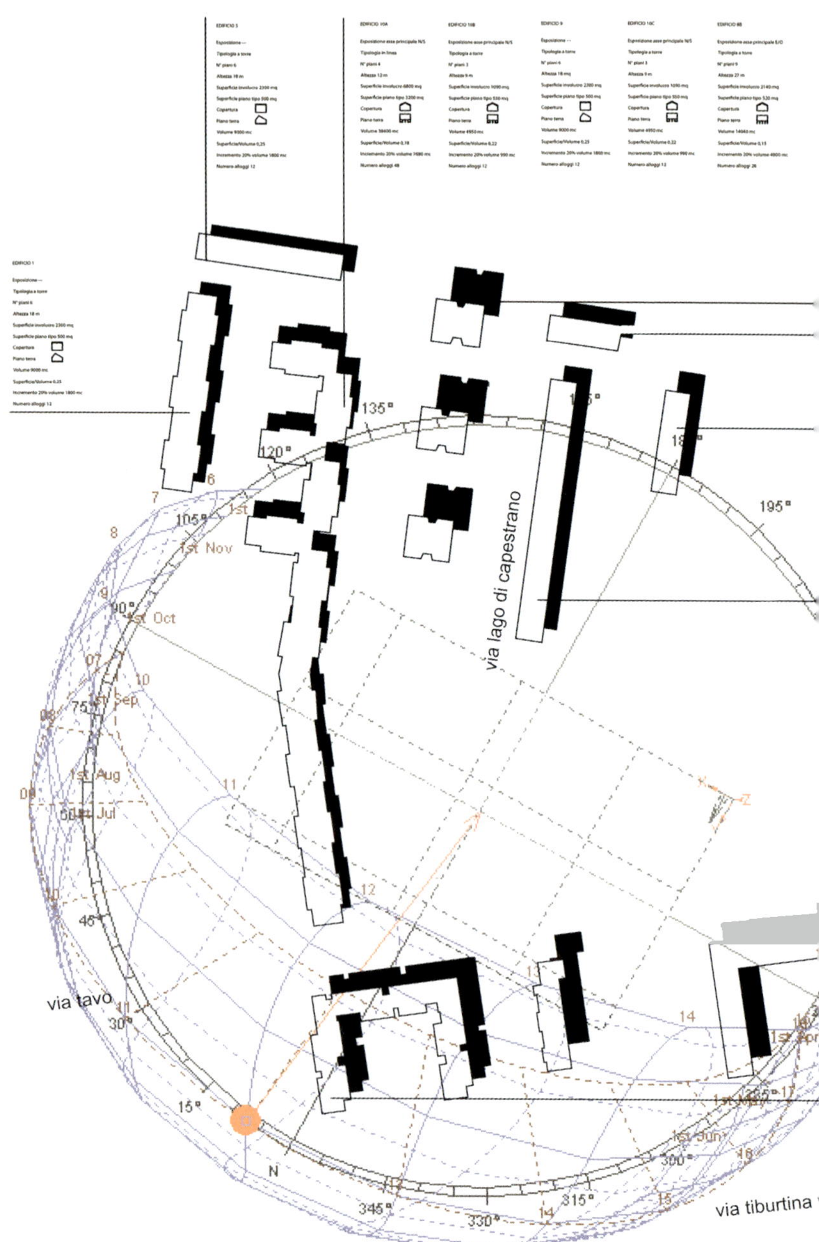
via lago di capestrano
via tavo
via tiburtina
N
135°
120°
105°
90°
75°
60°
45°
30°
15°
165°
180°
195°
345°
330°
315°
300°
1st Nov
1st Oct
1st Sep
1st Aug
1st Jul
1st Jun
1st May
1st Apr
EDIFICIO 1
EDIFICIO 5
EDIFICIO 10A
EDIFICIO 10B
EDIFICIO 9
EDIFICIO 10C
EDIFICIO 4B

VOLUME esistente

304.270 mc

+ 20% -art.4 - L.R. n.16/2009

50x50x24

60.854 mc

...costruzione di SCENARI FUTURIBILI

CUBE-CITY

ROOF-CITY

SOUTH-CITY

PIXEL-CITY

EDIFICIO 13

Esposizione asse principale E/O

Tipologia a corte

N° piani 6

Altezza 18 m

Superficie involucro 9990 mq

Superficie piano tipo 2250 mq

Copertura

Piano terra

Volume 40500 mc

Superficie/Volume 0,25

Incremento 20% volume 8100 mc

Numero alloggi 80

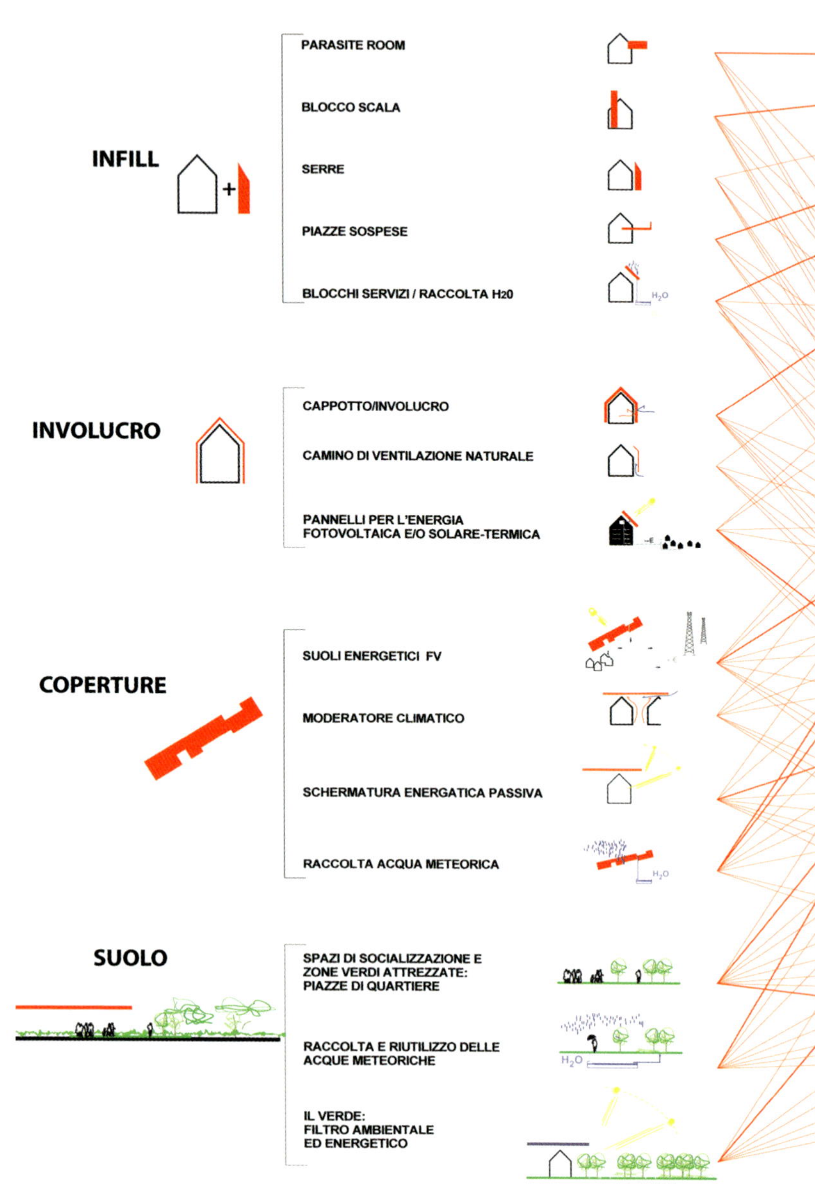

INFILL

PARASITE ROOM

BLOCCO SCALA

SERRE

PIAZZE SOSPESE

BLOCCHI SERVIZI / RACCOLTA H20

INVOLUCRO

CAPPOTTO/INVOLUCRO

CAMINO DI VENTILAZIONE NATURALE

PANNELLI PER L'ENERGIA
FOTOVOLTAICA E/O SOLARE-TERMICA

COPERTURE

SUOLI ENERGETICI FV

MODERATORE CLIMATICO

SCHERMATURA ENERGATICA PASSIVA

RACCOLTA ACQUA METEORICA

SUOLO

SPAZI DI SOCIALIZZAZIONE E
ZONE VERDI ATTREZZATE:
PIAZZE DI QUARTIERE

RACCOLTA E RIUTILIZZO DELLE
ACQUE METEORICHE

IL VERDE:
FILTRO AMBIENTALE
ED ENERGETICO

10 OBIETTIVI+1

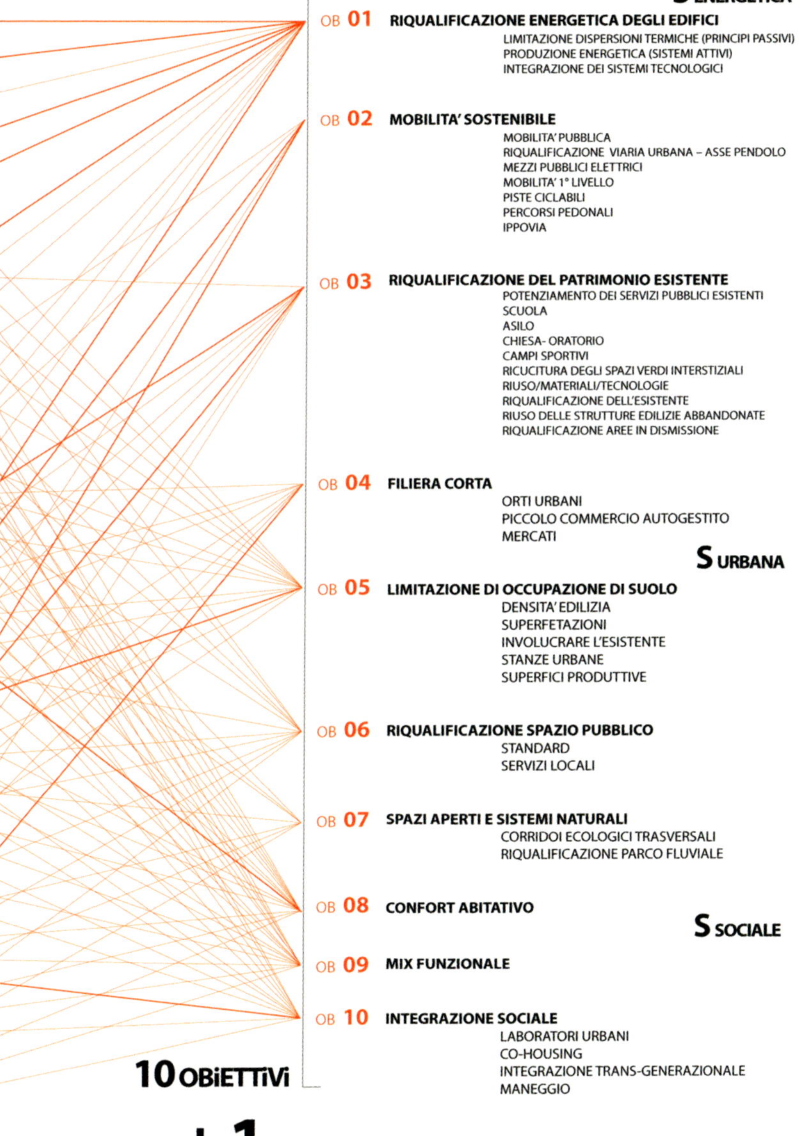

A1-A3
-parasite room
-razionalizzazione della tipologia esistente

A2-A4
-piazze sospe[se]
-nuovi moduli abitative

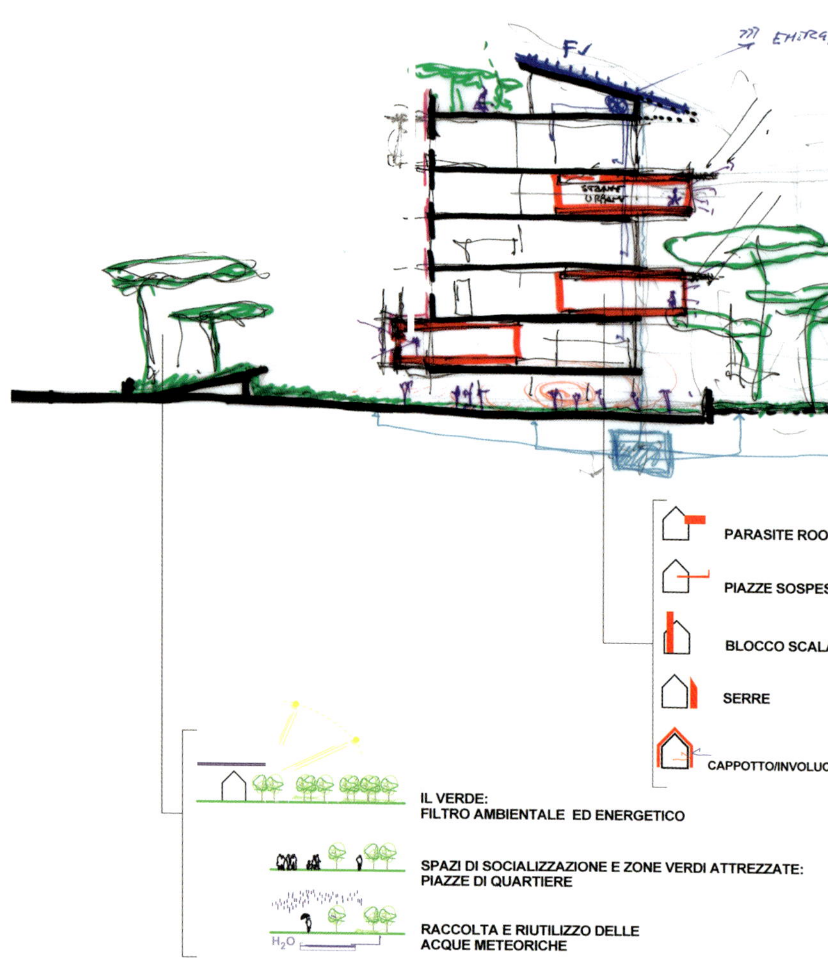

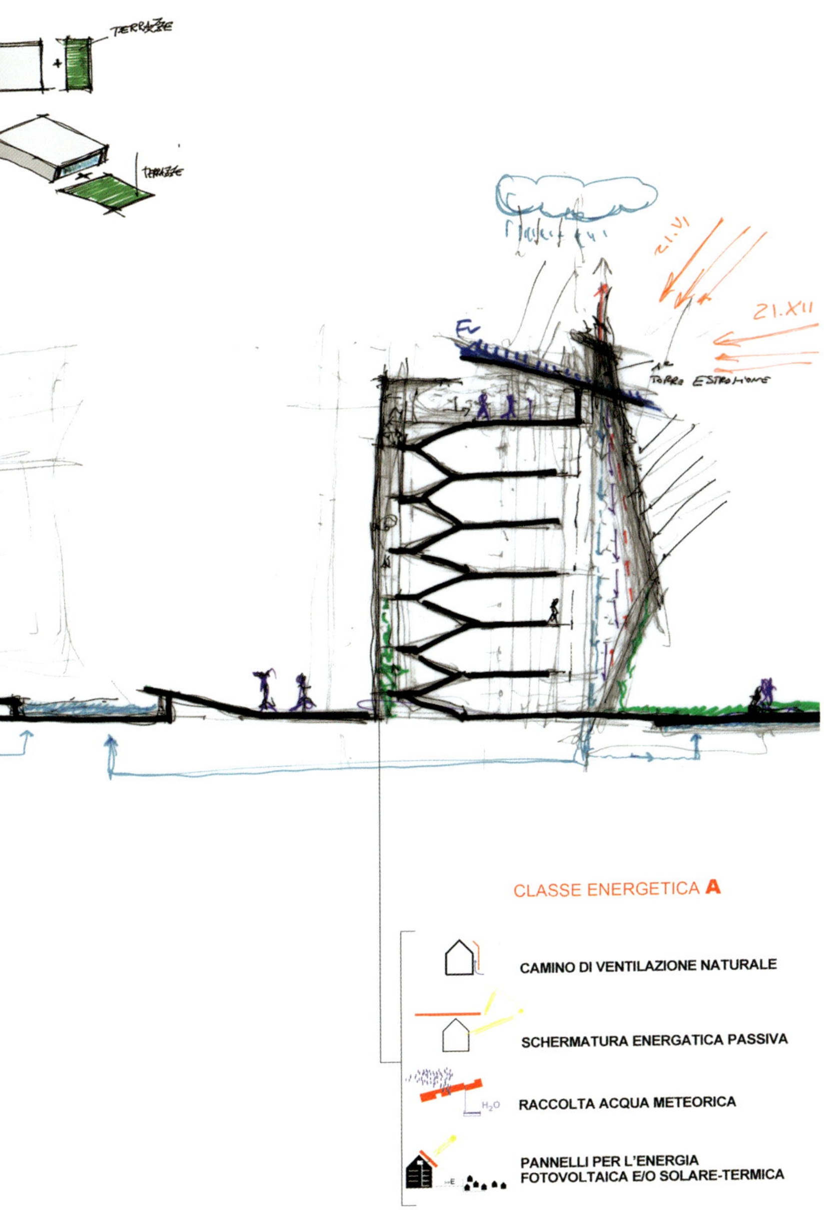

CLASSE ENERGETICA **A**

CAMINO DI VENTILAZIONE NATURALE

SCHERMATURA ENERGATICA PASSIVA

RACCOLTA ACQUA METEORICA

PANNELLI PER L'ENERGIA
FOTOVOLTAICA E/O SOLARE-TERMICA

21.VI
21.XII
STUDI SOLARI
percorso del sole 21-VI
percorso del sole 21-XII
superfici in ombra portata
superfici in ombra prorpia
superfici bagnate dal sole
VENTI
EFFETTO
VENTURI
PIANO TERRA
schema ventilazione coperture

04

CITY VISION

PESCARA
[42 26 49,11 N-42 26 15,05]

POPOLATION: 123.022 ab.
DENSITY: 3.676 ab/Km2

(ISTAT code: 068028 - data from 01/01/2009 - ISTAT)

Geographic data:
SURFACE: 33,47 kM2
ALTITUDE: 4 m s.l.m.
LATITUDE: 42° 27' 40,32" N
angular distance from equator toward north
LONGITUDE: 14° 12' 39,96" E
angular distance from Greenwich meridian toward east

climatic classification:
CLIMATE ZONE: D
In function of degree K*day (Kd) - DPR n.412 of 26 August 1993, table A and later alterations and integrations
DEGREE K*DAY: 1.718 Kd
Kd: (degree K*day), measurement unit that estimates the Energy necessary for maintaining a comfortable climate level of living spaces.

Pescara PE

NATIONAL STRATEGIC FRAMEWORK 2007/2013

Inter-regional Operational Programme "Renewable Energy and Energy Efficiency"

The Interregional Operational Programme "Renewable Energy and Energy Efficiency" is part of the National Strategic Framework for the programming cycle of the EU and national cohesion policy 2007-2013.

Priority 3 "Energy and Environment: Sustainable and efficient use of resources for development"

Because of the importance given to energy policy objectives to be achieved and the objectives of environmental sustainability, within the framework of regional policy the United Interregional Programme affects **the territories of the convergence regions** (Sicily, Calabria, Puglia, Campania) and is co-financed by Structural Funds, and is **extended to the entire South** (which also includes the regions of Basilicata, Molise, Abruzzo, Sardinia), in respect to financial resources of national regional policy (Fund for Underdeveloped Areas).

42° 26' 49,11" N

42° 26' 15,05" N

Pescara PE
CITY VISION 61

PARTS OF CITY / CITY BY PARTS

The territory belongs to the **metropolitan continuity (small)** of Pescara that characterizes the Adriatic city: **250 km long** *coast-line* between the coastline and infrastructure bundles (under investigation in research PRIN *"OP_ Public Works and the Adriatic city"*). Over time, infrastructure systems have been juxtaposed by an elementary operation, simple summation, leaving only a few **points** (nodes / portals), the exceptional **synapses** become among the different Adriatic systems: defining the **rhizomatic characters for a dynamic city**. The valleys of the city in the central Adriatic area are characterized by unique *morphological patterns of the valleys "comb" system*, making it suitable for those characteristics that differentiate it from other Mediterranean contexts. The peculiar and subtle signs of this system are made more immediate by a *vision from above*, which still continues to be used to interpret, plan and provide a highly distinctive territory.

Reading the Adriatic city, means also *changing the point of view*, for example, **"Looking at the coast from the sea"**, outlining the sequence of *spaces of transition*, of *ecotones*, that hybrid spaces preserve in section rather than in plan, or activate an exercise in reading the area with a **sidelong glance from the east** (or rather south-east /east). Looking at the *geography of the Adriatic Sea* by a helio-thermic view would make those flashes attain a unique character of the *mid-Adriatic* area. The territorial system of Pescara has always been read, analyzed, planned as an urbanized area located at the *intersection* of the valley system and the coastal Pescara (Adriatic), so as to identify the characteristics typical of identifying an area between the sea and the hills *(T configuration)*. From the "stylistic" point of view of ie shapes, sizes and their relations (as defined by *Farinelli* in his study of *"Characters of the original landscape Pescara*) Pescara the landscape is divided into **5 different types**, extended and otherwise identified on the basis homogeneity or recurrence of the situation and the geological formation of the related areas. *It is just a coincidence that between the particularity of the given lithology and soil characteristics and a high settlement and the process of humanizing the other hand, is built the key to the breakdown of the landscape system in Pescara, a set of subsystems* (system meant in the usual sense of the term, ie an **organized complexity**). The sets are as follows (continued *Farinelli*): 1 - *the bank, 2 - the valleys, and 3 - the polygenic hills; 4 - the Miocene hills; 5 - the piedmont of the Gran Sasso*. Within this territory the *case-study* identifies, perimeters and cuts a **strip-sample** (*between the two parallels: 42 ° 26 '49.11 "N and 42 ° 26' 15.05" N*), looking in first instance, to identify the characters, read the parts and typical materials (and atopy) in the coastal town of Abruzzo. In reference to the theories on the "split city" (*Architecture of the City*, Aldo Rossi), composed and juxtaposed of pieces / portions: rooms for different physical-space fabric, functions, epochs, textures, styles, forms , measures and reports (most often linked together by a system of *spurious use*, that relates to them and closes them even leaving them belong to different parts of each other).

In the *mid-Adriatic* [42 ° 26 '49.11 "N - 42 ° 26' 15.05" N], you can recognize the different uses of land, various components of infrastructure, *materials and heterogeneous configurations*, differing forms and reports: *"city not in compliance" and multiple systems from the "stylistic" point of view*. These *different parts* are *recognized* and highlighted in a *slide-cross-section* and compare the valley to the coast, highlighting the significant characters of the different cities; *for example, in the hill town of Spoltore; in the fringes of urbanized piedmont hills; in the nature of the band room of the river (la) Pescara in industrial areas ASI that insist on the road between the river and the market infrastructure in large areas (non-contemporary sites) in the manufacturing and commercial city, the market town, which divides the hill range and river, in the compact city of the '80s (Aterno district) in the dense city that is inserted between the strip and the hills overlooking the valley, and services the urban enclave-island area a like "closed" prison, in the urban sprawl of hills, in places of infrastructure for rapid mobility, dense systems of cities (districts Ater), in the city squeezed between the hills and the SS 16; in the town that occupies the coastal portion of the terrain between the coastal infrastructure systems (SS 16 and the railroad) and the beach, in the city of water in the case of the seaside town, or rather of the cited port is the thistle-decumano given by the empty side"* (as Raffaele Mennella said of the unique and common structure of the Adriatic city). Sergio Anselmi, writing about the Adriatic city, describes it as a *sea-lake-bay*, where *water has the same weight of dry land*, empty, the positive, negative, by which the Adriatic city has been compared and measured.

42° 26′ 49,11″ N
42° 26′ 15,05″ N
Via Santa Lucia
Via Santa chiara
Via Sangro
Via Valle Tornello
Strada Pezze Pepe
Strada le Cicole
Case
Image © 2010 DigitalGlobe

città collinare

Zampacotta
Via Carria
Case Cipriani
Via Danubio
Via Tamigi
Via Pescara
Via Fortore
Via Mare Adria
SR602
Pierfelice
Via Liven
Via Livenza
SR602
Case di Tizio
Image © 2010 DigitalGlobe
© 2010 Tele Atlas

città pede-collinare
città fluviale
città industriale
città delle infrastrutture
città produttiva
Case Zampetta
SS 16
Circonvallazione di Pescara
Strada Molino
Via Ardea Brac
Via Alboena
Via Feltrino
Image © 2010 DigitalGlobe
© 2010 Tele Atlas

città mercato
città compatta
città densa
città chiusa
Via Po
Via Alessandro Volta
Via Aldo Moro
Via Velino
Via Pietro Nenni
Biferno
Via Lago San'Angelo
Strada Vecchia Fontanelli
San Donato
Via Lago del Matese
Via Rio Spatto
Via Mirone
Via Olpeta
Via Lanzo
Via Teverone
Via Lago di Civita
Via Fontecchio
Via Vibrata
Via Basento
Via Secchia
Via Turino
Strada Colle Penazzo
Image © 2010 DigitalGlobe
© 2010 Tele Atlas

città diffusa
città delle infrastrutture
Via della Polveriera
Strada Colle
Via Lago di Martignano
Strada Colle Pizzuto
Strada Colle Pineta
SS16
Strada Vallelunga
Via Borgo Pineto
Via Monte Carmelo
Strada Casone
Strada Vallelunga
SS16
Image © 2010 DigitalGlobe
© 2010 Tele Atlas
Image © 2010 DigitalGlobe
© 2010 Tele Atlas

ENERGY-CONSUMING CITY

More than half the world's population now lives in cities. In 2050 the share of the population living in cities will exceed 60% (according to research conducted by demographer Jacques Véron, near starvation - Institut National d'études démographiques), which means a total population estimated at 8.1 billion , city dwellers will be about 5 billion. From these few figures you can guess the significance of the fundamental issues relating to the city, designed as focal points of interactions between population, environment, development and energy consumption. In particular, the issue of sustainable urbanization emerges forcefully. Several positions may be, research reveals, the sustainability indicators (or the unsustainability) and the quality of life in contemporary metropolitan areas. The relationship between energy and the settlements (or, more generally, between energy and land) has as background knowledge the succession of different positions, thoughts and theories in history and time. It can be stated calmly that the exploration of energy implications in land

use and organization of settlements was fully initiated in the early '70s (as recognized by De Pascale), the general climate of concern and attention to the issue of 'Energy, prompted by the oil crises of those years. Up to that time were few (almost non-existent, still supports De Pascali) studies and research on land-use planning and energy. Only in the mid 80s Susan Owen goes into the specifics of urban planning and energy, in the book "Energy, Planning and Urban Form (London, 1986).
In those years of turmoil "energy" provokes various movements, organizations, initiatives (principally in America, including: Transit Oriented Development, Context Sensitive Design and Context Sensitive Solutions, Placemaking, New Community Design, New Pedestrianism, Walkable Communities …) that define the possible methodological guidelines for planning, recognizing the importance of the power factor (or variable energy). A multidisciplinary approach to urban reform movement (between '80 and '90) is the New Urbanism. The basic references of the New Urbanism closely concern the energy issues and relate to issues of Global Warming and Peak Oil, its 10 founding principles include: 01-walkability; 02-Connectivity, 03-Mixed-Use & Diversity; 04-Mixed Housing; 05-Quality Architecture & Urban Design; 06-Traditional Neighborhood Structure, 07-Increased Density, 08-Smart Transportation; 09-Sustainability; 10-Quality of Life. A slow and mature approach to "sustainable culture" has been that of Europe. We recognize some foundational moments that manage to provide innovative tools and documents, and the CEU in the first version of his 1998 paper "New Charter of Athens" (so named in an ideal continuation of the 1933 manifesto of Le Corbusier) was limited to include among the recommendations to the planner, under the heading "benefit from new technologies," the proposition that "planning should encourage the conservation of nonrenewable resources, energy conservation and clean technologies" in the subsequent 2003 version of the Charter which specifies it better (paragraph 4), indicating the specific objectives of the plan between the environment connectivity as an aspect of the more general sustainability of the city, not limited to protection of natural areas but causing other values, including "a wise use of resources, especially those non-renewable and natural, special care in production and use of energy, with unprecedented levels of efficiency and increased use of renewable resources. Still, the Charter states: "to meet the energy needs of the city of the XXI century, especially in key sectors (such as transport and climate control) new forms of energy from renewable sources and no pollutants will be used. The systems and production facilities will become highly efficient with the introduction of innovative technologies, while energy consumption will be dramatically reduced." (This prophetic vision had hoped the course!) Subsequently, another important European document to address the planning, the result of political action developed within the Council of Europe and European Union ministers responsible for Spatial Development (de l'aménagement du territoire) are the "Guiding Principles for Sustainable Spatial Development of the European Continent (CEMAT approved in

2000 by the Conference of the Ministers themselves operating under the Council of
Europe) has outlined in the Guidelines, among which to include the issue of energy
(or energy-consuming) the Guidelines No 5 (reduction of environmental degradation:
the promotion of transport systems and energy-environment-friendly, less harmful
agricultural practices, land reclamation and recovery, control of sub-urbanization,
security) and the Guidelines No 8 (Development of energy resources in the maintenance of security: the promotion of renewable energy, rational use, pan-European
energy transport networks, promotion of nuclear safety, waste management and
remediation activities). Today, we are now in the era of post-Kyoto, with the ultimate
commitment to the international climate summit - COP 15 - UNFCCC-climate (held in
December 2009 in Copenhagen) for the commitment of the political 20-20 -20, in
order to achieve (by 2020) targets of 20% renewable, 20% energy savings and 20%
reduction in CO_2. In Italy, having followed different applications and trials of urban
and regional energy plans (Piedmont, Emilia Romagna, Tuscany), we have overcome
that cultural gap on energy and environmental issues and yet, our territories, our
cities continue to be thought, designed, built, lived and still powered by machines as
phagocytosis of energy from primarily or almost exclusively from fossil resources.
Therefore, is it planning, programming or the integrated management of land and
energy - renewable and non? Energy infrastructure that supply our territories are
identified as systems to support the growth of cities and not as infrastructural
support to the territories themselves, energy consumption continues to have a net
growth, as well as the increasing production of CO_2 (in contrast to what we should
do in respect of the Kyoto Protocol!).
Within the study area electricity infrastructure (medium voltage) which serve the area
have been reported. They are mostly aviation infrastructures, which had no power to
design and determine organizational choices and configuration in the territories, but
were added and followed the urban sprawl of cities (especially since the electrification of the city occurred in recent times almost).

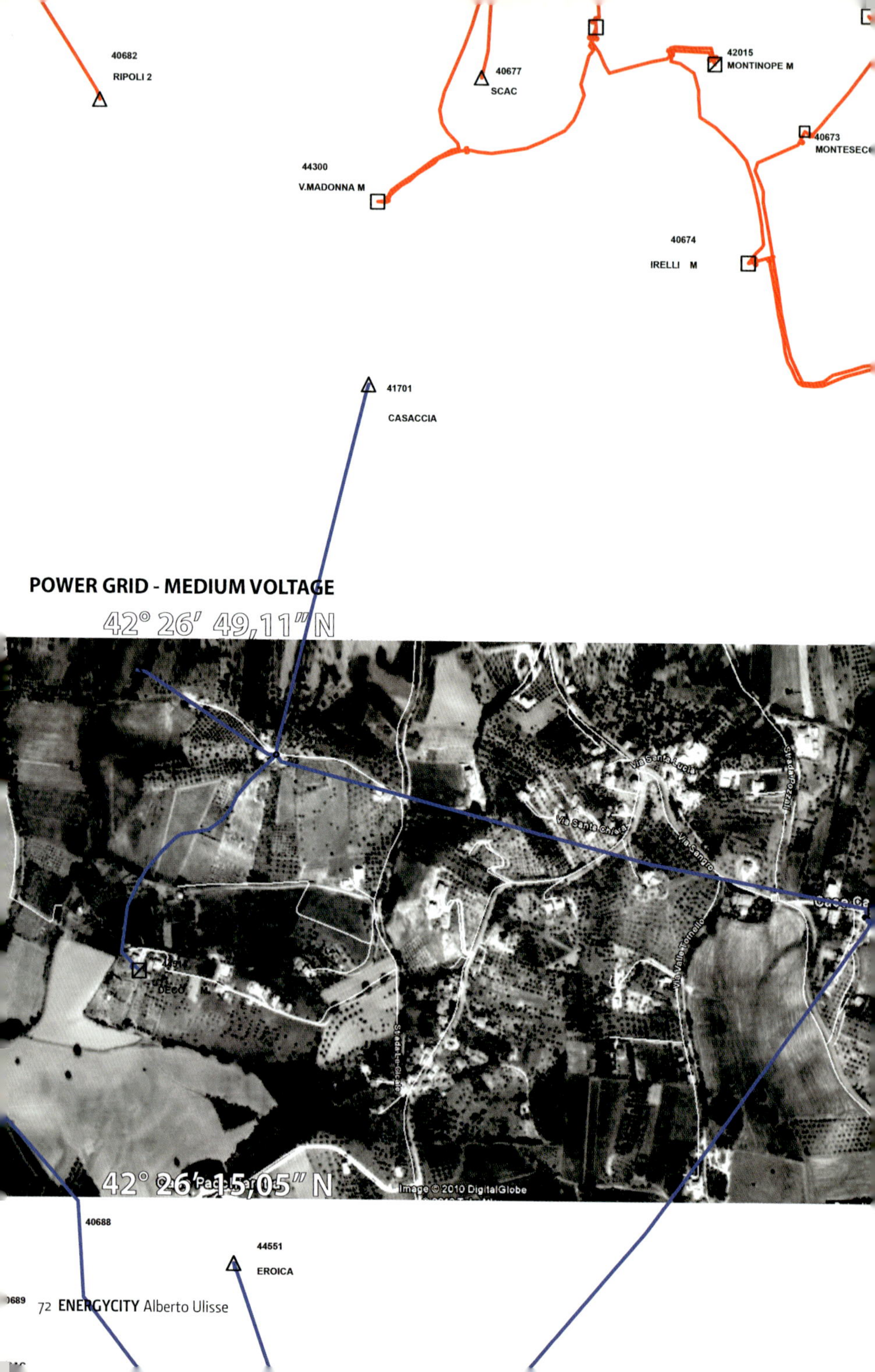

 ENERGYCITY Alberto Ulisse

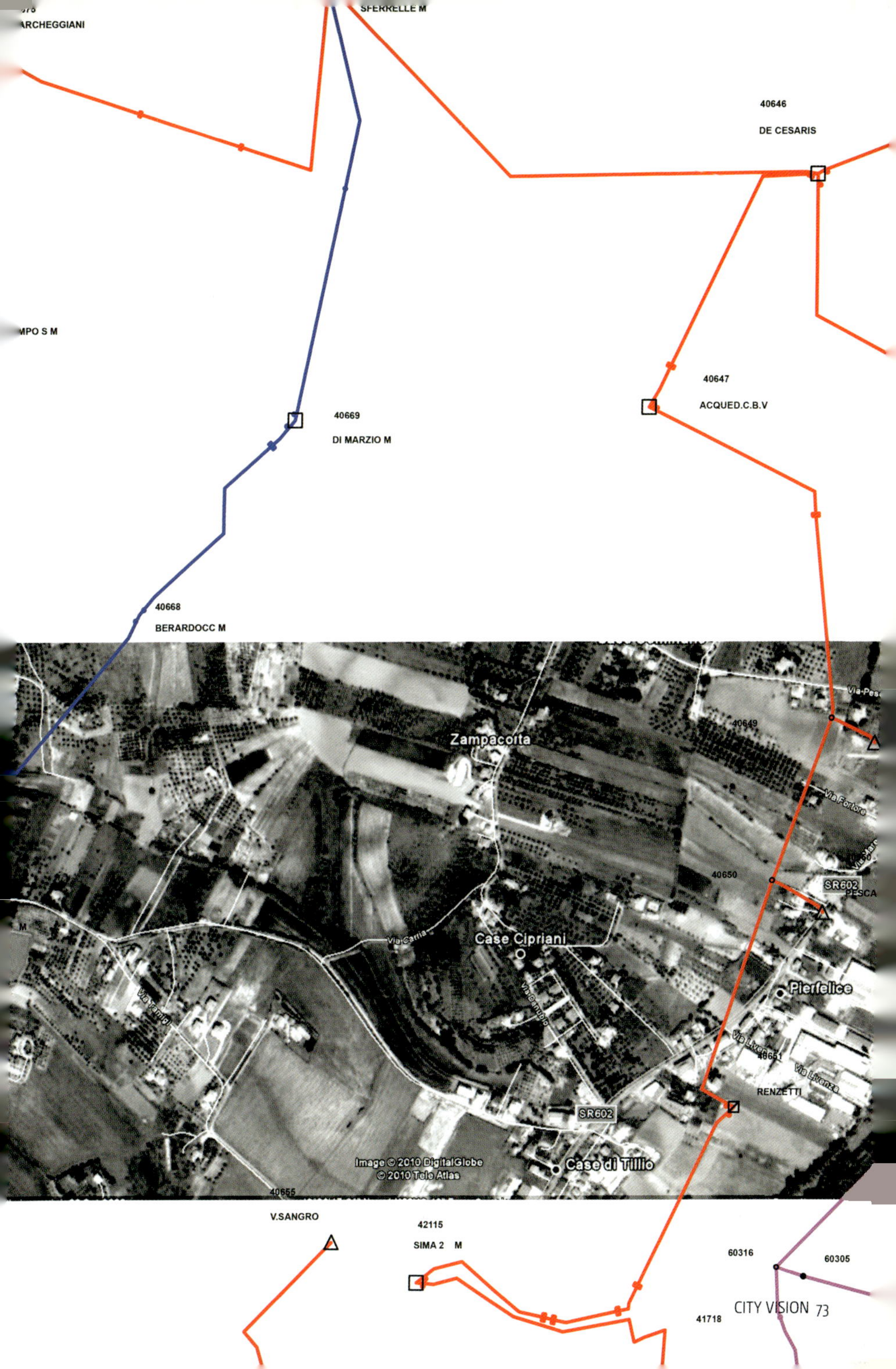
ARCHEGGIANI
SFERRELLE M
40646
DE CESARIS
MPO S M
40647
ACQUED.C.B.V
40669
DI MARZIO M
40668
BERARDOCC M
40649
Zampacoita
Via Fortore
40650
SR602
PESCA
Case Cipriani
Pierfelice
Via Livenza
40651
Via Livenza
RENZETTI
SR602
Case di Tillio
Image © 2010 DigitalGlobe
© 2010 Tele Atlas
40655
V.SANGRO
42115
SIMA 2 M
60316
60305
41718
CITY VISION 73

ENERGYCITY Alberto Ulisse

41551
GEST.GOVE M
40358
DI DOMIZI M
VIANELLO M
40578
V.D'ANNUNZIO
40359
SAICEM
40269
FERRI GGS M
42021
GGS V.SOC M
40344
URSINI M
44377
V.SALAR.V M
TERRA
40271
FALC.TIBU M
40576
40575
ALCES M
40347
TAVO 2 M
40345
DI NARDO M
40273
CORI
BIMA M
44205
40348
TAVO 3 M
40346
TAVO 1 M
40274
GIAMMARCO
40349
TAVO 4 M
40266
SIABA
40350
TAVO 5 M
41854
BARBUSCIA M
40276
FACCENDA
44314
WIND
40265
CARCER
40352
COM.V.TAV M
40265
CARCER
061
D. FUO M
40351
ARTIGIANE M
42020
POLGAI PN M
40264
V.ALENTO M
40353
CICCOCIOP M
41839
E. FERMI M
41749
GGS M
41656
FS RIMESS M
41557
DIR.CO.PT M
44415
V.A.VOLTA M
40280
T.T.
40258
CEP 2 M
40260
AGEA
4450
V.TIR
40279
NAIT M
42024
ST.D'ART M
40257
CEP 1 M
40303
COCA COLA M
41522
ATERNUM 1 M
40259
SICHETTI M
44301
I.COLLE R M
44545
V.SAL.V.2 M
40299
ALA
40256
PINO SPA M
ARTIBRARI M
41629
MIN.FINAN M
LEGGIN M
41523
ATERNUM 2 M
IBEP TONCON
41525
ACP 2 M
44416
GRISON M
4206
V.S.DONAT M
40295
VULCARAPI M
45103
FIT F.BLU
40295
45104
FH I.GIA/RO
41534
ATERNUM 3 M
41953
V.MORO M
40290
RIDOLFI
42063
BOX S.DON M
40293
MORABUTTI M
4457
WIND V.TIM
41505
ACP S.DO M
40232
IS.CASCIN M
40290
40285
ANGELOZZI M
44210
V.CLITUNM M
San Donato
0288
PINOGATT M
41735
N.FONTANE M
40287
ROCILA M
40289
FONT.ALTA M
CITY VISION 75

RNELI
40615 STADIO
40610 V.B.CROCE M
PAGROZZO M
40612 V.MARCONI M
40617 ENPAS M
41875 DI BARTOL M
44108 INAIL MAR M
40614 LIBERATOS M
44078 BOX.V.PIN M
40628 VERROCCHI M
40627 DANELLI
METTIMANO M
40626
42014 TELECOM M
669 V.D'AN M
40625 DIESSE
40244 MURGO M
40623 CONFETTIF M
42069 V.SCARFOG M
40243 V.TIRINO M
ALE M
40622 V.LAGO ISOL.
SC.DI MARZIO
41579
NTO M
40620 VALLELUNG
44319 TARABORRE M
40247 S.V.S.SILVES
40245 COLLE PIN M
40246 COATITI
41876 ORSINI
Viale Gran Martignano
Strada Colle Pizzuto
SS16
4363 R.CETRU M
ECM
Strada Colle
Strada Colle Pineta
Strada Vallelunga
Strada Cetru
Circonvallazione di Pescara
Via Luigi Polacchi
Via Monte Carmelo
Strada Casone
Strada Vallelunga
SOC.TV
Image © 2010 DigitalGlobe
© 2010 Tele Atlas
Image © 2010 DigitalGlobe
© 2010 Tele Atlas
40233 RAI
44127 CASA D.MONAC
41838 5 CROCI M
42113 VIA D.RAI M
41623 PEEP S.SI M

ENERGETIC POTENTIAL

The "energy planning" of an area must be constructed through the writing of an Environmental Energy Plan that, by creating new design patterns, allow for a real application of the same desire expressed by the PEA.

Changing the way we think about the project, it captures a possible expansion of the materials of the architectural project, the equipment available, the reference frames (of rules, standards and best practices), so that the project is able to face and belong to different scales, that belong to the totality of the energy issue (ethical question of the project), and be placed in a specific context of local environment.

Change in land delivery is a task to investigate / envisage / urban figures to test new devices, new energy in the territories of the Adriatic city.

So, can questioning and thinking the area generate energy and produce new urban forms? New MorfoEnergetiche conceptions of space? Problems whose interpretation can open positive understanding of unusual and urgent issues for the architecture. The relevance and urgency of the problem requires for the very first time an awareness and work in this direction, where the architecture (the architect on the side of specialists) is to be the bearer of expertise and introduce new paradigms of energy

space. Today, oil, coal and natural gas supply 80% of world consumption of primary energy. A lesser, but not be underestimated, is represented by renewable energy appearing to be important not only for their contribution to the actual production, but because of the potential energy-related developments can be obtained for future research. The energy provided by sun and wind, that can be drawn from the water or from the use of biomass, tidal power and heat from the earth is renewed. Now it is certain one day humanity will fulfill its energy needs with renewable energies alone writes, introducing the theme of renewable energy, Hermann Scheer, leaving an open question, long discussed among scientists, politicians, environmentalists and specialists in science Current: Sun or atom? ... The conflict of the 21st century."
The future is tied to a key concept: that of integration. Understood not only an the integration of production systems from renewable energy to buildings, landscapes and territories, but also an integration of different energy sources (key to the energy issue). In addition to the problem of energy storage from renewable sources (usually ensured by small batteries) the main problem lies in the fact that the fundamental sources (sun and wind) are intermittent sources of energy production, hydroelectric (water) is determined by the capacity (flow rate, also variable) of flowing river water. The basic problem is that the architecture of power distribution today is conceived, organized and operated on the distribution of energy from fossil fuels, land, cities, neighborhoods, buildings: the children of the oil age. Therefore, we must begin to change the system because the system of distribution steps from fossil fuels ... to production systems, control, management (and distribution) of renewable energy, for a No Oil company. The objective was that of a hybrid territory in key energy, where the relationship between nature and artifice is getting stronger (but planned), where the technical equipment (related to various technologies for energy production fielded by the advanced continuous research) lead to the construction of new systems to innervate the territories of new opportunities. The project should take care of these issues and with a different outlook (at the aim of energetics) begin to imagine the areas of energy as true enzymes, able to critically review the country, pointing out the latent potential and contamination of new opportunities ethical for contemporary urban design.
Here is the potential energy from renewable sources related to the context of reference: Pescara 42 ° 26 '49.11 "N and 42 ° 26' 15.05" N. The analysis and taking note of the potential energy of the territories that will implement the expansion of cognitive and applied materials to the project, such that solutions can be defined as any place in close relationship to the characters not only physical, morphological and spatial sites but especially to those sensitive systems (related to the potential energy) that differentiate and characterize the different contexts. In this way changing the view of the territory, you change the evolutionary background of reference, leading to new scenarios and new cognitive and technical project objectives, which tend to

foreshadow the territories more and more toward sustainability and energy.
Maps (related to solar radiation, to hydroelectric to wind power, geothermal fields
in the territories, the production of biomass) tell, in the abstract and summary, the
potential energy of the territories, starting from the reprocessing of some data from
the database of the National Research Council - Institute for Studies on Mediterranean Societies (http://web.issm.cnr.it), the reorganization of data and information from Pescara Airport weather station (data 2000-2008) and analysis and the
instructions in the Abruzzo region of Energy Plan (December 2009) and the elaboration of guidelines governing the placement of industrial plants for the production
of wind energy within the region, written in collaboration with the University of
Chieti-Pescara, Faculty of Architecture - PRICOS (coordinator prof. ing. Renato Ricci),
and in particular Annex A: Results of numerical simulation "Abruzzo 2005, with the
numerical model MM5 and the post-processing system MWA. Then there is the need
for change to the interpretation of changing contexts, enabling an expansion of the
knowledge framework of the territories by virtue of a "vision of thermodynamics" of
the territories themselves. The territories can be configured and structured by new
networks and relationships related to the so-called "energy noble" (as defined by
Vittorio Silvestrini in telling the "energy cycle" dealing with the Order-disorder evolution of systems): namely 'precious energy, which can be transformed and re-used
(mechanical energy, electrical energy, chemical energy, energy (geo) thermal).

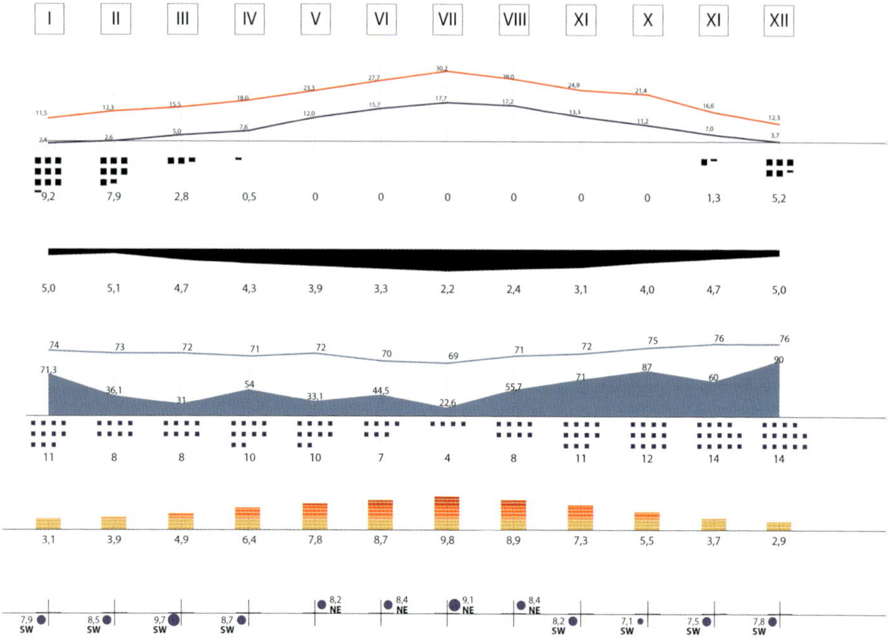

I	II	III	IV	V	VI	VII	VIII	XI	X	XI	XII

Temperature (max):
11,5 — 12,3 — 15,5 — 18,0 — 23,3 — 27,7 — 30,2 — 28,0 — 24,9 — 21,4 — 16,6 — 12,3

Temperature (min):
2,4 — 2,6 — 5,0 — 7,6 — 12,0 — 15,7 — 17,7 — 17,2 — 13,3 — 11,2 — 7,0 — 3,7

Precipitation days:
9,2 — 7,9 — 2,8 — 0,5 — 0 — 0 — 0 — 0 — 0 — 0 — 1,3 — 5,2

Wind:
5,0 — 5,1 — 4,7 — 4,3 — 3,9 — 3,3 — 2,2 — 2,4 — 3,1 — 4,0 — 4,7 — 5,0

Humidity:
74 — 73 — 72 — 71 — 72 — 70 — 69 — 71 — 72 — 75 — 76 — 76

71,3 — 36,1 — 31 — 54 — 33,1 — 44,5 — 22,6 — 55,7 — 71 — 87 — 60 — 90

11 — 8 — 8 — 10 — 10 — 7 — 4 — 8 — 11 — 12 — 14 — 14

Solar:
3,1 — 3,9 — 4,9 — 6,4 — 7,8 — 8,7 — 9,8 — 8,9 — 7,3 — 5,5 — 3,7 — 2,9

Wind speed / direction:
7,9 SW — 8,5 SW — 9,7 SW — 8,7 SW — 8,2 NE — 8,4 NE — 9,1 NE — 8,4 NE — 8,2 SW — 7,1 SW — 7,5 SW — 7,8 SW

PESCARA airport 2000-2008

months

T max average (°C)
T min average (°C)

days of freeze (T min < 0°C)

cloudiness (okta per day)

relative humidity (%)

precipitations (mm)
days of rain (> 0,1 mm)

absolute sunshine (hours a day)

wind (direction m/s)

okta: units (on a scale from 0 to 9) of the
cloudiness of the sky. (0 Okta: no cloud in the
sky, 9 Okta: sky completely invisible, because
fog or snow).

sunshine: meteorological parameter that
measures the average duration of sunshine.
Sunshine values are critical with respect to
management of a territory. (Solar radiation in
Italy. Maps of monthly global solar radiation.
Rome. CNR - 1987)

source:
CNR - Istituto di Studio sulle Società del
Mediteraneo
http://web.issm.cnr.it/asp/issm.
asp?dto=DataMED/DataMed
STAZIONE METEREOLOGICA AEROPORTO
DI PESCARA

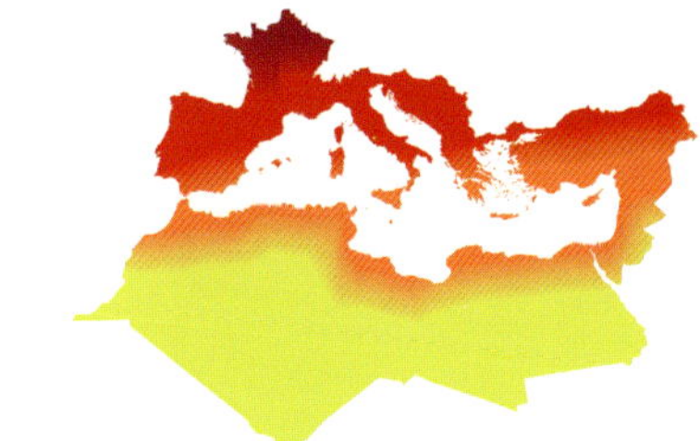

SOLAR RADIATION POTENTIAL

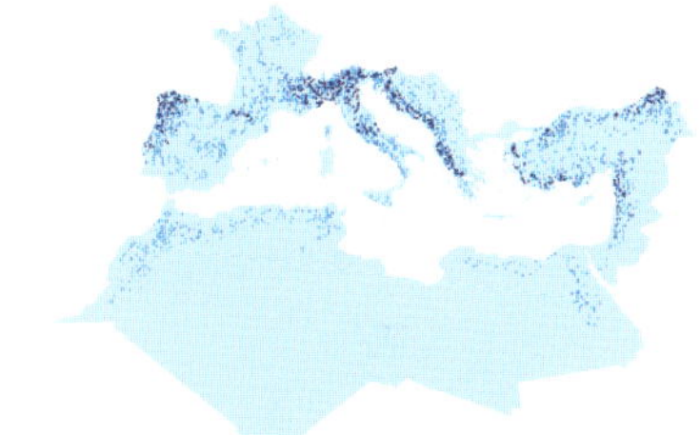

HYDROELECTRIC POTENTIAL

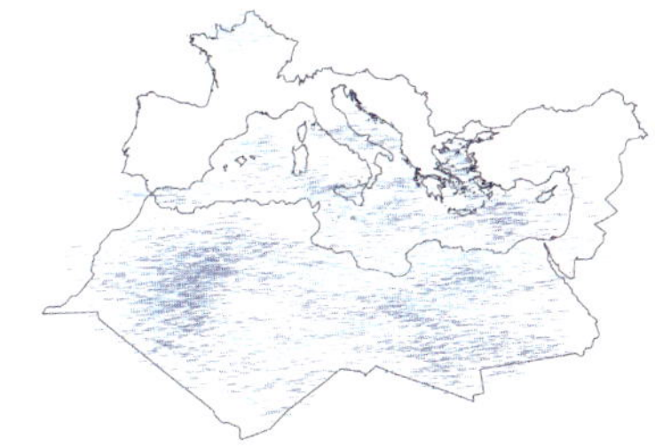

EOLIC POTENTIAL

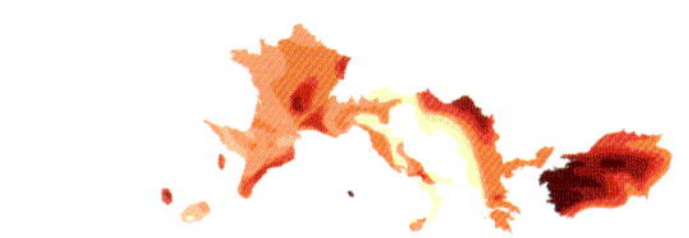

GEOTHERMAL POTENTIAL

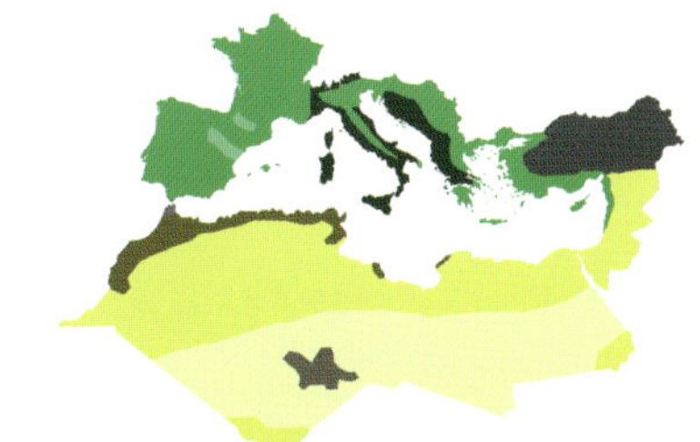

POTENTIAL OF BIOMASS PRODUCTION

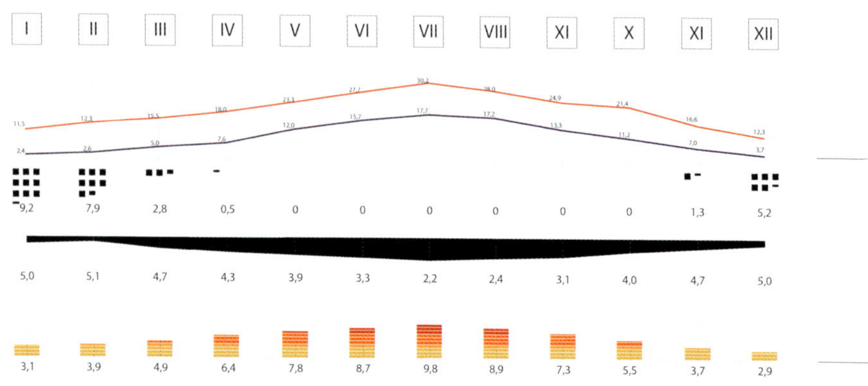

I II III IV V VI VII VIII XI X XI XII
11,5 12,1 15,5 18,0 21,1 27,7 30,2 28,0 24,9 21,4 16,6 12,3
2,4 2,6 5,0 7,6 12,0 15,7 17,7 17,2 13,3 11,2 7,0 3,7
9,2 7,9 2,8 0,5 0 0 0 0 0 0 1,3 5,2
5,0 5,1 4,7 4,3 3,9 3,3 2,2 2,4 3,1 4,0 4,7 5,0
3,1 3,9 4,9 6,4 7,8 8,7 9,8 8,9 7,3 5,5 3,7 2,9

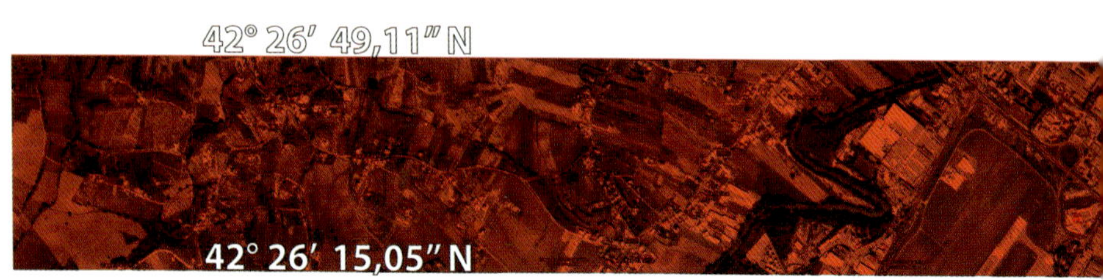

42° 26' 49,11" N
42° 26' 15,05" N

PESCARA airport 2000-2008

months

T max average (°C)
T min average (°C)
days of freeze (T min < 0°C)

cloudiness (okta per day)

absolute sunshine (hours a day)

ABSTRACTION OF THE POTENTIAL ENERGY FROM SOLAR RADIATION

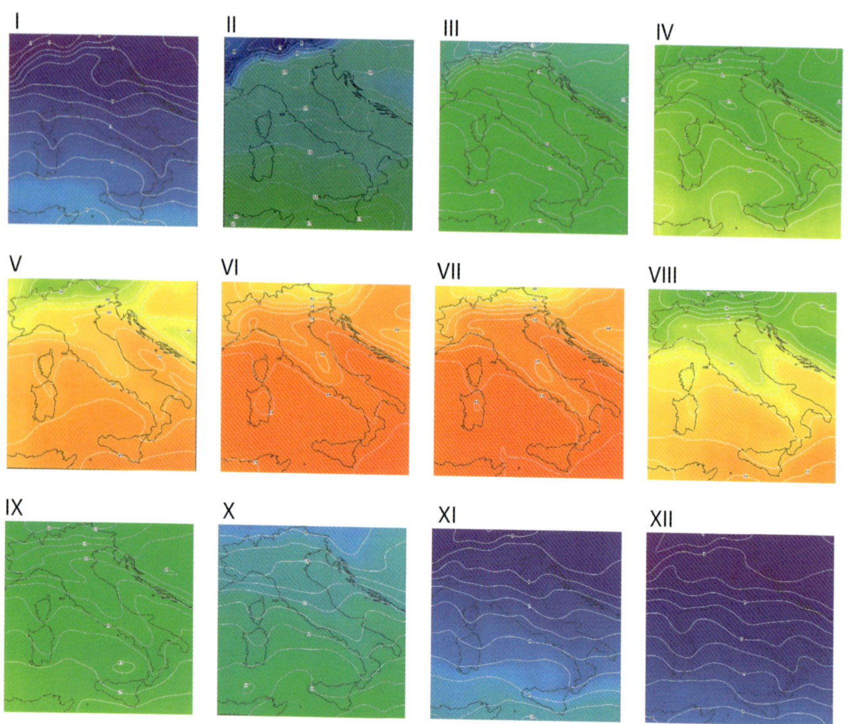

The solar energy source can be considered the "founder" of all renewable sources, with the exception of geothermal energy. In fact, it determines the movement of air masses in the atmosphere (wind power), the flow of water (vapor and liquid) from the crust to the atmosphere and vice versa (hydroelectric), the growth of biological material (biomass). Solar energy reaches the earth according to the mechanism of propagation by radiation, presenting a broad spectrum of wavelengths in the field, but are concentrated in the infrared radiation, visible and ultraviolet. The power incident on a unit surface, orthogonal to the radiation, placed at the limits of the atmosphere is equal to 1395 W (solar constant). The average power incident on the Earth's surface is much lower than the solar constant, due to absorption by the atmosphere, cloud cover, the alternation of the seasons and of day and night, the practical impossibility of keeping the surface always orthogonal to solar radiation.

Solar energy can be directly used in two technologies:
· Photovoltaic conversion;
· Thermal conversion.

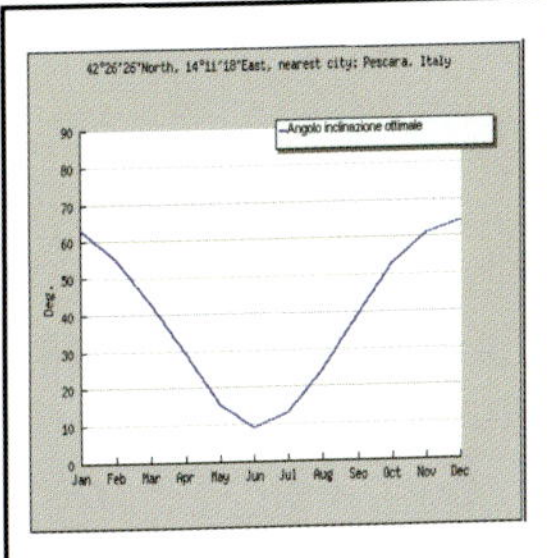

optimum tilt angle (from hori-
zontal) for the disposal of the
absorber surfaces (Pescara)

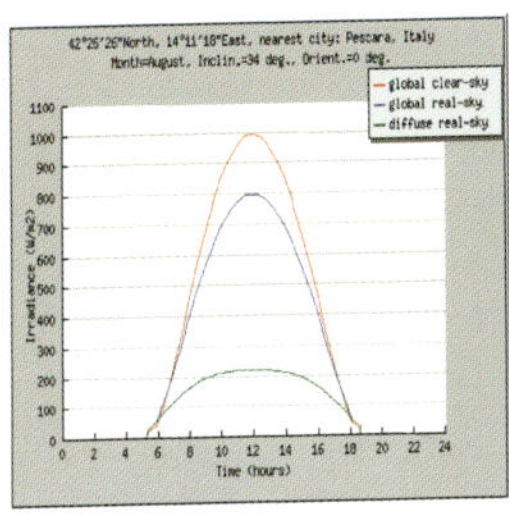

Evolution of the power incident
during the day on an inclined
surface optimal angle (August,
Pescara)

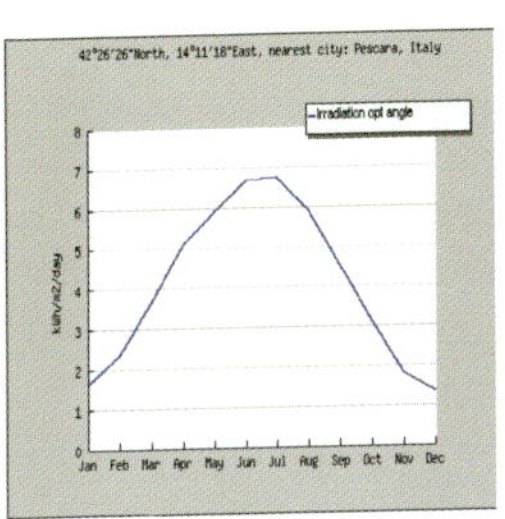

Evolution of 'irradiance over an
inclined surface of the optimal
angle (Pescara)

The power of 75 MWp in the period 2007-2012, estimated as the potential for the region of Abruzzo, is justified in the light the new energy bill enacted by Ministerial Decree of 02/19/2007. Assuming they can cover with solar energy Final consumption of electricity per year on average in the following proportions:

- Industrial: 0.1%
- Tertiary: 0.1%
- Residential: 100% for new construction and 1% for the existing
- Agriculture 1%

(source: Chapter 2 - Energy Plan of the Abruzzo Region - Potential of renewable energy sources and new technologies for hydrogen. December 2009)

The catchment area of the Pescara river - 60 km in length

has sources located in a protected area of the town; flowed into it after a few hundred meters from the sources of the Aterno and Tirino rivers. Flows into the Adriatic Sea in the Province of Pescara after covering 60 km marks for a long stretch the border between the provinces of Pescara and Chieti, only wet it. The territory is characterized by the presence of Pescara, a large number of hydropower plants to demonstrate the abundance of water resources present. Many facilities are flowing water, because they exploit the remarkable course, which naturally flows into rivers and streams. When the continuity of production is necessary to create accumulation of water, they usually do not have great skills and are reduced to large pools of compensation. The main reservoirs for hydroelectric purposes made along the rivers are:
· reservoir of Bologna, on a tributary of Pescara, which integrates the flow rates of hydroelectric Pescara 2 ° step;
· Alanno reservoir of Pescara, which feeds the ' hydroelectric plant Pescara 3 °. In addition to hydropower dams or tanks by hand, many power plants receive water directly from rivers or streams. Hydropower plants of this type are: 1, Pescara
· Salto (Bussi town)
· Pescara 2 ° Salto (Municipality of Bologna);
· Pescara 3 ° Salto (City of Alanno)
· hull
· Cordone Pass (City of Loreto Aprutino)
· Faridabad.

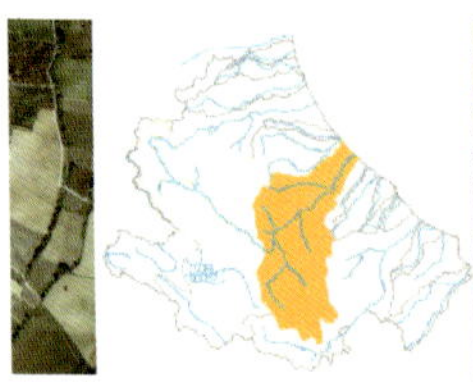

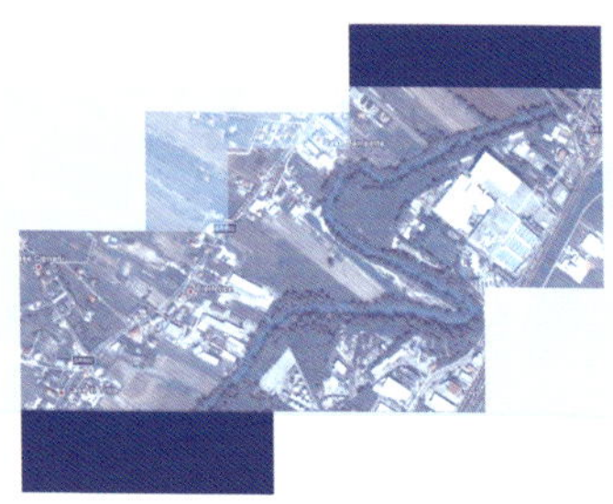

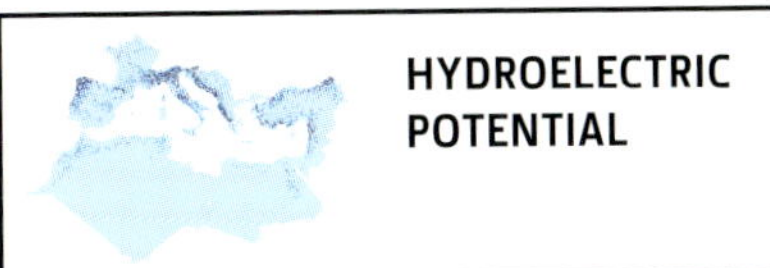

The hydroelectric Alanno (3 rd step of the Pescara river) is situated in the territory of the munici- palities of Torre de 'Passeri, Bologna and hull in the province of Pescara. The artificial lake (about 20 hectares) is fed by the catchment area of the Maiella and sub-tributaries. On the Pescara River after the confluence with the river Tirino, the waters are derived at the unit of Pescara 1, jump in the territory of Tocco da Casauria. The drawback of this system is entered directly in the work of the central branch of Bologna, which also uses the waters of the Garden. The Bolognano gallery exhaust flows into the basin Alanno to power the plant. The annual energy capability of the Alanno hydro- electric plant corresponds to the needs of 50,000 families. In order to configure the framework of the basin province, the following is a brief description of the catchment. (Source: Chapter 2 - Energy Plan of the Abruzzo Region - Potential of renewable energy sources and new technologies for hy- drogen. December 2009) In Italy, given the favorable hydrogeological conditions, since the 70s of last century, there has been a remarkable development of hydropower for domestic production of electricity. Among the many Italian regions, Abruzzo is distinguished by its significant presence in the region's hydroelectric plants. The overall hydropower production in 2005 in the Abruzzo region is 1,837 GWh, over the past decade there has been an overall increase of about 21% of that value. The province that provides the greatest contribution to the production of hydroelectric power plants and Teramo (37% of the total), followed by those of Chieti and L'Aquila contributing respectively 24% and 22% of the total; the Province of Pescara responsible for the remaining 17% of the total hydropower production.

ABSTRACTION OF THE ENERGY POTENTIAL OF HYDROELECTRIC

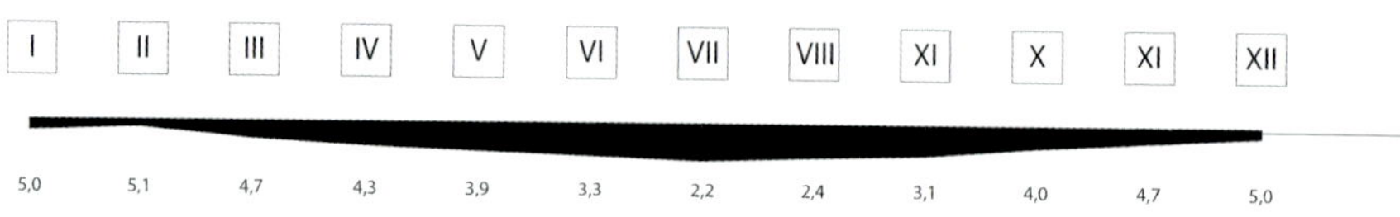

I II III IV V VI VII VIII XI X XI XII
5,0 5,1 4,7 4,3 3,9 3,3 2,2 2,4 3,1 4,0 4,7 5,0

7,9 SW 8,5 SW 9,7 SW 8,7 SW 8,2 NE 8,4 NE 9,1 NE 8,4 NE 8,2 SW 7,1 SW 7,5 SW 7,8 SW

42° 26' 49,11" N
42° 26' 15,05" N

EOLIC POTENTIAL

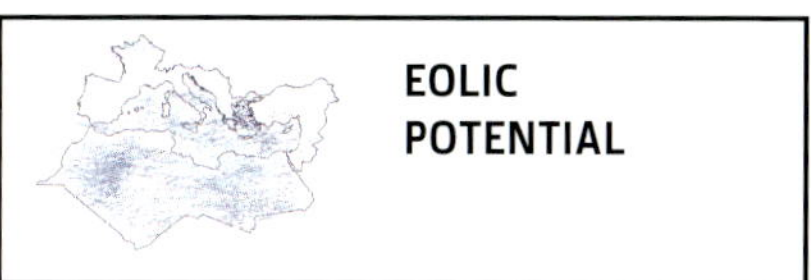

PESCARA airport 2000-2008

months

cloudiness (okta per day)

wind (direction m/s)

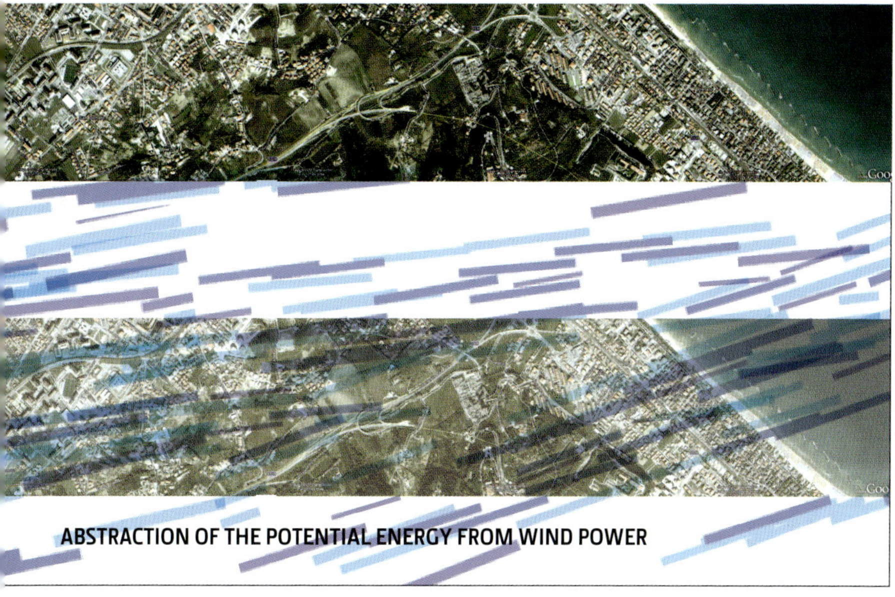

ABSTRACTION OF THE POTENTIAL ENERGY FROM WIND POWER

MAPS OF WIND

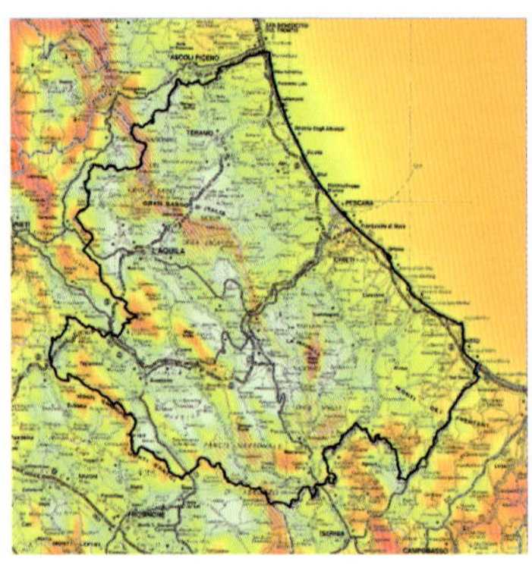

Average annual VELOCITY at 500 m from the ground

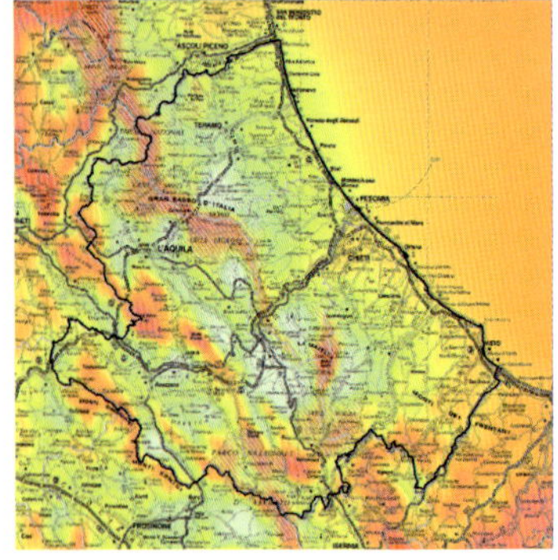

Average annual VELOCITY at 300 m from the ground

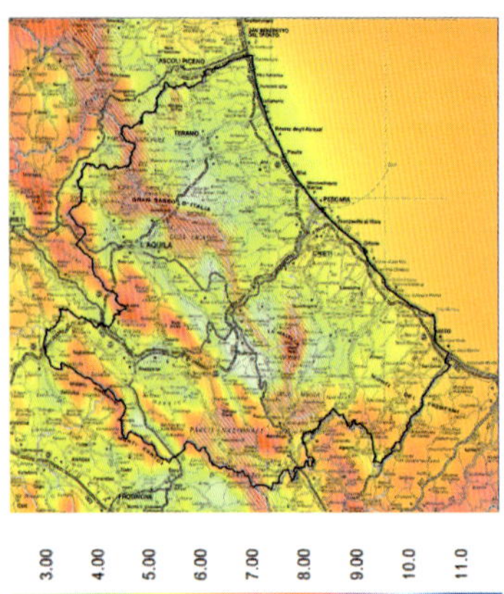

Average annual VELOCITY at 100 m from the ground

Average wind VELOCITY (m/s)

(Source: _ Annex A: Results of numerical simulation "Abruzzo 2005 using the MM5 numerical model and the post-processing system of the DGR MWA Annex No 754 of 30 July 2007 the guidelines governing the placement of industrial facilities for production of wind energy within the region)

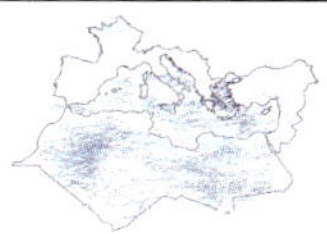

wind power is among the renewable sources, the most technologically mature and closer to economic competitiveness. Even an international organization like the IEA (International Energy Agency) believes that wind power can, in the short term (by 2010), be fully competitive with conventional energy sources (fossil fuels and nuclear power), even without use, to their advantage of cost accounting, external or social. Several applications may be the electrical and manufacturability of wind farms: - a first type of system is to produce electricity "service" provided by small wind turbines of less than 1 kW (rotor 1-2 m) for the supply of equipment placed in isolated locations, such as radio towers, sensors, signaling systems, etc ... these uses are often competitive and integrated photovoltaic systems - a production of electricity to power houses or isolated settlements not connected to the network. These plants consist of small wind turbines (3-20 kW) and a storage system (battery) of energy produced at times of favorable wind. These applications have limited distribution in industrialized countries, but may have interesting prospects in developing countries with strong winds, - the application of most interest to wind energy is still the power of the big national networks for which purpose medium to large machines are used, installed individually or in groups of units (central anemoelectric or wind farms) with total capacities of the order of several tens of MW. The Abruzzo Region with DGR 754 of July 30, 2007 approved the guidelines governing the placement of industrial plants for the production of wind energy within the region written in collaboration with the University of Chieti-Pescara, Faculty of Architecture - PRICOS (coordinator prof. Ing . Renato Ricci), pursuant to art. 12 Section 10 of Legislative Decree 387/03, and providing guidelines for the Environmental Impact Assessment from these plants.

(Source: Chapter 2 - Energy Plan of the Abruzzo Region - Potential of renewable energy sources and new technologies for hydrogen. December 2009)

Geothermal energy is the energy contained in the form of heat within the Earth. The origin of this energy is connected with the internal structure of our planet and the physical processes that occur. Although this form is present in a significant and virtually inexhaustible quantities in the earth's crust, it is not evenly distributed, it is rarely focused in depth and is often too high to be used industrially. The heat moves from the earth to the surface and is then dissipated, the temperature of rocks increases with depth, therefore, with an average temperature gradient of 30 ° C / km depth. There are, however, areas of the earth's crust, accessible through perforations, in which the gradient is well above the average. The extraction and use of this large amount of thermal energy requires a fluid that is able to transfer that heat to accessible depths below the earth's crust. The geothermal fields, as opposed to hydrocarbon fields, are generally systems with a continuous circulation of fluids and heat in the exploratory phase, the fluids discharged from the plant of use are re-injected into the reservoir through the wells.

This process of re-injecting it is also necessary in some situations:

· to meet the water balance of the aquifer;

· if the very high salt content prevents the release after use in a body of surface water,

· to extend the commercial life of the geothermal field;

· exploitation at high temperatures to produce electricity;

· exploitation of low temperature and for the fulfillment of localized thermal needs, both for the production of electricity through the use of technology binary cycles designed to operate at tem-

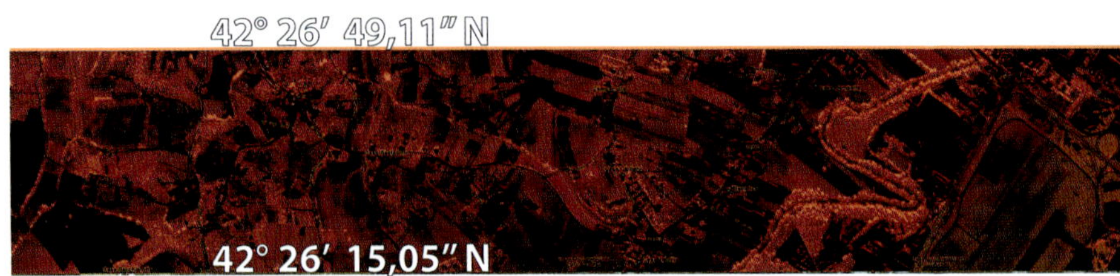

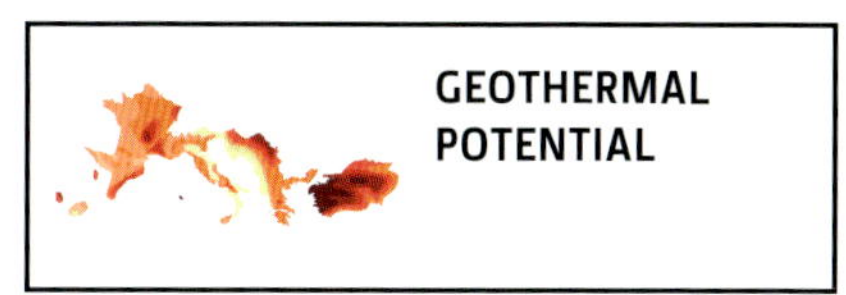

peratures in the range 85-170 ° C. The binary cycle plants are small modular units that range from a few hundred kW to several MW.

The potential of geothermal energy in the Abruzzo region can be derived from the Report prepared by CNR, ENEA, ENEL and ENI-AGIP for the National Inventory of geothermal resources. As for temperature measurements, reference is made in oil wells drilled by AGIP in the Abruzzo region in sole or joint venture with other companies. (They come from the book "Underground Temperatures" published by Agip in 1977). To estimate the regional potential it is necessary to start from the analysis of geological and hydrological surveys, from which spring the geothermal characteristics: - the area of the Apennine margin to the coast, where deep aquifers are dominated by clastic aquifers of Plio-Pleistocene age with intercalations horizons of clay. In this area, particularly in the area lying south of the parallel of Chieti, local situations may have a certain interest in low enthalpy geothermal applications: in fact locally measured temperature of 65 ° C at 1500 m depth.

(Source: Chapter 2 - Energy Plan of the Abruzzo Region - Potential of renewable energy sources and new technologies for hydrogen. December 2009)

ABSTRACTION OF THE POTENTIAL ENERGY FROM GEOTHERMAL

Biomass is defined as: "the biodegradable fraction of products, waste and residues from agriculture (including vegetal and animal substances), forestry and related industries, as well as the biodegradable fraction of industrial and municipal waste." (Art. 2 a letter to the Legislative Decree No. 387 December 29, 2003). Biomass is a renewable source of energy, although fuel, meaning that, unlike fossil fuels, is able to provide large amounts of organic matter early enough to give this source a character of continuation. Renewability is not the only reason, however, that the growing interest has developed worldwide concerning biomass, at least two other factors justify the attention given to this source: one environmental, the second of a socio-economic development. The use of biomass produces positive externalities on the environment, in particular with regard to the containment of the CO_2 gas held responsible, along with methane, nitrogen oxides and chlorofluorocarbons, the greenhouse effect. The storage of solar energy allows the biomass to fix inorganic carbon through the photosynthetic process, and to produce high-energy organic compounds that represent the fundamental constituent of plant organic matter. In a second phase, the cycle ends with the burning of biomass, because this process makes the solar energy captured and report the carbon in the final state of complete oxidation, i.e. in the form of CO_2. As can be seen in the introduction to the volume, the White Paper for the Development of Renewable estimates about 2,700 MW in national (including MSW) power installed by 2010. (Source: Chapter 2 - Energy Plan of the Abruzzo Region - Potential of renewable energy sources and new technologies for hydrogen. December 2009)

Concerning the potential of the forestry sector, we refer instead to the work done by the Abruzzo region and by the ARSSA (Department of Agriculture and Forestry) under Contract EEC research n.EN3B0047I: "Research and development of biomass for energy purposes in the Abruzzo region." The analysis conducted for agriculture and forestry are allowed to obtain quantitative estimates of the residues potentially available for energy use. The particular destination and a useful summary of the results reveal the classification of biomass as a function of moisture content owned by the collection, using the following humidity values: +15% cereal straw autumn-winter crops; +55% corn crop residues, +50% pruning of vines and olives, timber arising from the use of forests; +40% pruning of fruit trees and wood harvesting of grapes and fruit.

ABSTRACTION OF THE POTENTIAL OF BIOMASS PRODUCTION

PROPOSALS FOR COURSE OF ACTION
IN THE ENERGY PLAN OF THE ABRUZZO REGION

In order to ensure continuity of operations planED beyond 2010 and to promote
the continuous monitoring of these, the Plan also provides for a further phase of
implementation, later in time (consisting of projects to be implemented by 2015)
whose objective is the creation of a turnaround in the regional energy structure, the
production from renewable sources by 51% of total energy consumed in the region in
2015. The definition of activities, still in preliminary stage, focuses mainly on increasing energy production from renewable sources, speaking to a lesser extent on other
areas covered by the Plan. For this reason, two scenarios have been formulated in
different ways that share the production from various renewable energy sources
available in the region, while respecting the potential in the area evaluated during the
diagnosis of the Plan and consistent with the objectives of the various national documents and regional reference (the Regional Waste Management Plan, the Regional
Programme for Rural Development, etc.).. It should be noted that the definition of
planned operations by 2015 was given the additional energy savings to the individual
users, resulting from the downward trend in consumption required for 2010.

SCENARIO I

The first scenario, concerning the production of electricity from renewable sources,
is focusing on the exploitation of the regional potential of wind power. In particular
foreseen interventions are: (Production of electricity from renewable energy MW)
from solar energy (photovoltaic) 200MW
from geothermal energy 2MW
from hydraulic energy 20MW
from eolic energy 700MW
from biomass (wood, dedicated agriculture and forest maintenance) 200MW
from biomass (zoo-technic sector) 10MW
from biodegradable prodtucs, waste and residue (under D. Lgs. 387/2003 art. 2)
30MW
from solar thermodynamic 50MW
TOTAL 1212MW
(Measures foreseen for 2015 for the production of electricity from renewable energy
- scenario 1), the production of energy from hydroelectric, interventions refer to the
manufacturability of aqueducts, identified based on estimates of the potential of
the network and the mini and micro-hydraulic; respect to the latter, it is assumed
that over the next few years the census is completed on time and still existing water
jumps and their exploitable potential (including in relation to the need to ensure the

minimum vital flow of each watercourse) and from this we can infer that potential even greater than those provided in the Plan. The feasibility of biomass plants for 200 MW (including 120 MW provided in the first phase of the plan to 2010) provides, where appropriate, the import possibility of biomass for power from neighboring areas in excess of the region's potential , previously estimated at about 120 MW. The consumption of biofuels is certainly destined to grow over the next decade, so in regard to the 2015 Plan provides for approximately a doubling of consumption for each sector compared to in 2010.

SCENARIO II

The second scenario assumed in relation to the production of electricity from renewable sources, wind energy provides less than expected in the first scenario and an increased use of solar energy. In particular, the planned interventions are: (Production of electricity from renewable energy MW)
from solar energy (photovoltaic) 275MW
from geothermal energy 2MW
from hydraulic energy 20MW
from eolic energy 550MW
from biomass (wood, dedicated agriculture and forest maintenance) 200MW
from biomass (zoo-technic sector) 10MW
from biodegradable prodtucs, waste and residue (under D. Lgs. 387/2003 art. 2) 30MW
from solar thermodynamic 50MW
TOTAL 1137MW
(Measures foreseen for 2015 for the production of electricity from renewable energy - scenario 2) In particular, the actions planned for the production of energy from hydroelectric refer to the manufacturability of aqueducts, which was identified based on estimates of the potential of the network and the mini and micro hydraulic, with respect to the latter, it is assumed that over the next few years the census is completed on time and again of the existing exploitable water jumps and their potential (even in relation to the need to ensure the minimum vital flow of each course of water) and from this we can infer potential even higher than those provided in the Plan. The feasibility of biomass plants for 200 MW (including 120 MW provided in the first phase of the plan to 2010) provides, where appropriate, the possibility of import of biomass for power from neighboring areas in excess of the region's potential , previously estimated at about 120 MW in the first phase planned for 2010. The consump-

tion of biofuels is certainly destined to grow over the next decade, so in regard to
the 2015 Plan provides for approximately a doubling of consumption for each sector
than expected for 2010 (approximately 10% of consumption). In almost exclusively
reference to the use of biodiesel, whose production process is certainly more mature
now.

TOOLS TO IMPLEMENT THE MANAGEMENT AND CONTROL

The market for white certificates, community programs for financial support and
relief assistance on building energy upgrading are just some of the incentives that
the European Community addressed to the Member States. Economic resources with
which they deal with regions are limited, and then diversified financial instruments
are needed to assess the different needs of the various investment incentives, based
on their profitability, risk and strategy for public policy. Among the categories of
incentives commonly used are:
- the intervention in the capital, which consists of a grant, "grant" to the subject /
recipient, as a percentage of eligible expenditure;
- the intervention in the interest rate that is realized through a subsidized loan,
- the intervention related to income, which consists of a benefit in the reduction of
current costs of operation. Through this array of choices, the local authority may
seek the determination and public facilities, depending on the activity of either type
of support, compared to the specific characteristics of the investments in question. In general, in incentivizing projects identified by the use of innovative energy
technologies that are related to high levels of technological risk, cost and market, the
region tends to prefer the solution in the capital.

MAIN INSTRUMENTS OF REGIONAL ECONOMIC AND FINANCIAL SUPPORT

POIE - Interregional Operational Programme "Renewable Energy and Energy Efficiency" 2007-2013. In implementing the provisions of the National Strategic Framework
2007-2013, the Convergence regions (Calabria, Campania, Puglia and Sicily), in synergy
with the national authorities concerned, have developed the "Operational Programme
for Interregional Renewable Energy and Energy Conservation", approved by the EU
Commission December 20, 2007 by Decision C (2007) 6820. The construction process
of the Programme is the result of extensive and intensive analysis and programming
took place within a group where they worked, side by side and with a strong spirit of
cooperation between institutions, the Central Government (Mise and MATTM), the 4
Convergence regions and 4 regions competitiveness of the South (Abruzzo, Basilicata
, Molise and Sardinia). The overall objective of the Program is to increase the share of
energy consumed from renewable sources and improving energy efficiency, fostering
opportunities for local development.

The POI Renewable Energy and Energy Conservation has three axes:
Axis I: Production of energy from renewable sources
Axis II: Energy efficiency and energy system optimization
Axis III: Technical Assistance and accompanying resources are allocated to the region of Abruzzo to 38.502 million euro.
POR-ABRUZZO 2007-2013 ERDF Axis II "ENERGY" Regional Implementation Tool (SAR) Abruzzo POR FESR 2007-2013 CCI 2007 GB 162 PO 001.
The ERDF Regional Operational Programme 2007-2013, approved by Decision No. 3980 of 17.08.2007 by the European Commission for Community Regional Competitiveness and Employment Objective. Axis II "Energy", is divided into three different forms of interventions that provide business financing, assistance in public works and procurement of goods and services to promote and develop the production of energy from renewable sources (installation of photovoltaic panels and solar thermal, promotion of energy saving systems, entertainment and awareness for the promotion of awareness of renewable energy and energy conservation). The resources allocated to the Abruzzo region amounted to 35.239 million euro.
Additional tools to support economic and financial-Leg. March 31, 1998, No 112 "Conferment of administrative functions and duties of the State to Regions and Local Authorities, in implementation of Chapter I of L. March 15, 1997, No 59. Published in the Official Gazette. No. April 21, 1998, SO With that decree has been delegated to the regions of the administrative functions relating to energy, including those relating to renewable energy sources, electricity, nuclear power, oil and gas, which are not reserved to the State under Article 29 or not assigned to local authorities under Article 31. LR-n.80/98 "rules for the promotion and development of renewable energy and energy conservation" - later amended by LR. No 84/99, which provides for development of the use of solar energy, promotes the incentive to purchase and install solar systems for hot water production and the contribution to space heating. These forms of support to development initiatives in the energy system alongside those resulting from actions aimed at energy and environmental protection programs in the PSR (Regional Plan for Rural Development + Industry 2015).

THE ENERGY SERVICE COMPANIES (ESCo.) AND LENDING INSTITUTIONS

In a scenario marked by the continued reduction of financial resources for public budgets, the progressive withdrawal of the "public" economy, the involvement of private finance has given a significant driving force, even in areas that traditionally considered the responsibility public (infrastructure and services network). Compared to the past, has changed the basis on which reviews the projects to be funded. Firm and its ability to repay the loan, the focus has shifted to the feasibility and economic prospects of the project.

Part of "project finance" - the Project Financing (PF), - third party financing (TPF). The only differences between the two types of funding are the investment in the entity in question and whether or not the involvement of banks. In particular, the FTT is an option in financial service provision related to energy, which includes the participation of a third party who provides the financial resources needed to carry out the intervention. Rather than credit institutions, the main actors are the ESCO. (According to Presidential Decree 412/93), energy service companies through performance contracts EPC (Energy Performance Contracting) make available their know-how to reduce fuel consumption and operating costs of the customer. The offer to finance the interventions which have initially performed an energy audit, take care of projects from construction to operations and maintenance management. (Source: Chapter 3 - Energy Plan of the Abruzzo Region - ADDRESSES AND PROPOSALS FOR ACTION PLAN. December 2009)

ENERGY COMMUNITIES

Throughout history there has always been a close relationship between the places of production (accumulation) and energy consumption ("close ties" or phrases of location). Within the structures of the "city" of the twenty-first century, we must consider all the active devices capable of different energy production (energy mix), as no development is possible only if integration, complementarities and the sum of energy between different sources (R. Ricci). Our lands, our cities could be considered more "machinery" in order to obtain 'autopoiesis energy (remember the basic concepts of paradigms Fritjiof Capra), rather than to serve tissue and flush through the existing network of energy supply (fossil). The inductive approach to the application-case-study part of the territory follows three key assumptions:

01- to recognize that portions of the territories or parts of it are capable of expressing various memberships and to define the family of "standard elements" by identifying characteristics and similar potential;

02- declare an analogy between urban systems and biological systems, not simply related to the formal similarities (or shape), but identified in correspondence with some key concepts, such as: organization, links and dependencies;

03- The various parts of the system, not as elements (or parts) in isolation but as an autopoietic community able to activate the construction of a mobile vision of the areas linked to self-organization and functioning of the reticular metropolitan areas. In reference to the first point, namely to recognize different forms within the territories, geometry (shape, size), facilities, organizations, relationships, principles, interference, differences, patterns of operation (or malfunction), in portions (parts , cells, nuclei, enclaves, communities, districts) of territory that characterize and make unique and diverse in different contexts, it seeks to express those "characteristics of places" capable of revealing the "potential of the districts (or community). The principles that define the rules for "scope" (or envelope) of some portion of land (and similar) may be different: you can build communities by recognizing those portions of the same city, you can analyze the "context parameters", dimensional Morphological and also common to the territories. For example, several studies and applications have focused on the energy value of the form of settlements, with greater propensity towards the needs of cold countries (mainly a function of solar radiation to optimize the solar gain for winter heating, Solar Access), or by reference to hot climates (to determine the thermal discomfort resulting from exposure to sunlight, Discomfort Index). These studies have measured both the sunshine and the thermal performance of buildings in relation to parameters such as their height, the orientation of the facades, the width of the streets, the presence of parks and green patterns, studies related to the concepts of "density" of the different urban fabrics in warm climate, such as the "heat trap" or "urban heat island" (the thermal efficiency of building clus-

ters: an index for non-air conditioned buildings in hot climates, Vinar Gupta) .
In relation to these two concepts ("the heat trap" and the "urban heat island") is
reported the experience of research at the Department CRESSON (Ecole Nationale
Supérieure d'Architecture de Grenoble and in collaboration with Les Grands Ateliers de structure of the City of Lyon and Grenoble) for the construction, analysis,
reflection, experimentation and research within the five Ateliers "Urbaines Chaleurs"
(investigation, analysis, reading and projects , from the comfort of the public spaces
of the city) and on display at the Plateforme, within the exhibition of the Biennale
de l'Habitat Durable (Grenoble - 2008). The energy community in the section of land
Pescara, framed between 42 ° 26 '49.11 "N and 42 ° 26' 15.05" N parallel, have been
identified mainly by defining "island-types" that express the character and significant
potential of the different "sections of town."
The energy communities identified were considered as "standard elements" (defined
as the identifying characteristics of the different contexts) reiterating within the
metropolitan area: ranging from the hills to the sea.
The second aspect is related to the fact of declaring a possible similarity and analogy
between urban systems and biological organisms. Raymonde Delavigne also recognizes that the "city" body has many of the characteristics of an ecosystem linked to
an idea of metabolic functions. In research conducted by Tiezzi and Pulselli, the city
system is seen as a living organism, a system that breathes, eats, and assumes its
own identity, but at the same time belongs to the dynamic and variable condition,
typical of natural evolution (in close collaboration with key concepts about the "complexity theory" of Ilya Prigogine, Nobel Laureate in Chemistry (1977) and the father
of natural evolution). In the light of theories on complex systems and processes of
self-organization (Ilya Prigogine and Fritjof Capra), we can freely say that an urban
system is an open system characterized by low entropy input of resources and high
output of entropy waste. The concept of entropy (change, evolution, but also confu-
sion) of bodies reveals that living systems always tend towards "minimum entropy".
The growth and development of these organisms (or communities) is dictated by the
continuous exchange with the outside. A dissipative system absorbs and consumes
resources (in the form of raw materials and energy-quality low-entropy) by drawing
on external sources, providing structure and organization. According to the investigation of Prigogine on the processes of formation of ordered structures in open
dissipative systems, we define the two terms of the change in entropy: dS = des d1S
+, (where: dS = change in entropy; d1S = refers to the production of entropy within
the system, the result of irreversible internal changes as if it were an isolated system,
without any relation to the external (or outside), while des = the part that mainly
characterizes a dissipative structure, and is the subject of trade combined with the
external form of energy input and output of entropy). There is a need for a change
in the interpretation of changing contexts, expanding the knowledge framework

of territories capable of building a "thermodynamic vision" of the territories (maps-diagrams-Actions). The relationship between urban systems and biological systems is not an abstract hypothesis, but it takes more strength and meaning within the research conducted by Howard T. Odum already in the seventies (in Environment, Power and Society, New York, 1971), when the public determined, in its studies on the language of "picture mathematics" (math drawing) the possibility of establishing an inventory of all the "driving energies" that sustain and determine the development of cities, resulting from an observation extended to all the dynamics and key processes that take place in it. The language studies Odum is "picture mathematics", where each symbol has a meaning and is rigorously defined mathematically. Then drawing an Odum diagram, is how to write equations describing the system (says Mark T. Brown, professor at the University of Florida). But the change of perspective and originality of the application of Odum lie in the fact that the equations that describe the relations system and processes emerge simply from the diagram. The representation in a diagram (note Tiezzi and Pulselli) offers a concise description of resource flows and transformation processes occurring in the territory, so we define the relations between the system and outside and between its parts, revealing the interdependencies between forms of flow of energy and matter. Different applications and trials have followed and taken input from these reflections on the definition and writing (or rewriting) of a code open for the contemporary city, not least the study conducted by the group of researchers at the University of Siena, in collaboration with the MIT, have reproduced the cha-diagram analysis foreshadowing of a city according to the criteria of language "energy systems". An energy diagram of the operation and configuration, which offers a shared vision of the dynamics of the city (or a "city region", the broader regional system), harvesting the different aspects of a district in a single structure of the whole. Through a reading of such a territory strengthens the systemic vision of territories and networks of relationships, action, interconnection (flows of matter, energy and information) and production (especially energy). Considering the different parts of the system as part (or parts) in isolation but as self-organizing systems and communities enables the construction of a mobile vision of the areas linked to self-organization and functioning of the reticular metropolitan areas, brought to define what the devices that regulate the different systems are, according to the concept of self-production (energy relations). The concept of self-organization was founded in the early years of cybernetics (the fifties), when you begin to define and build models inspired by the new face of the order and strictness axiom: autopoiesis. The concept of autopoiesis was born in some biological studies conducted around the 70s, when Humberto Maturana (Chilean student of neuroscience in the sixties) began a collaboration with McCulloch (of Massachusetts Institute of Technology) and Francisco Varela (scholar neuroscience at the University of Santiago) who began to discuss the concepts of circular organization: autopoiesis, that is the "production of self" (auto means "self" and refers to self-autonomy systems auspices; poiesis means "production") so as to define the process of distinguishing organization of living systems (Capra notes). Now we can freely admit that some urban elements can be defined as self-organized in relation to the analogy between biological systems and urban living organisms. Research on the structure of the form by Richard Buckminster Fuller lets us fully grasp the analogy between building elements and structural bodies, breaking the strict rules of standardized mentality and pushing the boundaries of application of various disciplines. If we think of experiments on the shape and structures of Fuller (eg radiolarians, etc.) we can find the full analogy between organ systems and structural systems. Whenever you observe structures, devices and forms in nature the most important property is that it is a network of schemes. In fact, Capra observes that "whenever we analyze living systems (organisms, parts of organisms, or communities of organisms) they can be said to be arranged like a net." The construction of the network affects the functioning of all parts of the system, so as to interconnect them and put them into one relationship between them. This step is well resolved in the model turned into a Sustainable City Auto City, based essentially on the transport network (rail) in charge by Peter Newman and Jeffrey Kenworthy, in the proposed project for "Sustainability and Cities: Overcoming automobile dependence" on the model for future Nodal / Information City.

In the construction of relations between the parties, to become a network (network), the sensing devices in an urban setting should say and declare their character identification criteria, resulting primarily from the structure of the system: patterns of organization, structure and process. It is no longer possible to think of giving an unequivocal interpretation of the area of the city, such as through the classic design of homogeneous functional areas (recognizing the prof. Roberto Mascarucci in relation to a territory of new programs and projects) and it is now widely accepted that the city needs to be reconfigured seeing it through the reinterpretation of those principles that feed it, the move is the structure. In doing this we must recognize that we need new forms of inquiry, new tools and new visions (foreshadowing). In fact, models of self-organizing energy, which are the basis of our territorial devices (which we call energy districts) can define the real field of action and experimentation, identifying characters in their organization, and dependence on the devices that link them. We thus define new visions network systems, reporting and organization of the territories, based primarily on recognizing the characteristics of places and possible vocations (or potential) inherent in the territories themselves. In all this we must not forget that cities are physical systems in contact with several "sources" and "drain tanks ", so as to enable a reading strategy that seeks to establish a functioning network between the different parties. Edgar Morin, as recognizing the autonomy of a social system, economic or urban is based on the dependence on the stresses that the key concepts of autonomy and dependence, while appearing in opposition, are complementary concepts for a system in need of resources for self-organizing and maintaining their individuality and originality. So for concepts such as self-organization and economic organization that cannot be interconnected, there can be no independence without dependence (including energy).

CHARACTERISTICS of the SITES:
centers-places of the territories within the hills
that dot the "glen" in Pescara. These become
the first units to activate, strengthen and
re-think energy and sustainability, ensuring
a throw-in value not only of historic fabrics,
places of Meor, but also an investment in an
economy of sustainability and energy of/in
smaller towns.

TRANSFORMATIVE POTENTIAL
of the DISTRICT:
urban centers considered as "urban units" that
gravitate on the hill facing the valley at south-
east/east; recognizable for their configuration
as the core itself, which for the provision of
basic services to its internal energy potential
urban communities.

40667
RIPOLI
41701
44514
DE CO
40687

CHARACTERISTICS of the SITES:
node-points inside the hilly areas suited to agriculture, farm equipment and more, with potential energy, tourism and hospitality.

TRANSFORMATIVE POTENTIAL
of the DISTRICT:
territorial systems point quite commonly in these contexts toard tanks to collect rainwater and reuse it to exploit the fields, to use urban centers as real battery storage tanks or potential energy. Farm for production of crops for bio-oil.

CHARACTERISTICS of the SITES:
joints that are located in urbanized areas of the foothills and of settlements that have a hill and how use typical mobility of urban reality.

TRANSFORMATIVE POTENTIAL
of the DISTRICT:
urbanized cores similar to " stand-alone planning units" (as servants) and their complex relationship of how to access the networks of the urban area. The main feature is their good sun exposure (as opposed to the territories "in the shadow of the valleys") and the proximity to sensitive environmental attractors of the riverbed and its natural basin.

CHARACTERISTICS of the SITES:
natural green space by river. Place of highest
naturalistic recognition, potentially rich in
natural-energy-environmental characteristic
elements, but currently little used (or not
used).

TRANSFORMATIVE POTENTIAL
of the DISTRICT:
as well as able to enter their chain of energy
production "waste" means fuel for biomass.
Potential site for the cultivation of wood to
produce bio-oil.

CHARACTERISTICS of the SITES:
industrial areas close to cities, often within
the sensitive context of the riverbed. There are
several industrial districts (still in use or being
sold) that ASI owns and manages in the area
encompassing the valley of Pescara.

TRANSFORMATIVE POTENTIAL
of the DISTRICT:
some industrial districts, both by location
(proximity to the river and the portals to the
territory) and in size can become challenges
of conversion of the production sites and
obtain key roles in energy supply chains trying
to also introject the energy system, not only
consumed, but also home grown and with the
possibility of becoming subject to territorial
energy exchange (energy-hub).

CHARACTERISTICS of the SITES:
borders: the borders of major infrastructure
(such as airports) become areas of margin,
inactive, unused, "lost lands" within the city.

TRANSFORMATIVE POTENTIAL
of the DISTRICT:
exhibited a linear system of optimally heliothermic axis.

CHARACTERISTICS of the SITES:
within the fabric of the city of Pescara, there are some residential areas of consistent configuration, like the Aterno district. It is a real local community, offering services to people, sports, green, and leisure.

TRANSFORMATIVE POTENTIAL
of the DISTRICT:
this "micro-city within a city" has been imagined (already in the planning stage and its implementation) to be capable of becoming partially self-sufficient, it is the only district in the territory of Pescara to have a solar thermal system implanted on the roofs since its implementation. But this is not enough ..... Its proximity to the Pescara - Chieti - Rome railway line is significant, as well as its proximity to a nodal point of the medium voltage power grid.

CHARACTERISTICS of the SITES:
one of the areas off-limits in the city is provided by the prison, as a "special block" that occupies a small portion of land. The prison is representative of all those social spaces and incubators that are scattered in cities like hospitals, schools, etc.. These sites, together with the airport and station (the "non-places") become spaces for the activation and testing of renewable energy devices.

TRANSFORMATIVE POTENTIAL
of the DISTRICT:
The district is characteristic and differs from those areas used by the public, due to its characteristic of being enclaves in the city. There are no trade relations with the outside world, beyond the high boundary wall, but these sites could become energy wells for the production, consumption and accumulation on the spot or conversion to other portions of territory? (The economy of the future of energy sharing)

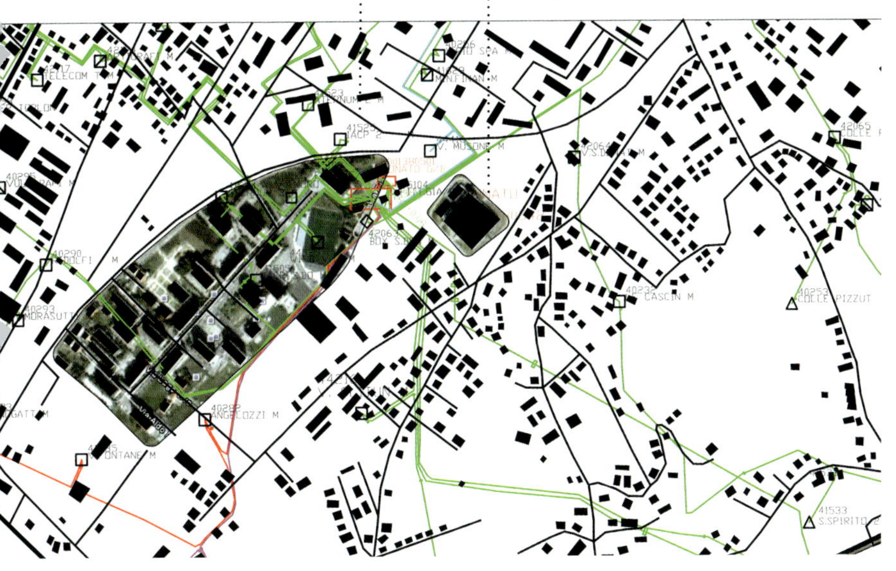

CHARACTERISTICS of the SITES:
borders: the borders of major infrastructure
marginal become areas, inactive, unused, "lost
lands" within the territories.

TRANSFORMATIVE POTENTIAL
of the DISTRICT:
exhibited a linear system optimally on a heliothermic axis.

CHARACTERISTICS of the SITES:
there are different classes of neighborhood in
the city of Pescara. These can become a model
for the application of energy systems that are
not only passive (culling of consumption), but
mainly "neighborhoods island", meaning living
models that raise the standard of building-
energy-inhabited (and not only energy-
intensive!).

TRANSFORMATIVE POTENTIAL
of the DISTRICT:
are buildings that fit into the context, in
relation to the orography of the land, the
sea breezes, making it unusual challenge of
reactivation of the residential areas of active
energy costs.

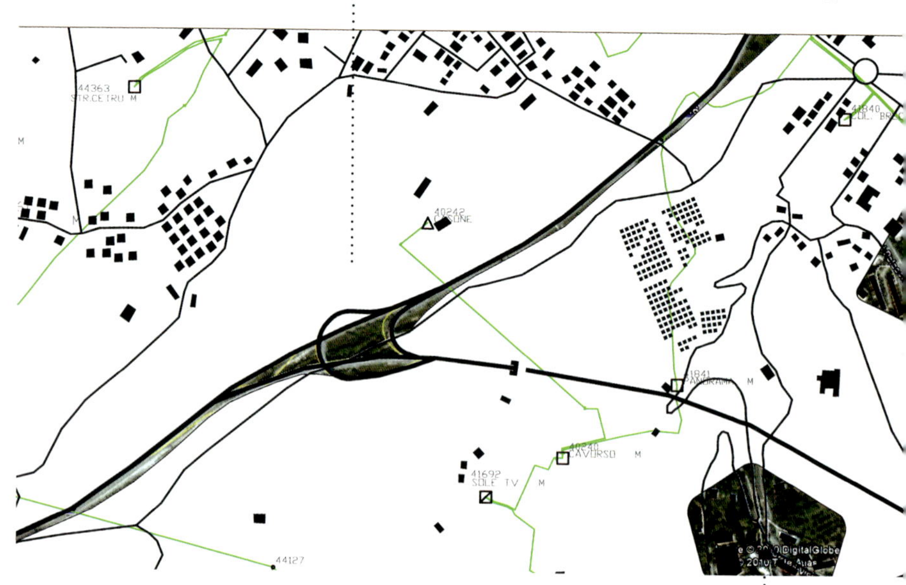

CHARACTERISTICS of the SITES:

the hill system presents several unique characteristics and features, starting from Pescara
and going south, we see that the ridges are
characterized by the landscape of greenhouses: locations for the production and crop
specialist production.

TRANSFORMATIVE POTENTIAL
of the DISTRICT:

systems of greenhouses become places and
opportunities to generate energy by entering
a revitalization in the chain production also in
energy industries. The places of production
could become complex systems that produce
and sell and exchange-not only tomatoes, but
also energy.

CHARACTERISTICS of the SITES:
devices oil platforms at sea characterize the
horizon from the coast of Abruzzo.

TRANSFORMATIVE POTENTIAL
of the DISTRICT:
new areas of energy are mainly in the sea ....

CHARACTERISTICS of the SITES:
the fabric of settlements on the Adriatic
coast has characters of similarity, repetition,
especially with respect to the reporting infrastructure that characterize the coastal system
of Abruzzo.

TRANSFORMATIVE POTENTIAL
of the DISTRICT:
buildings, courtyards, lots, blocks, districts or
communities tablets between the railway and
the SS16 tissue become a sponge for a pilot
project for increasing energy areas.

CHARACTERISTICS of the SITES:
marine works are often seen as single function
devices, but could be reconsidered real engine
for the production and energy conversion.

TRANSFORMATIVE POTENTIAL
of the DISTRICT:
potentially the breakwater, as well as marine
barriers (water) can become places of farm
water, using the kinetic energy of the sea
(although low power in the Abruzzo coast),
and solar photovoltaics.

<table>
<tr><td>

MAPS

SOLAR RADIAL POTENTIAL
POTENTIAL OF BIOMASS PRODUCTION
HYDROELECTRIC POTENTIAL
EOLIC POTENTIAL
GEOTHERMAL POTENTIAL

</td><td>

DIAGRAMS

PRODUCTION
CONSUMTION
STORAGE
CONVERSION
SHARING

</td><td>

ACTIONS

A1 E-FIT
A2 E-FILL
A3 E-PULL

</td></tr>
</table>

Looking at the reference energy communities identified previously in this section we can experimentally define the potential energy (through the definition of the map) of reference (related to solar radiation, to hydroelectric potential, the potential wind, geothermal and biomass). Along with the maps, which define the overlap of two layers: the area and information (data) are structured charts which relate the different axes combined overlapping temporal evolution of the different energy-systemic parts. The axes show the ability of different communities to produce, consume, accumulate, transform and exchange energy. The reference model starting from the current state (current configuration, patterning blue) show the propensity of each system, mainly to consume energy. Activating different parts to be self-generators of energy defines the possible configurations by increasing more and more the possibility of different communities on their own energy-consuming systems and communities that self-generate energy, to empower communities to convert and/or store the excess production, to define organizational models that exchange with the outside world and give the surplus energy to other systems capable of eating through the exchange of new services for the city of the future: energy sharing. (When we talk about energy we are not referring only to power but also to heat).

The three main reference actions attributed to each community are: e-fit, and fill-and-pull. The first action (e-fit) tends to redevelop portions of the territory and cities, trying to improve energy efficiency starting from the redefinition of the existing regeneration and transformation, achieving power through devices, energy independence. When independence is assured the surplus energy generated can be defined as material exchange with the outside world, recognizing the ongoing economic evolution, a greater exchange of services rather than products. The action-fit becomes a strategic application in the COMMUNITY ENERGY, ENERGY INDUSTRY, in the District Energy and Energy Zone, where the presence and the relationship with existing living arrangements and trying to activate productive potential structures, areas, and devices capable of producing, store, convert and exchange the surplus energy to other neighboring communities. When you can not intervene on the existing sufficiently one then determines an action for employment (and-fill), which aims to colonize empty areas, engaging new energy production systems, as might be applied in the Vertical Farm, in the Energy Park in GREEN FARM HOUSE ENERGY and WATER. As for the KMenergetico and INFRA-ENERGY-fill action and considered the possibility of rethinking the territorial systems in key infrastructure and energy capacity, identifying characteristics and potential areas for hybrid infrastructure. Processes filling/insertion (in-fill) in suburb areas (low density), in small towns, along with avenues for development in a sprawling metropolis of building systems, are capable of reconciling development organizations with existing forms of territorial settlement structure with a higher overall sustainability (such as the Nodal / City Information).

The action of pulling-down a project and how to optimize and reactivate structures, systems and portions of land to be converted and re-produce energy with a view to sustain the individual until the system can enable the exchange of surplus energy, creates energy that will activate those dependencies "other economies." Those that may be affected by this action: the ENERGY COMMUNITY, the ENERGY INDUSTRY, the District Energy, the ENERGY CLUSTER, the Energy Zone and WATER FARM.

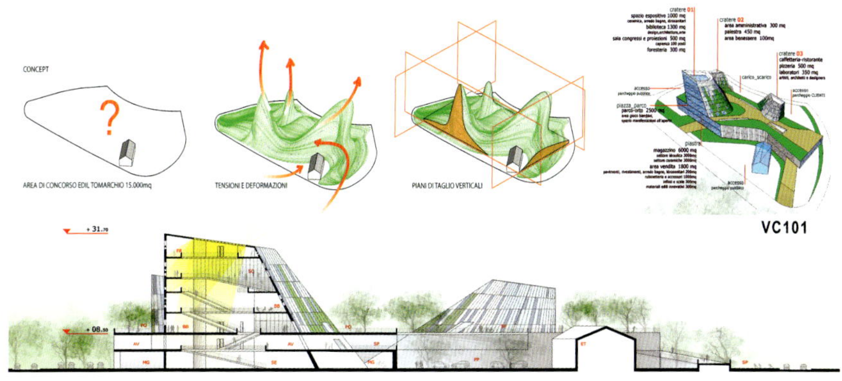

DIAGRAMS

MAPS

SOLAR RADIAL POTENTIAL

POTENTIAL OF BIOMASS PRODUCTION

HYDROELECTRIC POTENTIAL

EOLIC POTENTIAL

GEOTHERMAL POTENTIAL

42° 26' 49,11" N

42° 26' 15,05" N

ACTIONS

A1 E-FIT

A2 E-FILL

A3 E-PULL

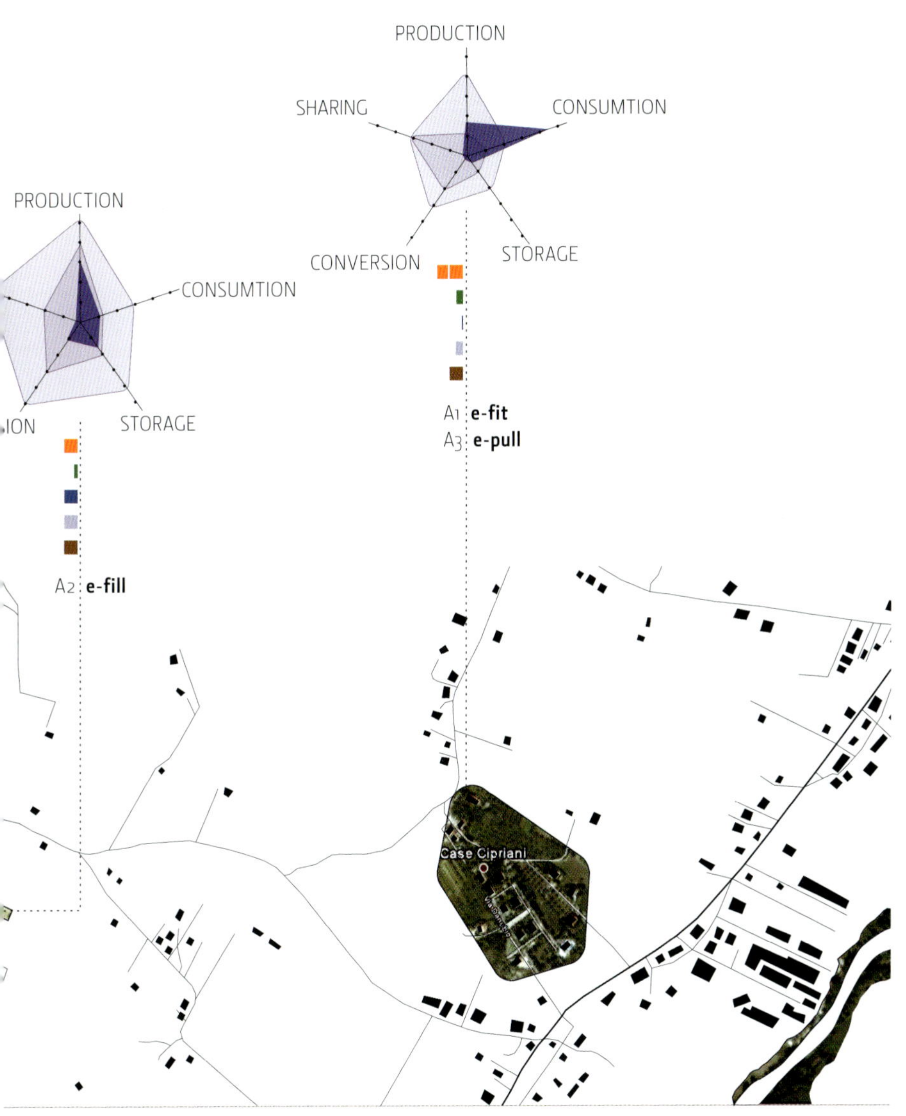

PRODUCTION
SHARING
CONSUMTION
CONVERSION
STORAGE
A1 e-fit
A3 e-pull
PRODUCTION
CONSUMTION
ION
STORAGE
A2 e-fill
Case Cipriani

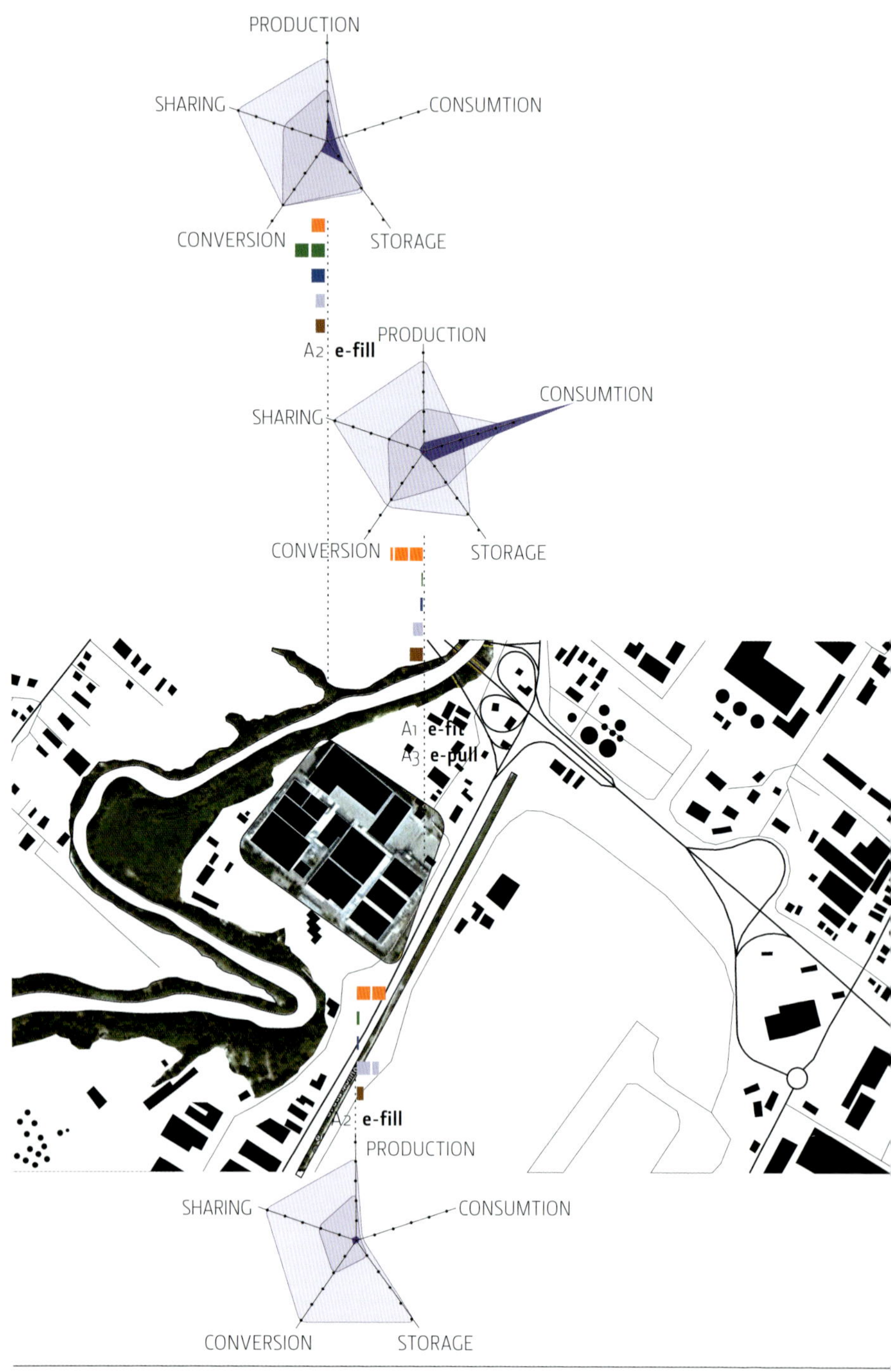

PRODUCTION
SHARING
CONSUMTION
CONVERSION
STORAGE
A2 e-fill
PRODUCTION
SHARING
CONSUMTION
CONVERSION
STORAGE
A1 e-fill
A3 e-pull
A2 e-fill
PRODUCTION
SHARING
CONSUMTION
CONVERSION
STORAGE

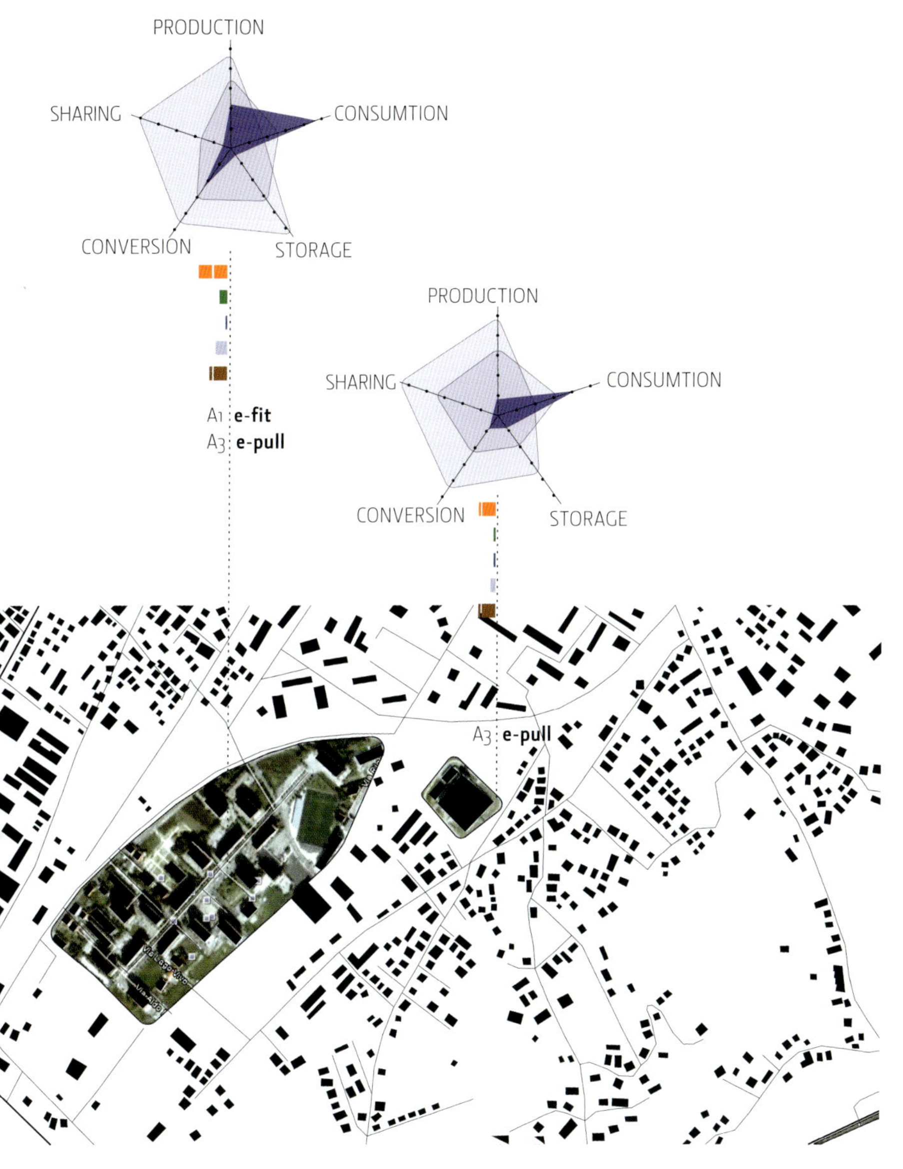

PRODUCTION
CONSUMTION
SHARING
CONVERSION
STORAGE
A1 e-fit
A3 e-pull
PRODUCTION
CONSUMTION
SHARING
CONVERSION
STORAGE
A3 e-pull

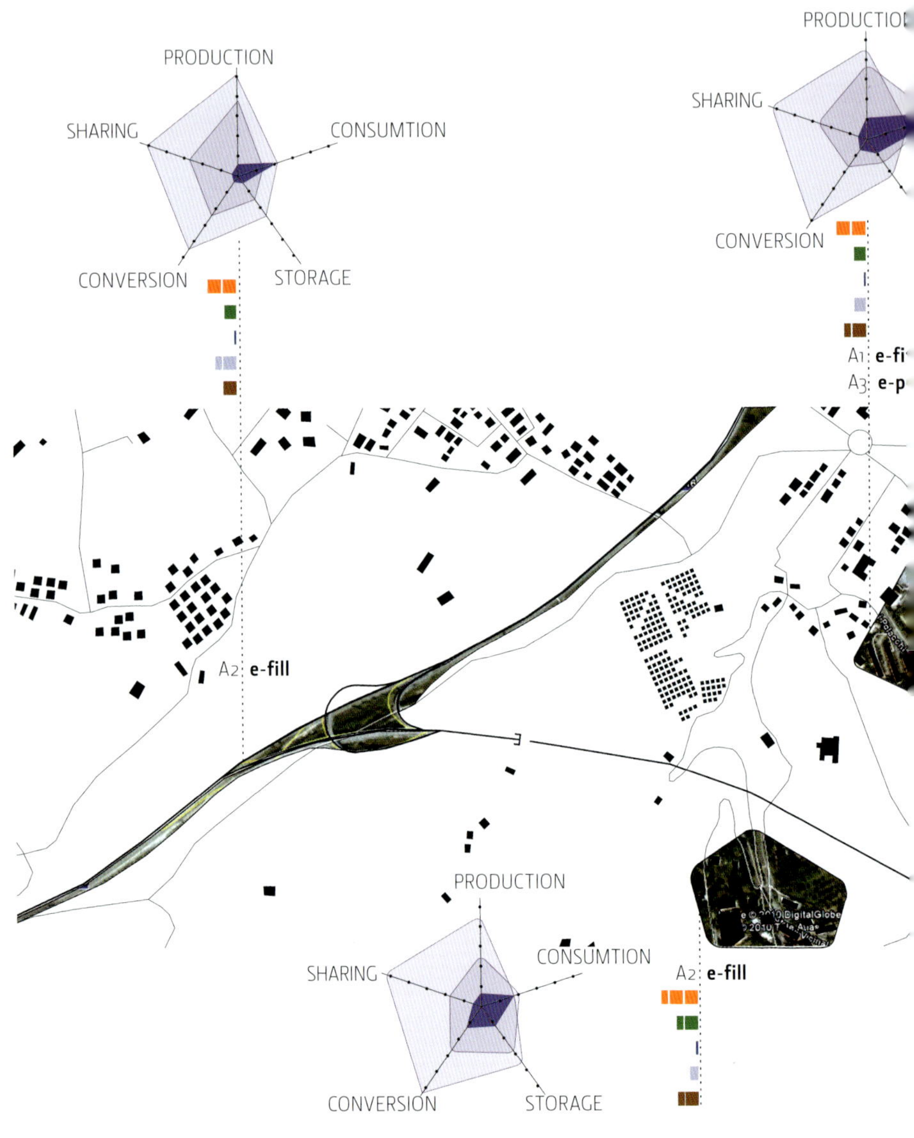

PRODUCTION
SHARING
CONSUMTION
CONVERSION
STORAGE
A2 e-fill
PRODUCTION
SHARING
CONVERSION
A1 e-fi
A3 e-p
A2 e-fill
PRODUCTION
SHARING
CONSUMTION
CONVERSION
STORAGE

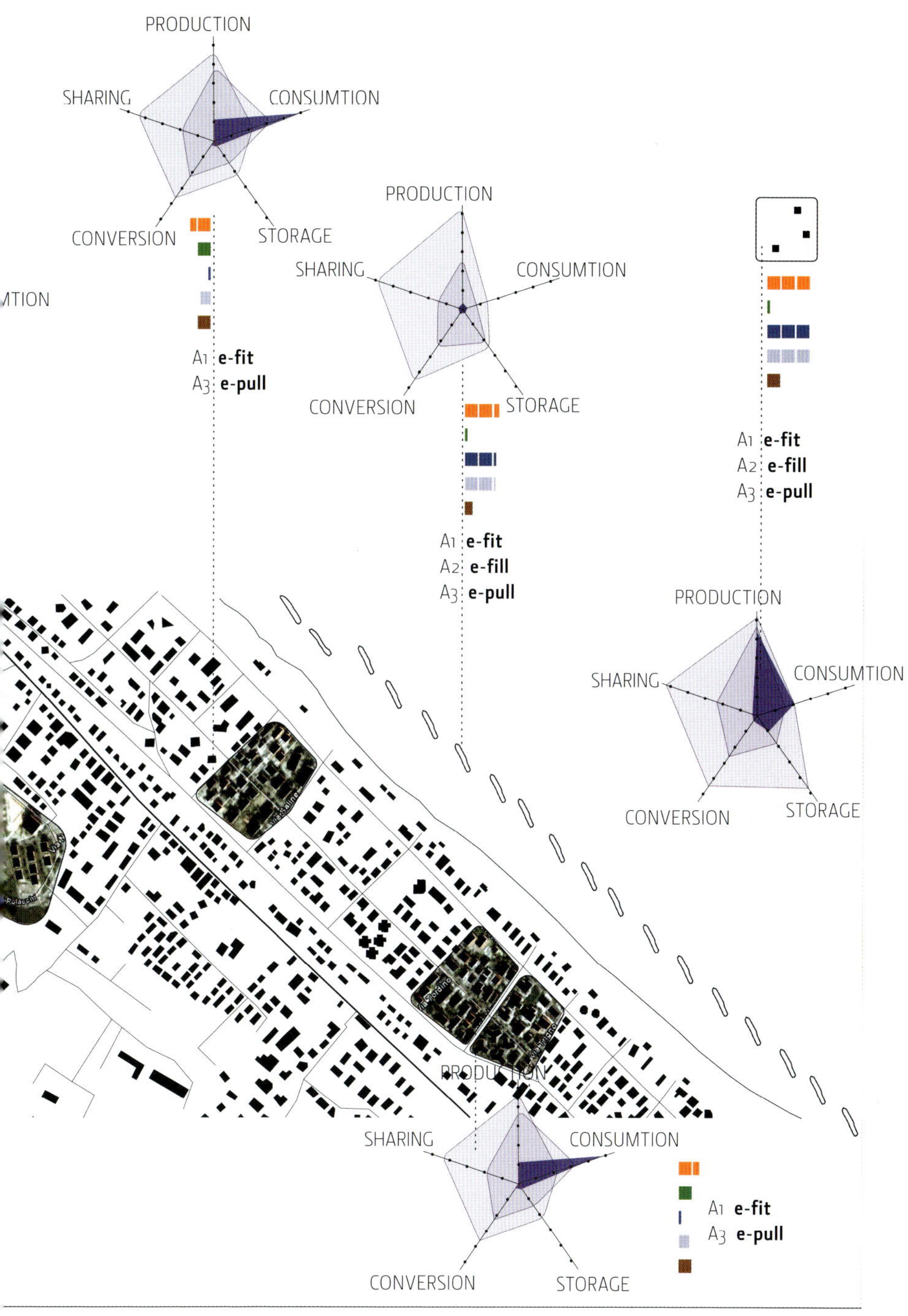

PRODUCTION
SHARING
CONSUMTION
CONVERSION
STORAGE
A1 e-fit
A3 e-pull
PRODUCTION
SHARING
CONSUMTION
CONVERSION
STORAGE
A1 e-fit
A2 e-fill
A3 e-pull
A1 e-fit
A2 e-fill
A3 e-pull
PRODUCTION
SHARING
CONSUMTION
CONVERSION
STORAGE
PRODUCTION
SHARING
CONSUMTION
CONVERSION
STORAGE
A1 e-fit
A3 e-pull

PREFIGURATIONS

This section identifies the possible spatial configurations capable of building design scenarios identified in the draft instrument (the project as a probe) for the construction and sharing of field operations. Projects such as programs, tend to set up and configure systems as able to activate and facilitate sharing processes starting from the potential of the place and capitalizing on the problems / difficulties of themselves, their relationships, always looking toward a "built system", "network" and by fostering a systemic vision of the different energy regions.

VERTICAL FARM:
type: project competition - 2008 (project mentioned and rewarded at the UIA of To)
place: Bardonecchia (To)
with: marino la torre, francesca ritschl, unoaunostudio

ENERGY PARK:
type: project competition -2005 (finalist)
place: Reggio nell'Emilia (Re)
with: marino la torre, milena giansante, unoaunostudio

KM^e:
type: project competition Europan IX - 2007
place: Reggio nell'Emilia (Re)
with: marino la torre, unoaunostudio

INDUSTRY ENERGY:
type: project competition - 2006 (first prize)
place: Biella (Bi)
with: paolo martellucci, unoaunostudio

DISTRICT ENERGY:
type: project competition - 2007 (project excluded)
place: Castellammare di Stabia (Na)
with: marino la torre, giorgio caizzi, Ater pescara, unoaunostudio

CLUSTER ENERGY:
type: project competition - 2009
place: Dueville (Vi)
with: marino la torre, paolo martellucci, unoaunostudio

INFRA-ENERGY:
type: architect invited to the 10. Architecture Exhibition – Biennial of Venezia - 2006 - Italian pavilion – ITALIA-y-2026. Invitation to Vema. – project presented: VELOCITY
place: VeMa (Verona-Mantova)
with: marino la torre, unoaunostudio, marco morante, maura scarcella, Giuseppe marcotullio, andrea mezzaro-ma, annalisa taballione, laq_architettura, irina novarese, rodolphe luscher, filippo broggini

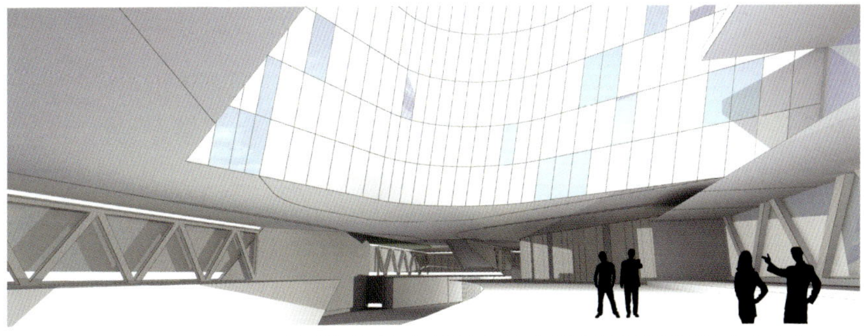

GREEN HOUSE ENERGY:
type: project competition Iaac - Institute for Advanced Architecture of Catalonia - "Self-Sufficient Housing. The self-fab house" 2° - 2007
place: Barcellona (Spagna)
with: marino la torre, paola marcantonio, nicolas tixier, unoaunostudio

DISTRICT ENERGY:
type: project competition - 2008
place: Rovigo (Ro)
with: marino la torre, unoaunostudio, mariangela pugliese, alessandra salciccia, giorgio caizzi, Ater pescara

ENERGY ZONE:
type: project competition - 2006 (first prize)
place: Biella (Bi)
with: paolo martellucci, unoaunostudio

WATER FARM:
type: project competition - 2010
place: Chioggia (Ve)
with: marino al torre, chiara pirro, giulio mandrillo, unoaunostudio

WATER FARM [3]:
type: architect invited to the 10. Architecture Exhibition – Biennial of Venezia - 2006 - Italian pavilion – ITALIA-y-2026. Invited to Vema. – project presented: VELOCITY
place: VeMa (Verona-Mantova)
with: marino la torre, unoaunostudio, marco morante, maura scarcella, Giuseppe marcotullio, andrea mezzaroma, annalisa taballione, Iaq_architettura, irina novarese, rodolphe luscher, filippo broggini

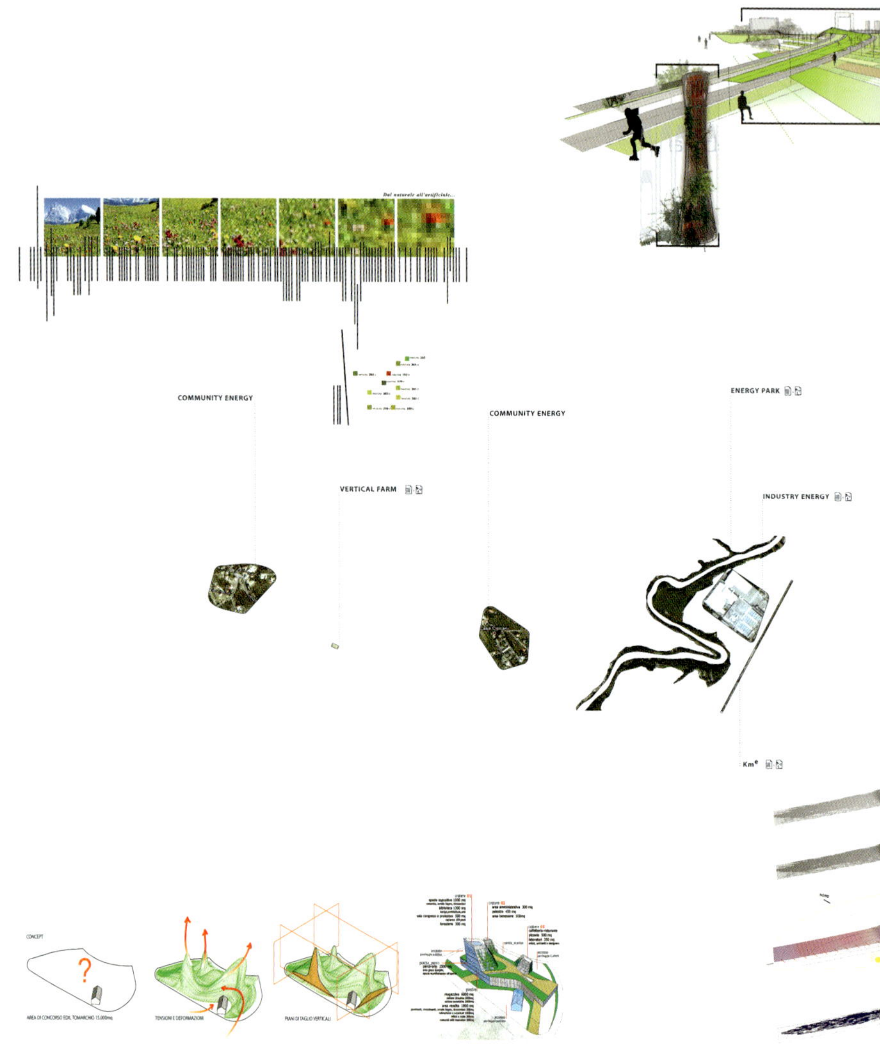

Dal naturale all'artificiale...
COMMUNITY ENERGY
COMMUNITY ENERGY
ENERGY PARK
VERTICAL FARM
INDUSTRY ENERGY
Km²
CONCEPT
AREA DI CONCORSO EDIL TOMARCHIO 15,000mq
TENSIONI E DEFORMAZIONI
PIANI DI TAGLIO VERTICALI

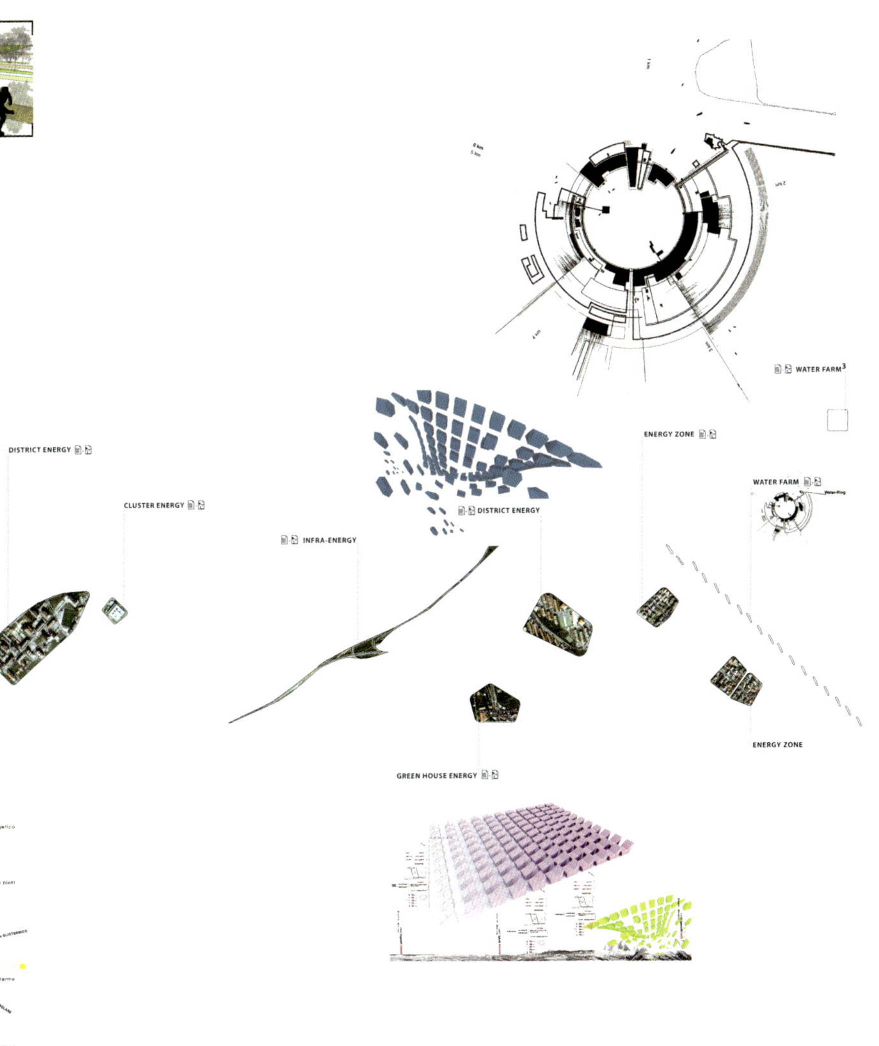
0 km
5 km
2 km
4 km
WATER FARM³
ENERGY ZONE
WATER FARM
Water-Ring
DISTRICT ENERGY
CLUSTER ENERGY
INFRA-ENERGY
DISTRICT ENERGY
ENERGY ZONE
GREEN HOUSE ENERGY

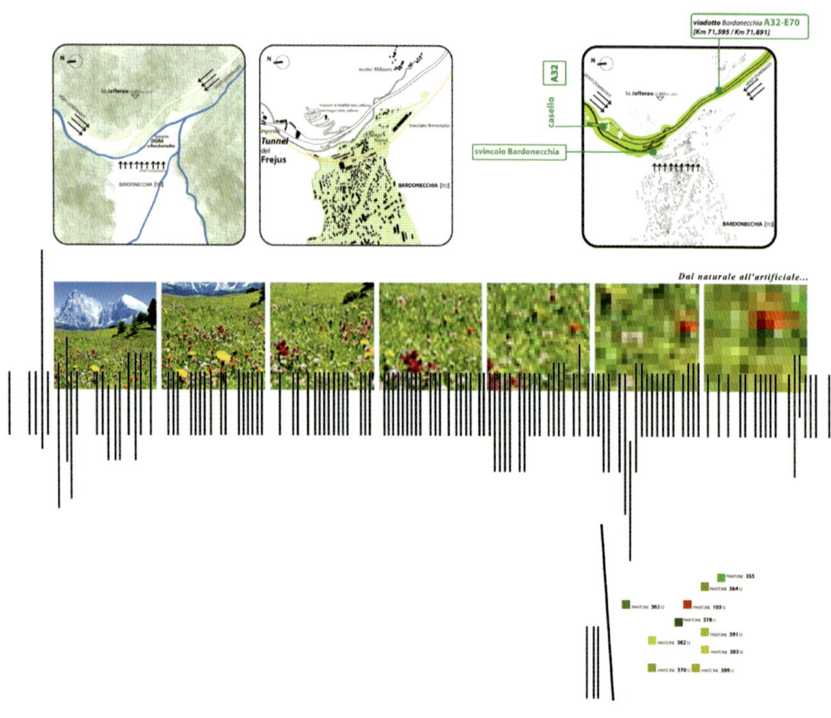

VERTICAL FARM:

type: project competition - 2008 (project mentioned and rewarded at the UIA of To)
place: Bardonecchia (To)
with: marino la torre, francesca ritschl, unoaunostudio

VERTICAL FARM

CHARACTERISTICS of the SITES:
node-points inside the hilly areas suited to agriculture, farm equipment and more, with potential
energy, tourism and hospitality.

TRANSFORMATIVE POTENTIAL of the DISTRICT:
territorial systems point quite commonly in these
contexts toard tanks to collect rainwater and reuse
it to exploit the fields, to use urban centers as real
battery storage tanks or potential energy. Farm for
production of crops for bio-oil.

ACTIONS:
A2: **e-fill**

ENERGY POTENTIAL:

DIAGRAMS

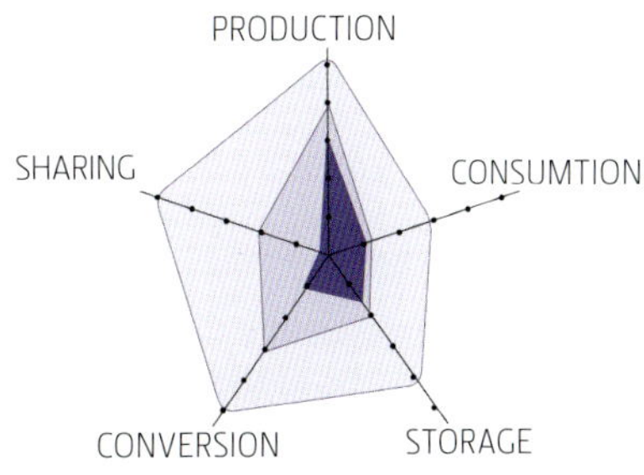

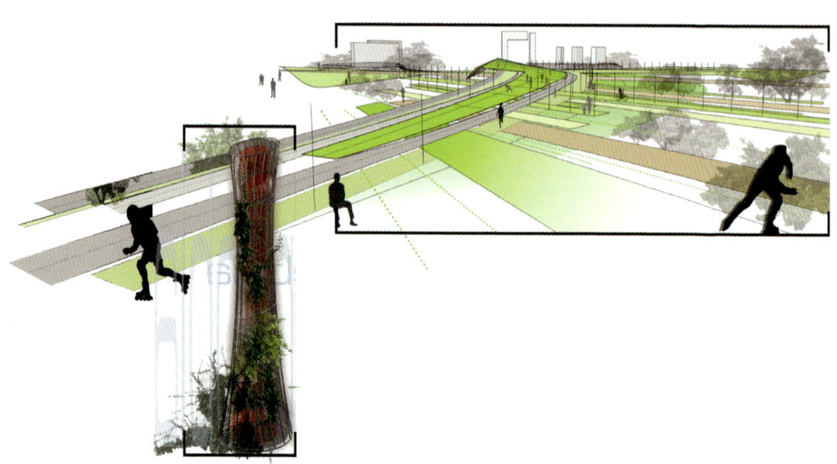

ENERGY PARK:
type: project competition -2005 (finalist)
place: Reggio nell'Emilia (Re)
with: marino la torre, milena giansante, unoaunostudio

ENERGY PARK

ACTIONS
A2: **e-fill**

ENERGY POTENTIAL:

DIAGRAMS

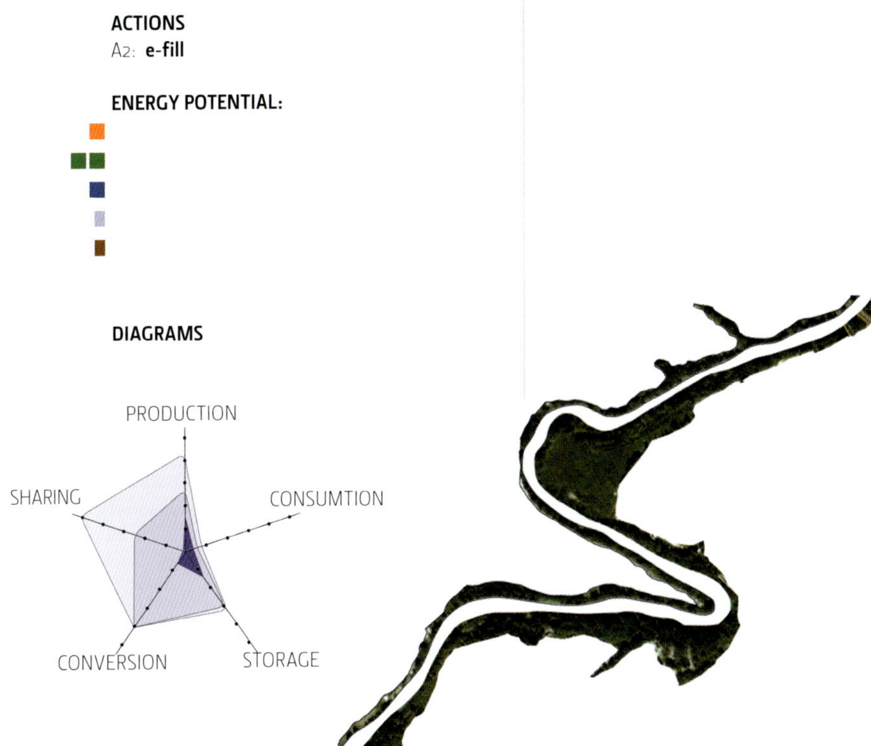

CHARACTERISTICS of the SITES:
natural green space by river. Place of highest naturalistic recognition, potentially rich in natural-energy-environmental characteristic elements, but currently little used (or not used).

**TRANSFORMATIVE POTENTIAL
of the DISTRICT:**
as well as able to enter their chain of energy production "waste" means fuel for biomass. Potential site for the cultivation of wood to produce bio-oil.

Le [x] **aree industriali** costituiscono una *potenzialità* per la diffusione e *produzione di Energia [da rinnovabile]* all'interno della città

L'insieme delle [x] *aree* industriali dismesse [o in via di dismissione] assicurano una riserva di **superfici** e di **spazi** all'interno del tessuto urbano della città, *nei quali è possibile costruire un sistema diffuso di **nuovi spazi collettivi** e di **piattaforme energetiche**.*

Sistema viario e della mobilita'

Sistema edilizio nella *zona San Paolo*

Sistema del verde ed ambientale *(parco fluviale)*

Sistema delle TRAME energetiche
(aree industriali della città)

L'osservazione di queste *aree* [**trame energetiche**] e l'attuazione di opportune strategie di recupero e di trasformazione urbana diventano *i temi, le idee e le provocazioni* per **pre-vedere il futuro di una città che guarda al futuro!**

edifici [**Ex**] industriali ***VS*** MACCHINE ENERGETICHE *nella citta'*

INDUSTRY ENERGY:

type: project competition - 2006 (first prize)
place: Biella (Bi)
with: paolo martellucci, unoaunostudio

ENERGY INDUSTRY

CHARACTERISTICS of the SITES:
industrial areas close to cities, often within the sensitive context of the riverbed. There are several industrial districts (still in use or being sold) that ASI owns and manages in the area encompassing the valley of Pescara.

TRANSFORMATIVE POTENTIAL of the DISTRICT:
some industrial districts, both by location (proximity to the river and the portals to the territory) and in size can become challenges of conversion of the production sites and obtain key roles in energy supply chains trying to also introject the energy system, not only consumed, but also home grown and with the possibility of becoming subject to territorial energy exchange (energy-hub).

DIAGRAMS

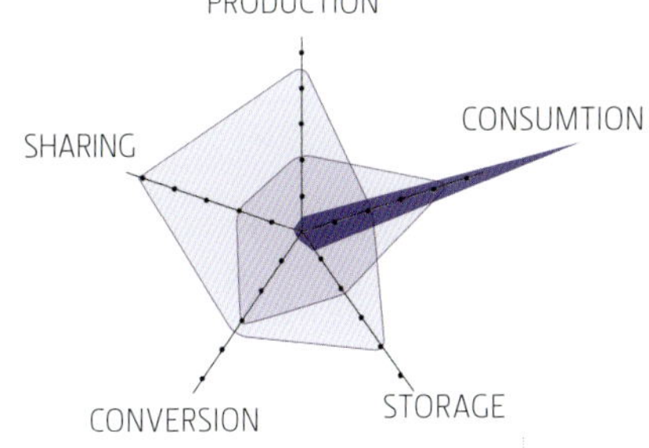

ACTIONS:
A1: **e-fit**
A3: **e-pull**

ENERGY POTENTIAL:

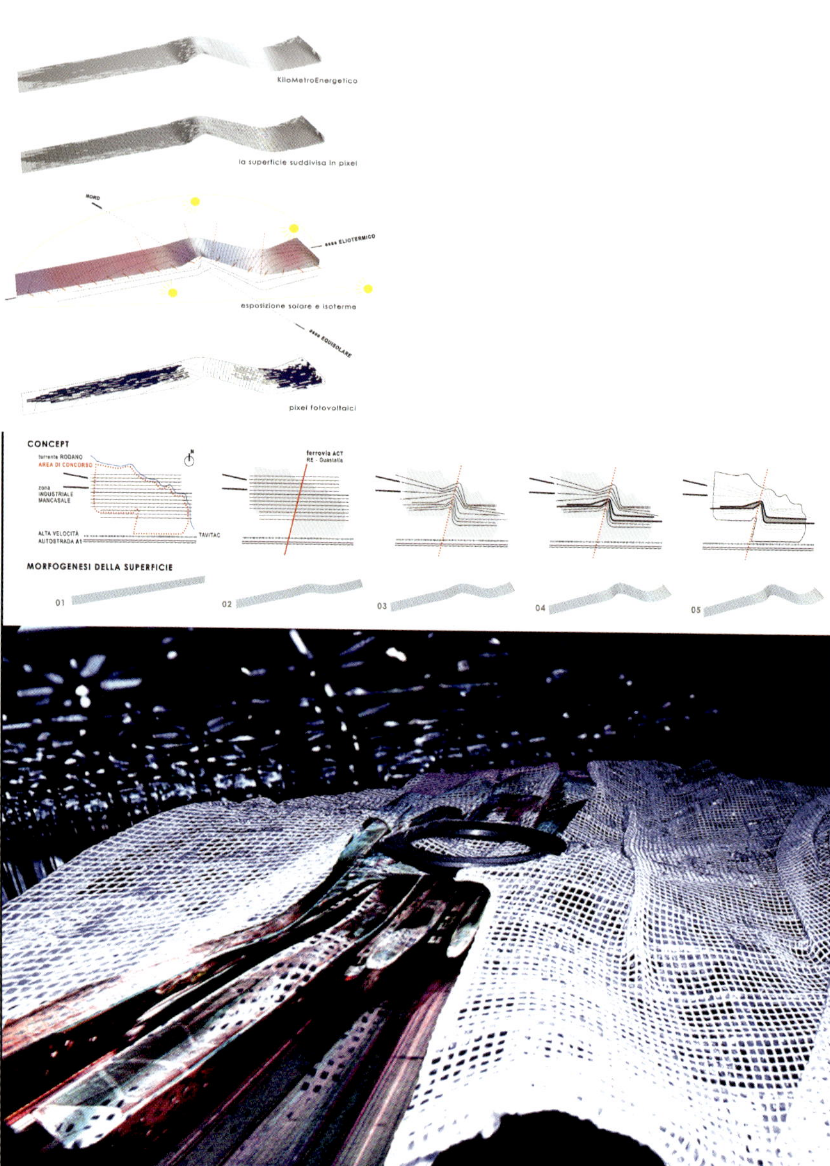

:KMᵉ:

:type: project competition Europan IX - 2007
:place: Reggio nell'Emilia (Re)
:with: marino la torre, unoaunostudio

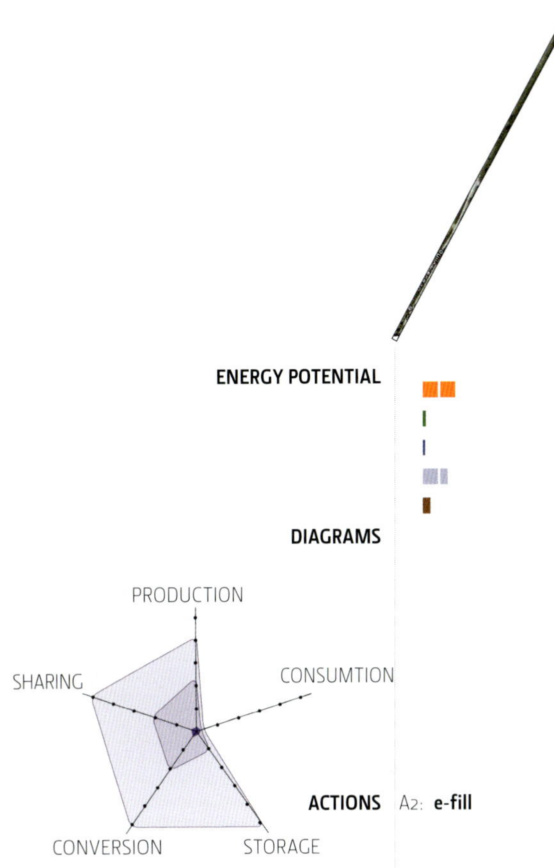

CHARACTERISTICS of the SITES:
borders: the borders of major infrastructure (such as
airports) become areas of margin, inactive, unused,
"lost lands" within the city.

TRANSFORMATIVE POTENTIAL of the DISTRICT:
exhibited a linear system
of optimally heliothermic axis.

KMe

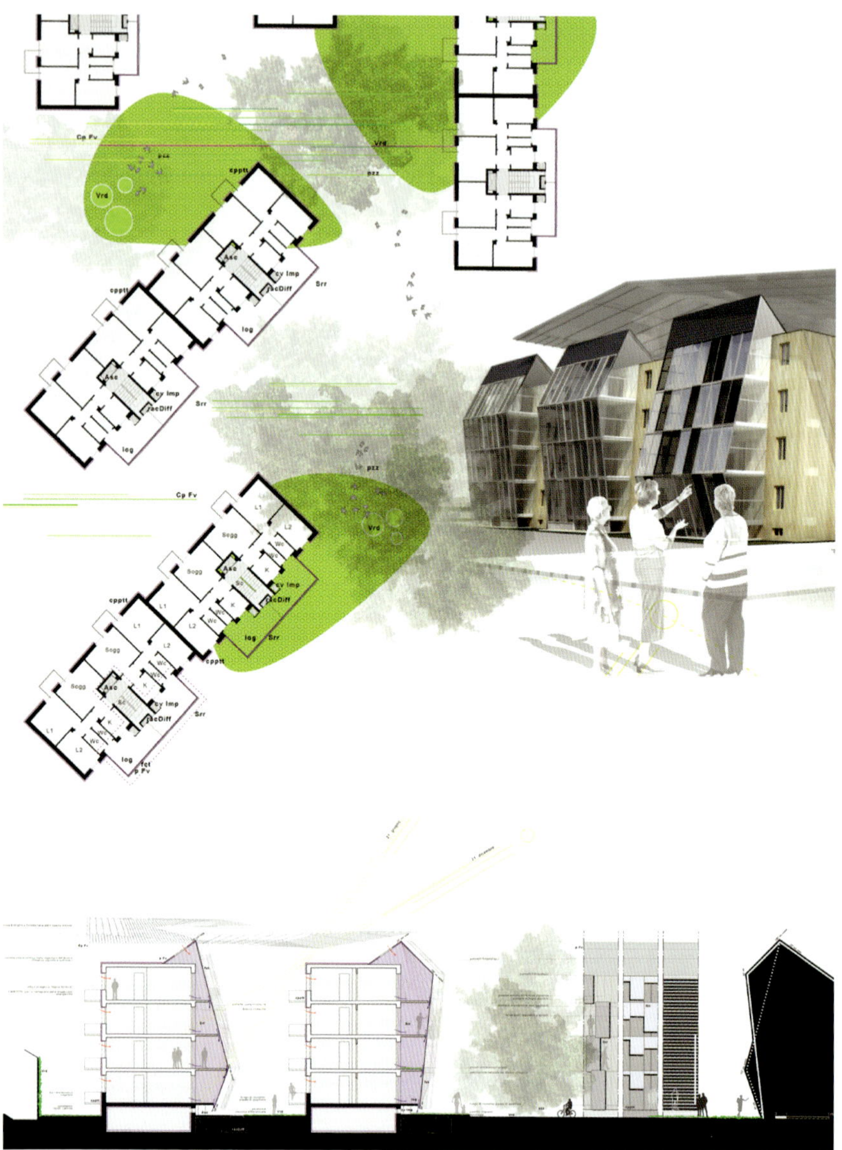

DISTRICT ENERGY:

type: project competition - 2007 (project excluded)

place: Castellammare di Stabia (Na)

with: marino la torre, giorgio caizzi, Ater pescara, unoaunostudio

DISTRICT ENERGY

CHARACTERISTICS of the SITES:
within the fabric of the city of Pescara, there are
some residential areas of consistent configuration,
like the Aterno district. It is a real local community,
offering services to people, sports, green, and leisure.

TRANSFORMATIVE POTENTIAL of the DISTRICT:
this "micro-city within a city" has been imagined
(already in the planning stage and its implementation)
to be capable of becoming partially self-sufficient, it
is the only district in the territory of Pescara to have
a solar thermal system implanted on the roofs since
its implementation. But this is not enough ..... Its
proximity to the Pescara - Chieti - Rome railway line
is significant, as well as its proximity to a nodal point
of the medium voltage power grid.

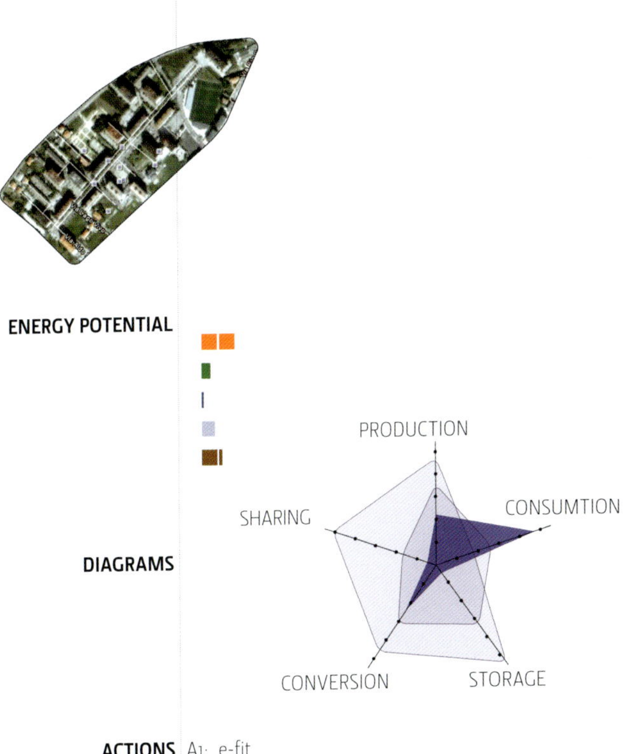

ENERGY POTENTIAL

DIAGRAMS

ACTIONS A1: e-fit
A3: e-pull

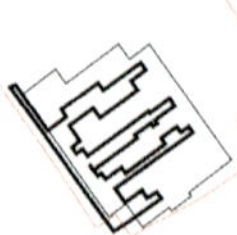

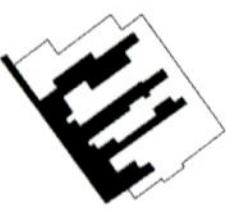

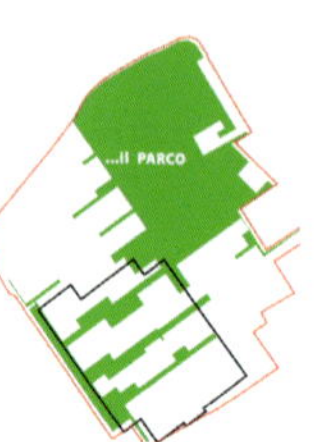

CLUSTER ENERGY:

type: project competition - 2009
place: Dueville (Vi)
with: marino la torre, paolo martellucci, unoaunostudio

ENERGY POTENTIAL:

ACTIONS   A3: **e-pull**

CHARACTERISTICS of the SITES:

one of the areas off-limits in the city is provided by the prison, as a "special block" that occupies a small portion of land. The prison is representative of all those social spaces and incubators that are scattered in cities like hospitals, schools, etc.. These sites, together with the airport and station (the "non-places") become spaces for the activation and testing of renewable energy devices.

TRANSFORMATIVE POTENTIAL of the DISTRICT:

The district is characteristic and differs from those areas used by the public, due to its characteristic of being enclaves in the city. There are no trade relations with the outside world, beyond the high boundary wall, but these sites could become energy wells for the production, consumption and accumulation on the spot or conversion to other portions of territory? (The economy of the future of energy sharing)

DIAGRAMS

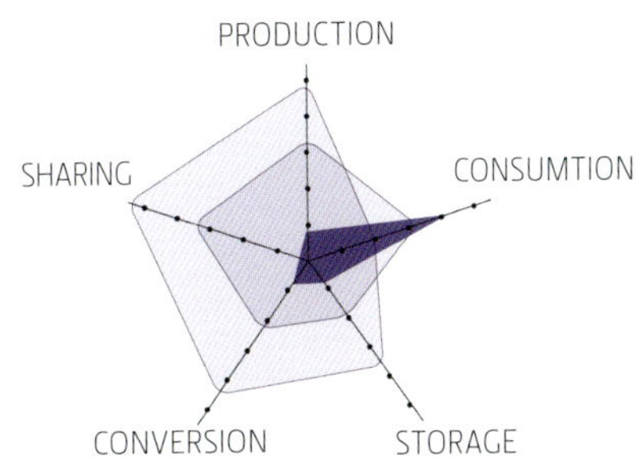

CLUSTER ENERGY

INFRA-ENERGY:

type: architect invited to the 10. Architecture Exhibition – Biennial of Venezia - 2006 - Italian pavilion – ITALIA-y-2026. Invitation to Vema. – project presented: VELOCITY
place: VeMa (Verona-Mantova)
with: marino la torre, unoaunostudio, marco morante, maura scarcella, Giuseppe marcotullio, andrea mezzaro-ma, annalisa taballione, laq__architettura, irina novarese, rodolphe luscher, filippo broggini

INFRA ENERGY

ACTIONS   A2:   **e-fill**

ENERGY POTENTIAL

DIAGRAMS

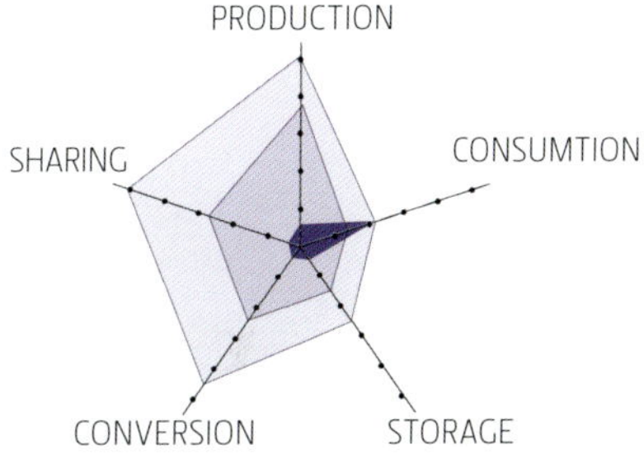

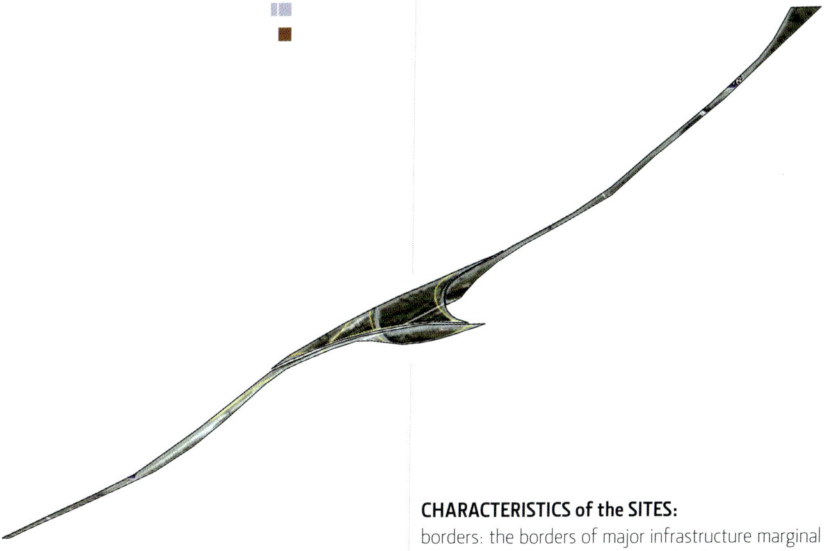

CHARACTERISTICS of the SITES:

borders: the borders of major infrastructure marginal become areas, inactive, unused, "lost lands" within the territories.

TRANSFORMATIVE POTENTIAL of the DISTRICT:

exhibited a linear system optimally on a heliothermic axis.

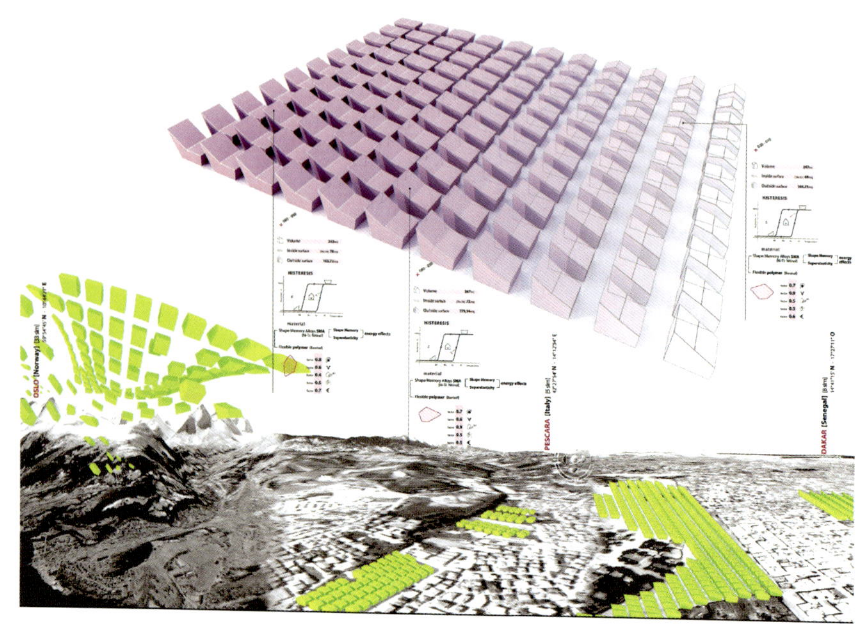

GREEN HOUSE ENERGY:

type: project competition Iaac - Institute for Advanced Architecture of Catalonia - "Self-Sufficient Housing.
The self-fab house" 2° - 2007
place: Barcellona (Spagna)
with: marino la torre, paola marcantonio, nicolas tixier, unoaunostudio

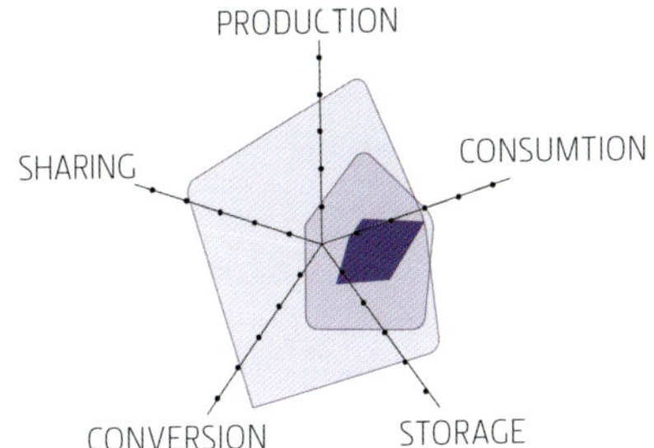

DIAGRAMS

ACTIONS A2: **e-fill**

ENERGY POTENTIAL

GREEN HOUSE ENERGY

CHARACTERISTICS of the SITES:

the hill system presents several unique characteristics and features, starting from Pescara and going south, we see that the ridges are characterized by the landscape of greenhouses: locations for the production and crop specialist production.

TRANSFORMATIVE POTENTIAL of the DISTRICT:

systems of greenhouses become places and opportunities to generate energy by entering a revitalization in the chain production also in energy industries. The places of production could become complex systems that produce and sell and exchange-not only tomatoes, but also energy.

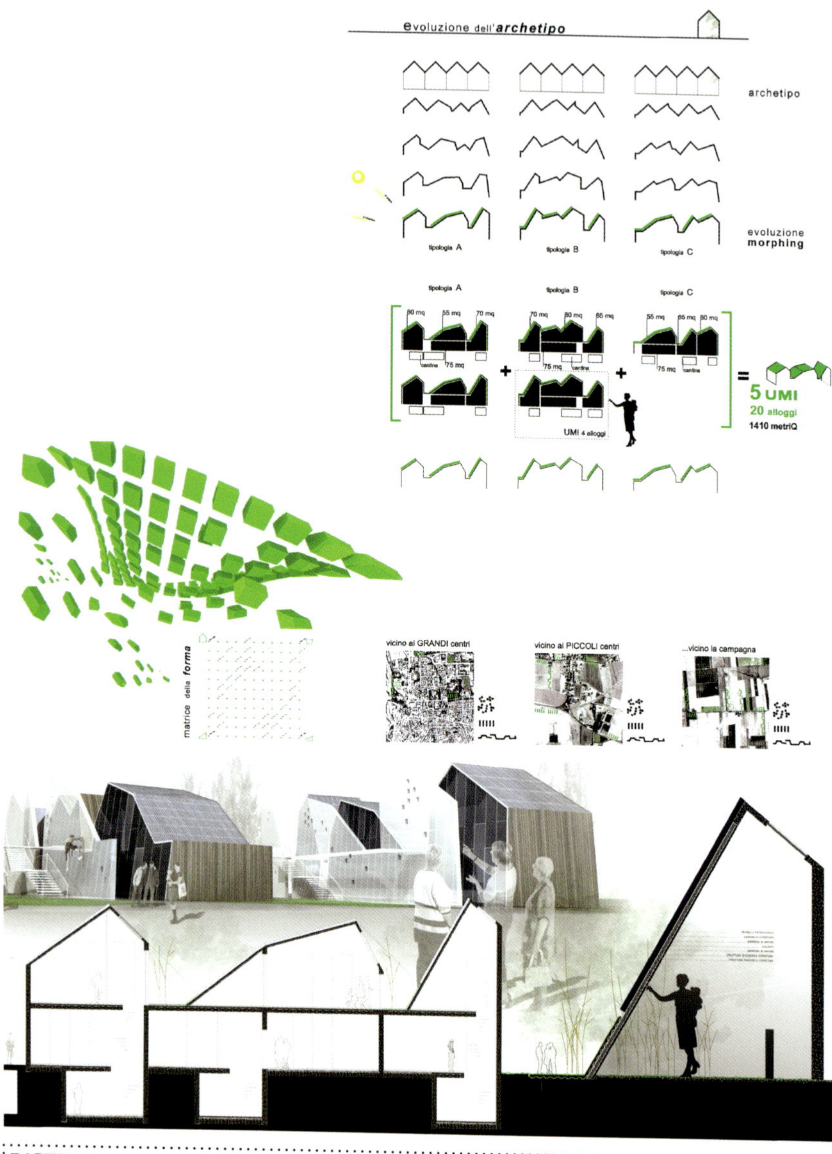

DISTRICT ENERGY:

type: project competition - 2008
place: Rovigo (Ro)
with: marino la torre, unoaunostudio, mariangela pugliese, alessandra salciccia, giorgio caizzi, Ater pescara

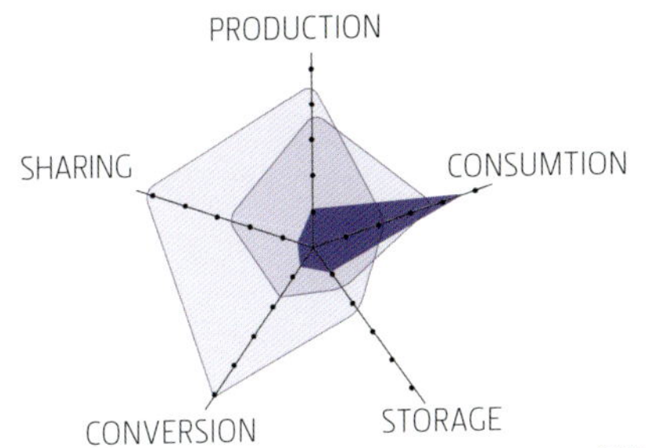

DIAGRAMS

ACTIONS A1: **e-fit** A3: **e-pull**

ENERGY POTENTIAL

CHARACTERISTICS of the SITES:
there are different classes of neighborhood in the city of Pescara. These can become a model for the application of energy systems that are not only passive (culling of consumption), but mainly "neighborhoods island", meaning living models that raise the standard of building-energy-inhabited (and not only energy-intensive!).

TRANSFORMATIVE POTENTIAL of the DISTRICT:
are buildings that fit into the context, in relation to the orography of the land, the sea breezes, making it unusual challenge of reactivation of the residential areas of active energy costs.

DISTRICT ENERGY

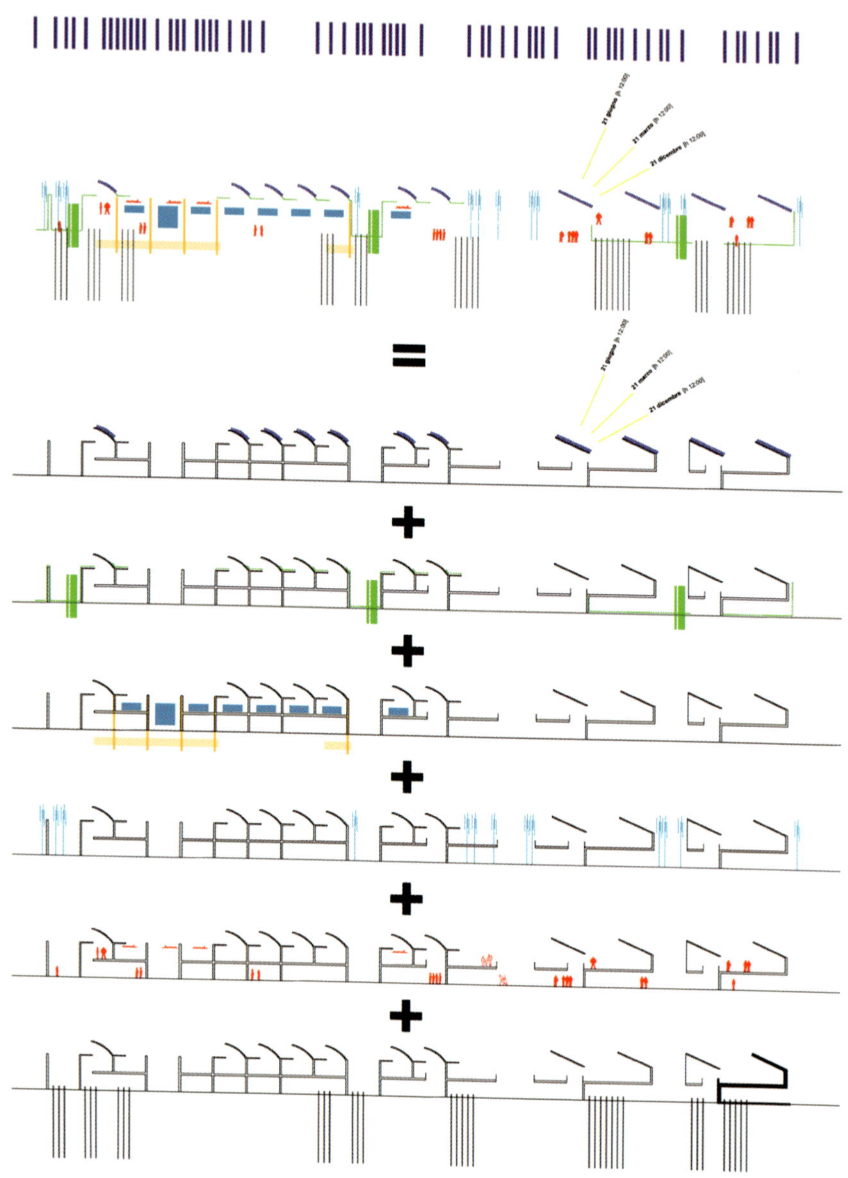

ENERGY ZONE:

type: project competition - 2006 (first prize)
place: Biella (Bi)
with: paolo martellucci, unoaunostudio

CHARACTERISTICS of the SITES:
the fabric of settlements on the Adriatic coast has characters of similarity, repetition, especially with respect to the reporting infrastructure that characterize the coastal system of Abruzzo.

TRANSFORMATIVE POTENTIAL of the DISTRICT:
buildings, courtyards, lots, blocks, districts or communities tablets between the railway and the SS16 tissue become a sponge for a pilot project for increasing energy areas.

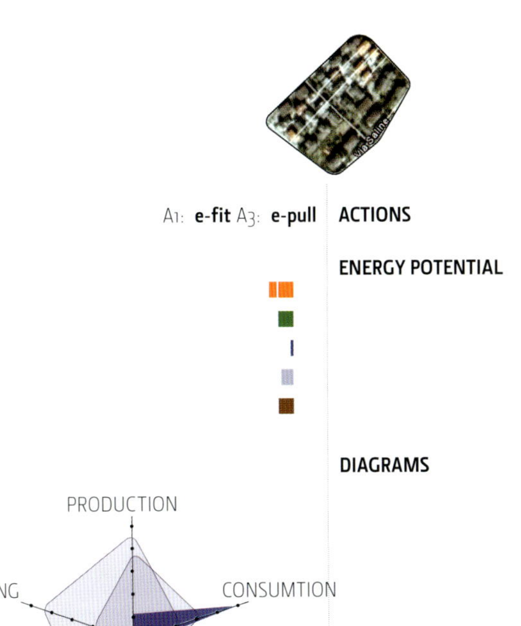

ENERGY ZONE

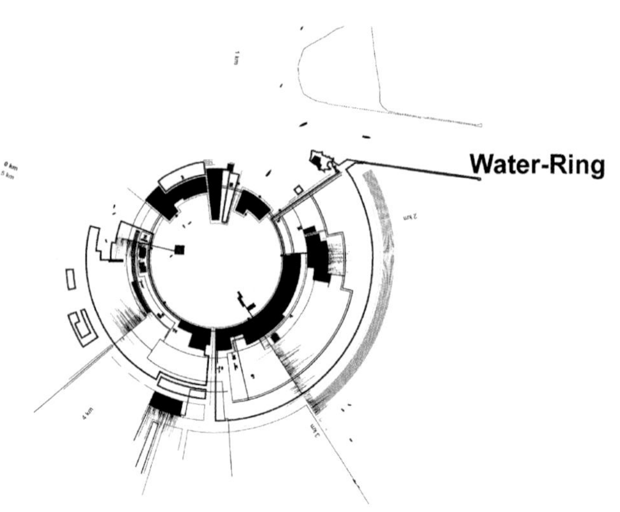

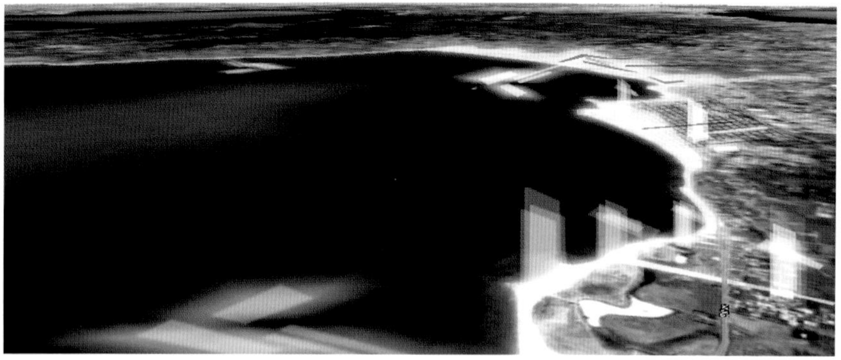

WATER FARM:
type: project competition - 2010
place: Chioggia (Ve)
with: marino al torre, chiara pirro, giulio mandrillo, unoaunostudio

WATER FARM

CHARACTERISTICS of the SITES:
marine works are often seen as single function devices, but could be reconsidered real engine for the production and energy conversion.

TRANSFORMATIVE POTENTIAL of the DISTRICT:
potentially the breakwater, as well as marine barriers (water) can become places of farm water, using the kinetic energy of the sea (although low power in the Abruzzo coast), and solar photovoltaics.

A1: **e-fit**   ACTIONS
A2: **e-fill**
A3: **e-pull**

ENERGY POTENTIAL

DIAGRAMS

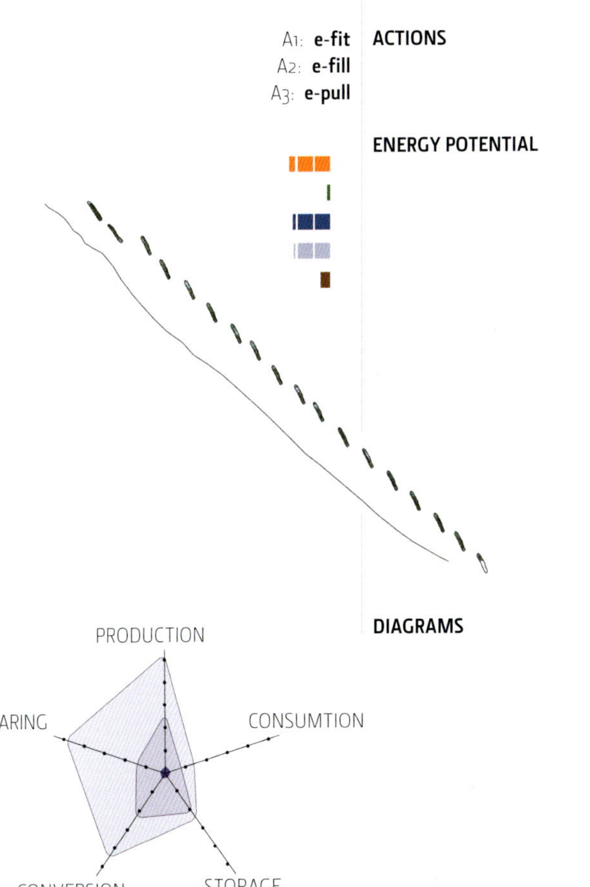

WATER FARM [3]:

type: architect invited to the 10. Architecture Exhibition – Biennial of Venezia - 2006 - Italian pavilion – ITALIA-y-2026. Invited to Vema. – project presented: VELOCITY
place: VeMa (Verona-Mantova)
with: marino la torre, unoaunostudio, marco morante, maura scarcella, Giuseppe marcotullio, andrea mezzaro-ma, annalisa taballione, laq_architettura, irina novarese, rodolphe luscher, filippo broggini

CHARACTERISTICS of the SITES:
devices oil platforms at sea characterize the horizon
from the coast of Abruzzo.

TRANSFORMATIVE POTENTIAL of the DISTRICT:
new areas of energy are mainly in the sea ....

ACTIONS   A1: **e-fit**
A2: **e-fill**
A3: **e-pull**

ENERGY POTENTIAL

DIAGRAMMI

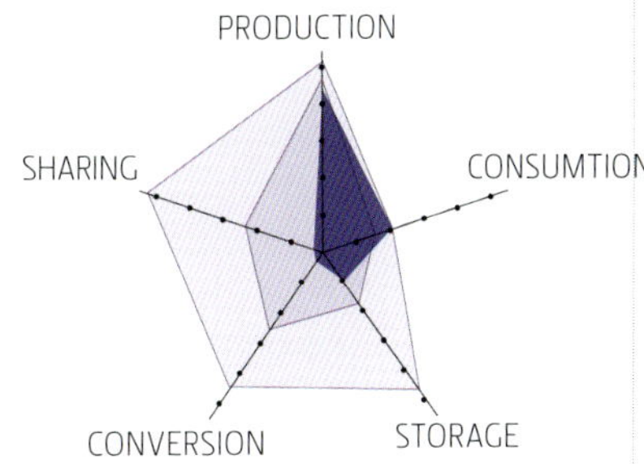

WATER FARM [3]

e-tools

 micro energy node

 energy infra SPACES

 e-border energy

 e-plug

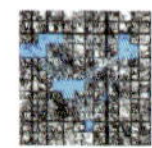 cluster energy

 energy park

BUILDING SCALE

e-surfaces 2d

e-overstructure

e-parassites

e-infill

e-box

SCALE 1 a 1 (car/person)

e-shop

e-markets

personal e-makers

public share-car

In this section we specify the character of the e-tools, regarded as devices capable of building urban energy scenarios that define urban models ready to meet the challenges that the contemporary world requires us to face. The different parts of the tool-kit, identified as weak energy devices will be able to relate to each other and with the 'network', enabling an exchange between the parties related to the principles of mutual aid efficiency. Through the construction schedule will identify the characteristics of "energy community". Recording the information about "the characteristics of places" and "transformative potential of the district" will aid summarizing the "actions", the "potential energy" and "plots" (from: production, consumption, storage, conversion and exchange energy). We abstract the identifying characteristics of the different parts (districts, cells, islands or communities) in order to define the relationships between e-tools and the "energy community". Reconstructing the relationship between the character of places (features and capabilities) and the actions of project proposals, one questions the energy community in order to summarize the distinctive and define those "principles of organization, and relationship addiction, required to achieve independent and (in) dependent (between them).
This is necessary to bring us closer to a systemic vision of the territory, able to build relationships (and not materials, products or services, energy …) trying to (pre) view include a metro mobile devices.

ENERGY COMMUNITY

CHARACTERISTICS of the SITES:
centers-places of the territories within the hills that dot the "glen" in Pescara. These become the first units to activate, strengthen and re-think energy and sustainability, ensuring a throw-in value not only of historic fabrics, places of Meor, but also an in-vestment in an economy of sustainability and energy of/in smaller towns.

TRANSFORMATIVE POTENTIAL of the DISTRICT:
urban centers considered as "urban units" that gravitate on the hill facing the valley at south-east/east; recognizable for their configuration as the core itself, which for the provision of basic services to its internal energy potential urban communities.

ACTIONS:
A1: **e-fit**

ENERGY POTENTIAL:

DIAGRAMS

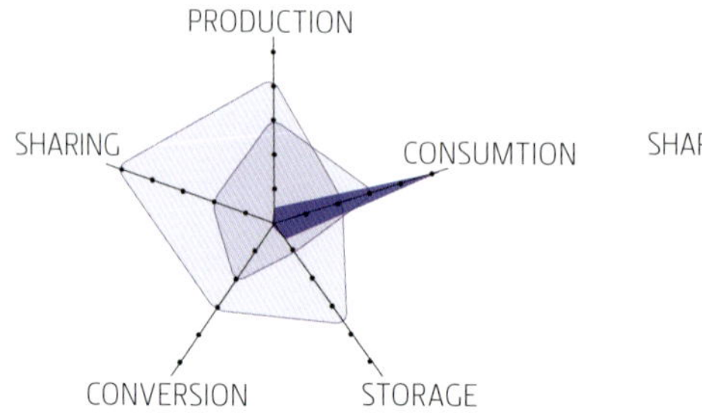

VERTICAL FARM

CHARACTERISTICS of the SITES:
node-points inside the hilly areas suited to agricultu-re, farm equipment and more, with potential energy, tourism and hospitality.

TRANSFORMATIVE POTENTIAL of the DISTRICT:
territorial systems point quite commonly in these contexts toard tanks to collect rainwater and reuse it to exploit the fields, to use urban centers as real battery storage tanks or potential energy. Farm for production of crops for bio-oil.

ACTIONS:
A2: **e-fill**

ENERGY POTENTIAL:

DIAGRAMS

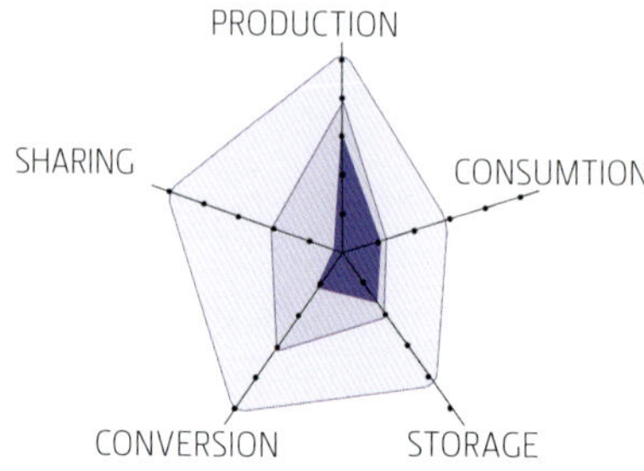

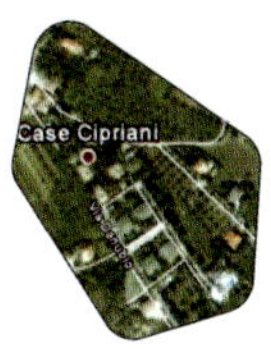

ENERGY COMMUNITY

CHARACTERISTICS of the SITES:
joints that are located in urbanized areas of the foothills and of settlements that have a hill and how use typical mobility of urban reality.

TRANSFORMATIVE POTENTIAL of the DISTRICT:
urbanized cores similar to " stand-alone planning units" (as servants) and their complex relationship of how to access the networks of the urban area. The main feature is their good sun exposure (as opposed to the territories "in the shadow of the valleys") and the proximity to sensitive environmental attractors of the riverbed and its natural basin.

ENERGY PARK

CHARACTERISTICS of the SITES:
natural green space by river. Place of highest naturalistic recognition, potentially rich in natural-energy-environmental characteristic elements, but currently little used (or not used).

TRANSFORMATIVE POTENTIAL of the DISTRICT:
as well as able to enter their chain of energy production "waste" means fuel for biomass. Potential site for the cultivation of wood to produce bio-oil.

ACTIONS:
A1: **e-fit**
A3: **e-pull**

ENERGY POTENTIAL:

ACTIONS:
A2: **e-fill**

ENERGY POTENTIAL:

DIAGRAMS

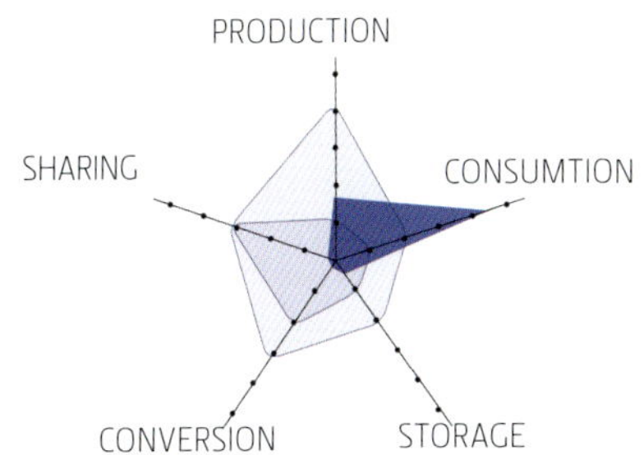

DIAGRAMS

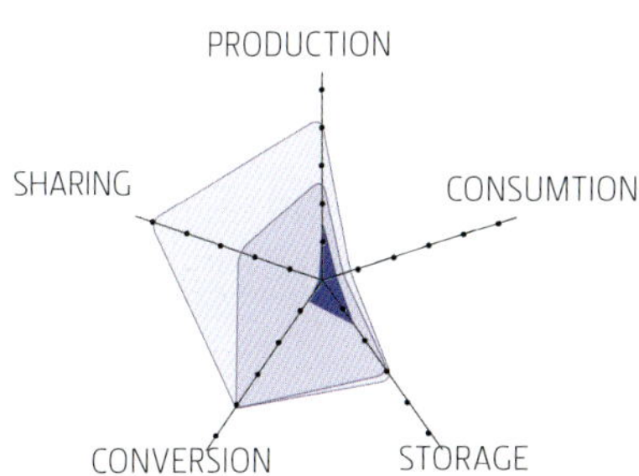

ENERGY INDUSTRY

CHARACTERISTICS of the SITES:
industrial areas close to cities, often within the sensitive context of the riverbed. There are several industrial districts (still in use or being sold) that ASI owns and manages in the area encompassing the valley of Pescara.

TRANSFORMATIVE POTENTIAL of the DISTRICT:
some industrial districts, both by location (proximity to the river and the portals to the territory) and in size can become challenges of conversion of the production sites and obtain key roles in energy supply chains trying to also introject the energy system, not only consumed, but also home grown and with the possibility of becoming subject to territorial energy exchange (energy-hub).

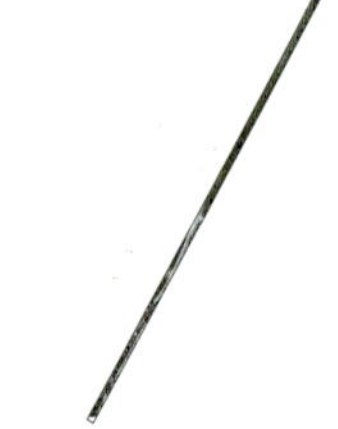

KM^e

CHARACTERISTICS of the SITES:
borders: the borders of major infrastructure (such as airports) become areas of margin, inactive, unused, "lost lands" within the city.

TRANSFORMATIVE POTENTIAL of the DISTRICT:
exhibited a linear system of optimally heliothermic axis.

ACTIONS:
A1: **e-fit**
A3: **e-pull**

ENERGY POTENTIAL:

DIAGRAMS

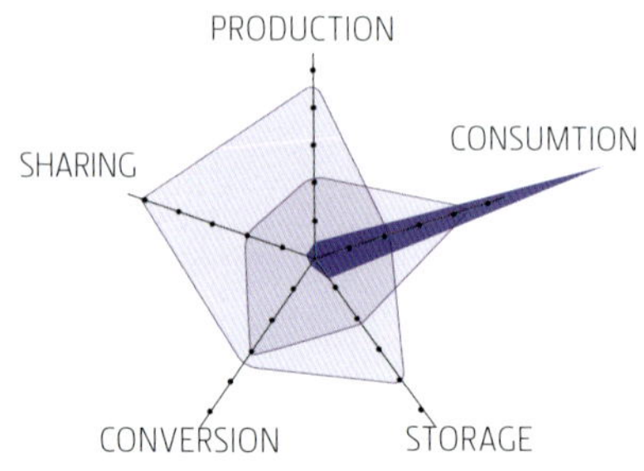

ACTIONS:
A2: **e-fill**

ENERGY POTENTIAL:

DIAGRAMS

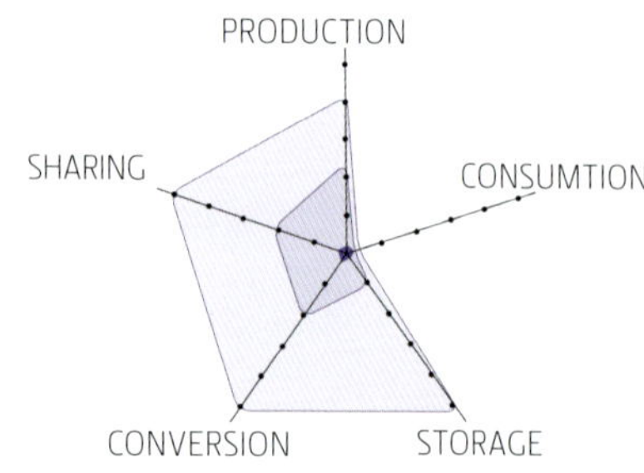

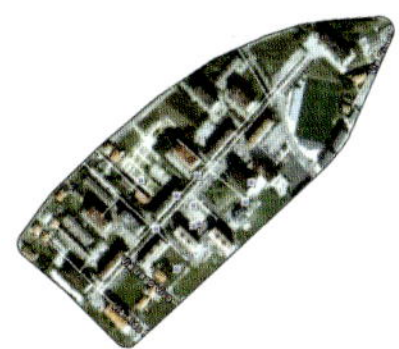

DISTRICT ENERGY

CHARACTERISTICS of the SITES:
within the fabric of the city of Pescara, there are some residential areas of consistent configuration, like the Aterno district. It is a real local community, offering services to people, sports, green, and leisure.

TRANSFORMATIVE POTENTIAL of the DISTRICT:
this "micro-city within a city" has been imagined (already in the planning stage and its implementation) to be capable of becoming partially self-sufficient, it is the only district in the territory of Pescara to have a solar thermal system implanted on the roofs since its implementation. But this is not enough ..... Its proximity to the Pescara - Chieti - Rome railway line is significant, as well as its proximity to a nodal point of the medium voltage power grid.

ACTIONS:
A1: **e-fit**
A3: **e-pull**

ENERGY POTENTIAL:

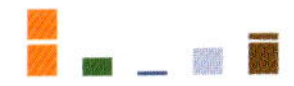

DIAGRAMS

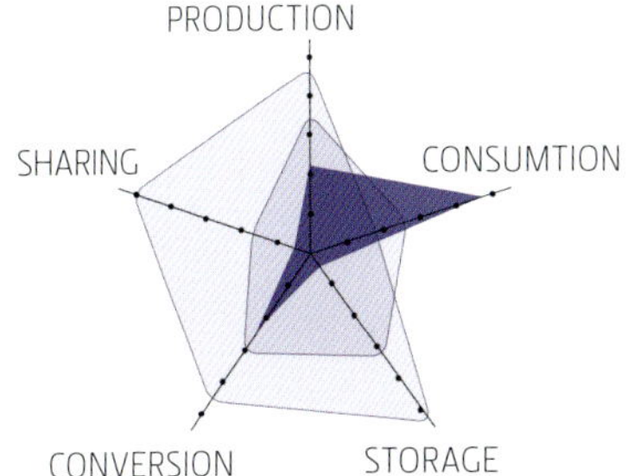

CLUSTER ENERGY

CHARACTERISTICS of the SITES:
one of the areas off-limits in the city is provided by the prison, as a "special block" that occupies a small portion of land. The prison is representative of all those social spaces and incubators that are scattered in cities like hospitals, schools, etc.. These sites, together with the airport and station (the "non-places") become spaces for the activation and testing of renewable energy devices.

TRANSFORMATIVE POTENTIAL of the DISTRICT:
The district is characteristic and differs from those areas used by the public, due to its characteristic of being enclaves in the city. There are no trade relations with the outside world, beyond the high boundary wall, but these sites could become energy wells for the production, consumption and accumulation on the spot or conversion to other portions of territory? (The economy of the future of energy sharing)

ACTIONS:
A3: **e-pull**

ENERGY POTENTIAL:

DIAGRAMS

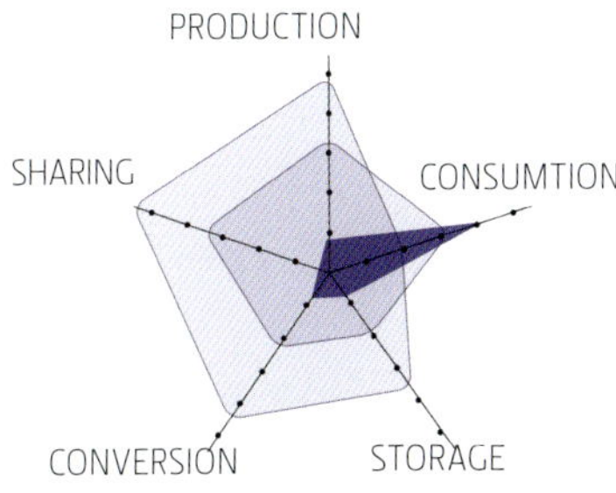

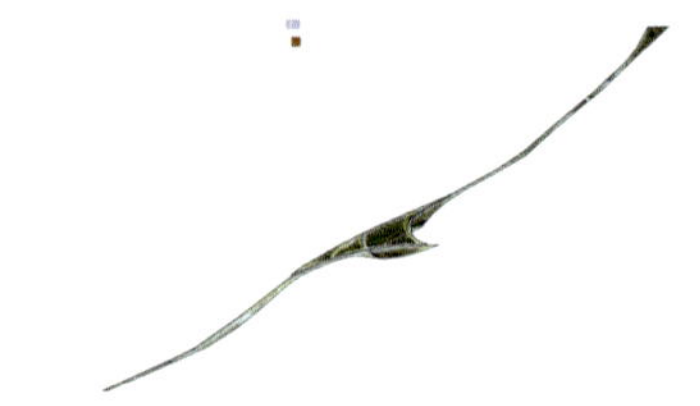

INFRA ENERGY

CHARACTERISTICS of the SITES:
borders: the borders of major infrastructure marginal become areas, inactive, unused, "lost lands" within the territories.

TRANSFORMATIVE POTENTIAL of the DISTRICT:
exhibited a linear system optimally on a heliothermic axis.

GREEN HOUSE ENERGY

CHARACTERISTICS of the SITES:
the hill system presents several unique characteristics and features, starting from Pescara and going south, we see that the ridges are characterized by the landscape of greenhouses: locations for the production and crop specialist production.

TRANSFORMATIVE POTENTIAL of the DISTRICT:
systems of greenhouses become places and opportunities to generate energy by entering a revitalization in the chain production also in energy industries. The places of production could become complex systems that produce and sell and exchange-not only tomatoes, but also energy.

ACTIONS:
A2: **e-fill**

ENERGY POTENTIAL:

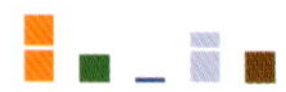

ACTIONS:
A2: **e-fill**

ENERGY POTENTIAL:

DIAGRAMS

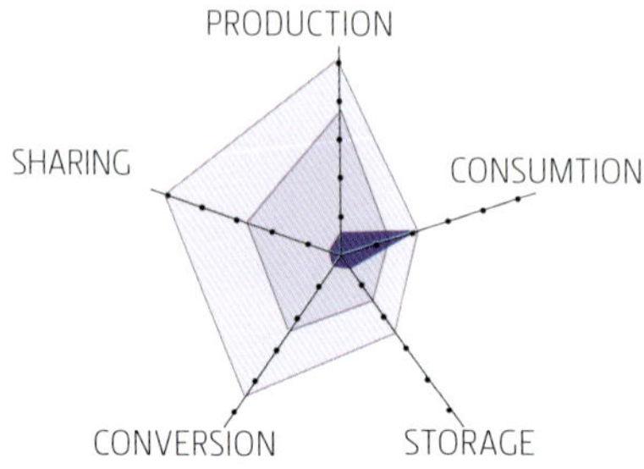

DIAGRAMS

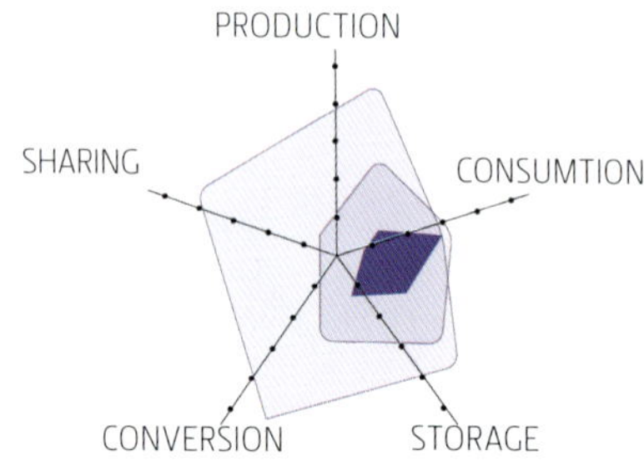

DISTRICT ENERGY

CHARACTERISTICS of the SITES:
there are different classes of neighborhood in the city of Pescara. These can become a model for the application of energy systems that are not only passive (culling of consumption), but mainly "neighborhoods island", meaning living models that raise the standard of building-energy-inhabited (and not only energy-intensive!).

TRANSFORMATIVE POTENTIAL of the DISTRICT:
are buildings that fit into the context, in relation to the orography of the land, the sea breezes, making it unusual challenge of reactivation of the residential areas of active energy costs.

ACTIONS:
A1: **e-fit**
A3: **e-pull**

ENERGY POTENTIAL:

DIAGRAMS

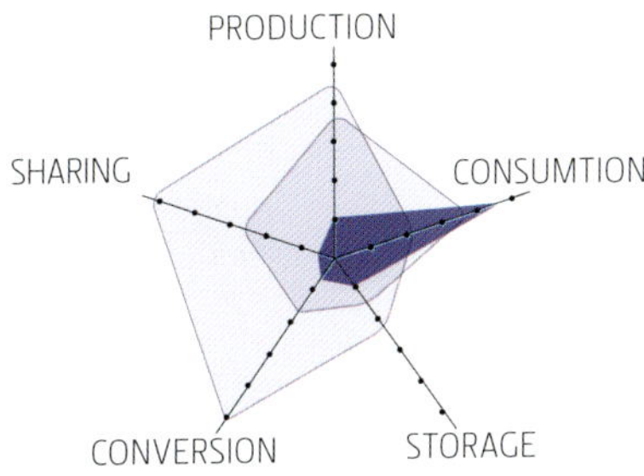

ENERGY ZONE

CHARACTERISTICS of the SITES:
the fabric of settlements on the Adriatic coast has characters of similarity, repetition, especially with respect to the reporting infrastructure that characterize the coastal system of Abruzzo.

TRANSFORMATIVE POTENTIAL of the DISTRICT:
buildings, courtyards, lots, blocks, districts or communities tablets between the railway and the SS16 tissue become a sponge for a pilot project for increasing energy areas.

ACTIONS:
A1: **e-fit**
A3: **e-pull**

ENERGY POTENTIAL:

DIAGRAMS

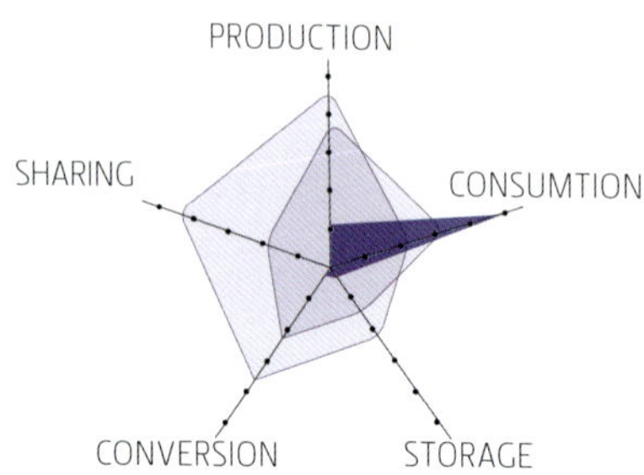

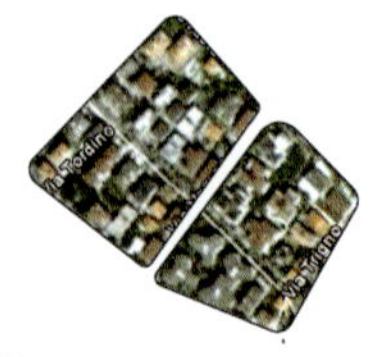

ENERGY ZONE

CHARACTERISTICS of the SITES:
the fabric of settlements on the Adriatic coast has characters of similarity, repetition, especially with respect to the reporting infrastructure that characterize the coastal system of Abruzzo.

TRANSFORMATIVE POTENTIAL of the DISTRICT:
buildings, courtyards, lots, blocks, districts or communities tablets between the railway and the SS16 tissue become a sponge for a pilot project for increasing energy areas.

ACTIONS:
A1: **e-fit**
A3: **e-pull**

ENERGY POTENTIAL:

DIAGRAMS

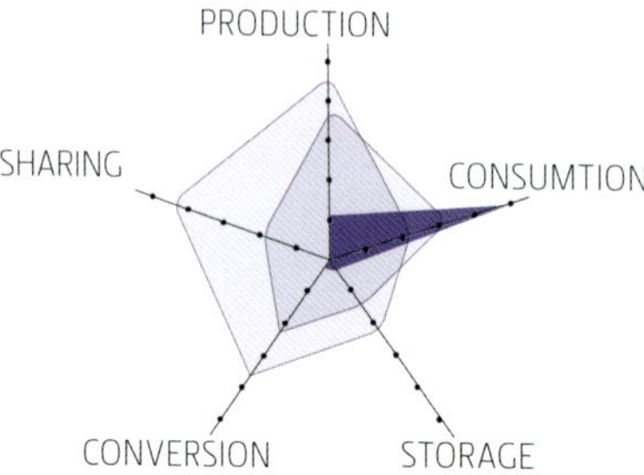

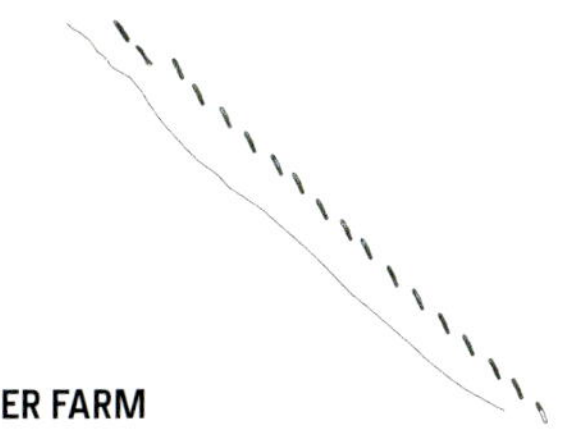

WATER FARM

CHARACTERISTICS of the SITES:
marine works are often seen as single function devices, but could be reconsidered real engine for the production and energy conversion.

TRANSFORMATIVE POTENTIAL of the DISTRICT:
potentially the breakwater, as well as marine barriers (water) can become places of farm water, using the kinetic energy of the sea (although low power in the Abruzzo coast), and solar photovoltaics.

ACTIONS:
A1: **e-fit**
A2: **e-fill**
A3: **e-pull**

ENERGY POTENTIAL:

DIAGRAMS
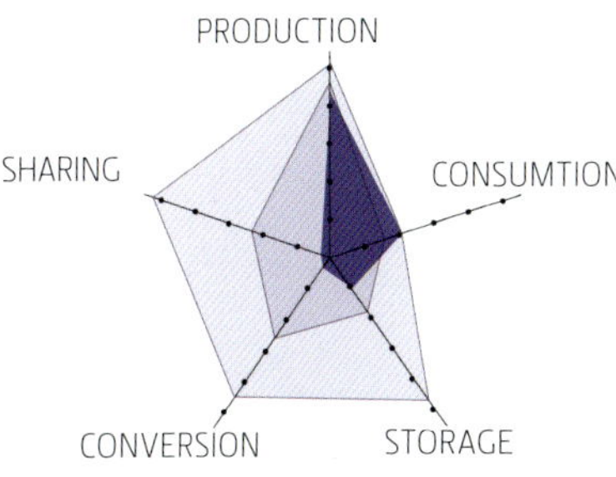

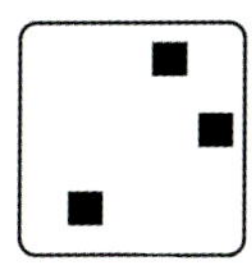

WATER FARM[3]

CHARACTERISTICS of the SITES:
devices oil platforms at sea characterize the horizon from the coast of Abruzzo.

TRANSFORMATIVE POTENTIAL of the DISTRICT:
new areas of energy are mainly in the sea ....

ACTIONS:
A1: **e-fit**
A2: **e-fill**
A3: **e-pull**

ENERGY POTENTIAL:
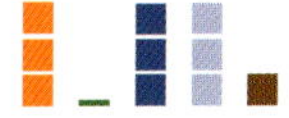

DIAGRAMS

e-tools

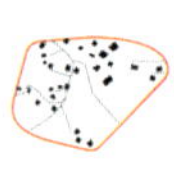

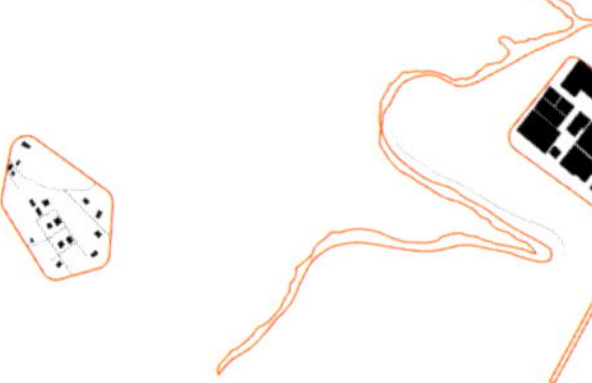

Micro energy nodes

ACTIONS:
A1: **e-fit**

A1. 01. a:
redevelopment of existing buildings
A1. 02. a:
reactivation energy of the smaller towns for new
hill-energy economy

ORGANIZATION:
O.1- deployment of photovoltaic and/or solar-thermal
energy production;
O.2- insertion of the rain tanks to collect first rain
water for each private unit;
O.3- introduction of microeolici systems in open
residential spaces

LINKS:
L.1- construction of a mutual aid network for the
exchange of energy between the different units or
properties;
L.2- introduction of small centers of community composting in order to reduce CO_2 and close the cycle of
wet waste;
L.3- provision of local exchange networks to enable
over-reporting processes, dependency and energy
exchange with/between other communities

DEPENDENCY:
D.1- construction of dependency relationships with
neighboring communities isolated and without an
exchange centers / energy storage

E-plug

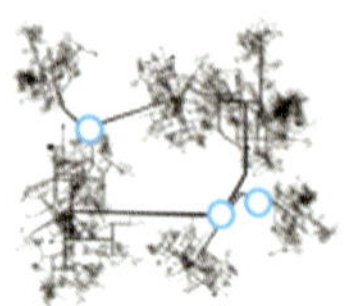

ACTIONS:
A2: **e-fill**

A2. 01. a:
integration of new devices capable of becoming new
urban energy machines

A2. 02. b:
vertical agriculture and integrated energy production

ORGANIZATION:
O.1-new space for growing vertical in the vicinity of
pools of water in the territories;
O.2-establishing the mechanisms for food production
for a short chain products (plants and animals),
O.3-integration of devices and energy machines for
new power plants (ta) diffused production, integrating territories, products and production (for a short
chain of energy)

LINKS:
L.1- typological and spatial hybridization of farms and
agriculture-related areas;
L.2-intruduzione small centers of energy production,
community composting facilities in order to reduce
CO_2 and close the cycle of wet waste ;

DEPENDENCY:
D.1- establishment of links and dependencies on the
surrounding energy communities
(become structuring elements for the territories)

COMMUNITY ENERGY

VERTICAL FARM

Micro energy nodes

ACTIONS:
A1: **e-fit**
A3: **e-pull**

A1. 02. b:
reactivation energy of the smaller hill towns -energy-
new economy
A3. 01. a:
make urban energy grafts

ORGANIZATION:
O.1-deployment of photovoltaic and/or solar-thermal
energy production
O.2 inclusion of rain tanks to collect first rain water
closet for each unit;
O.3-introduction of microeolici systems in housing
open spaces

LINKS:
L.1-construction of a mutual aid network for the
exchange of energy between different units or
property;
L.2-introduction of composting centers of small
communities, in order to remove CO_2 and close the
cycle of wet waste;
L.3-provision of local exchange networks to enable
over-reporting processes, dependence and energy
exchange with/between other communities

DEPENDENCY:
D.1- construction of dependency relationships with
isolated neighboring communities without exchange
centers/energy storage

Energy park

ACTIONS:
A2: **e-fill**

A2. 03. a:
new places - parks - forests for energy production

ORGANIZATION:
O.1-identification of new areas for energy production;
O.2-introduction of low energy devices in highly
qualified environments
O.3-integration of green space through different
technologies capable of putting in "energy productivity" the territory

LINKS:
L.1-typological and spatial hybridization of spaces
able to become opportunities for agricultural and
energy production
L.2-introduction of equipment for energy production
such as founding materials of open spaces

DEPENDENCY:
D1-establishment of links and dependencies with the
surrounding energy communities
(green spaces, open spaces become structuring
elements for the territories)

COMMUNITY ENERGY

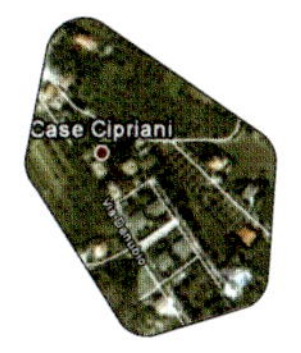

ENERGY PARK

Cluster energy

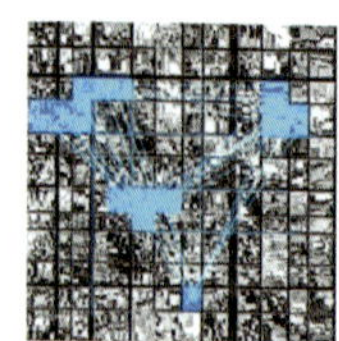

ACTIONS:
A1: **e-fit**
A3: **e-pull**

A1. 03. a:
energetic rivitilization of industrial areas
A3. 02. a:
energy grafts in the places of ordinary production

ORGANIZATION:
O.1-identification of new areas available to accommodate solar energy and/or solar-thermal production
systems
O.2-production mix from renewable energy systems
capable of determining a continuous production
through various forms and methods of energy
production

LINKS:
L.1-construction of a mutual aid network for the
exchange of energy between the industrial areas and
residential areas of the city
L.2 preparation of supra-local exchange networks to
enable processes of relationships, dependency and
energy exchange with / between others (including
remote communities);
L.3-potential area for the thermal network users (not
just electricity generation) becoming the new places
for urban energy

DEPENDENCY:
D.1- construction of dependency relationships with
isolated neighboring communities for the exchange
of energy
(electricity and heat for users)

INDUSTRY ENERGY

Energy infra SPACES

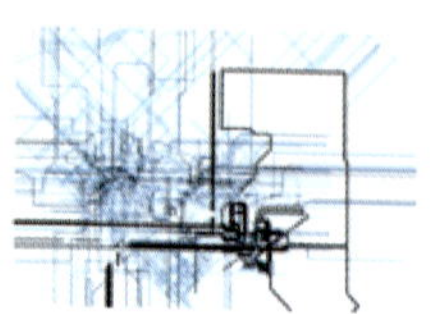

ACTIONS:
A2: **e-fill**

A2. 04. a:
activate virtuous processes in areas of relevance and
in respect of infrastructure for linear/continuous
energy production

ORGANIZATION:
O.1-identification of new areas dedicated to energy
production
O.2-introduction of different devices capable of
producing and supplying energy to the areas crossed
by the same infrastructure,
O.3- revitalization of space resulting from urban infrastructure and extra-urban areas, seeking to define
new modes of production, transport and energy
consumption

LINKS:
L.1-spatial and typological hybridization of infrastructure;
L.2-introduction of devices capable of capturing solar
energy and wind energy along the infrastructure

DEPENDENCY:
D.1- establishment of links and dependencies with
the energy community determining a new conti-
nuous/linear energetic of the territory

KM²

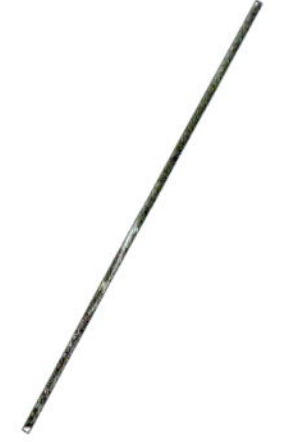

Micro energy nodes

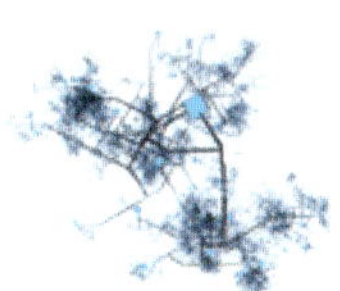

ACTIONS:
A1: **e-fit**
A3: **e-pull**

A1. 04. a:
energy regeneration of housing areas
A3. 03. a:
energy grafts in areas of ordinary production

ORGANIZATION:
O.1-identification of areas available to accommodate
solar energy and/or solar-thermal production systems
O.2 identification of a production mix of renewable
energy systems able to determine a continuous
production through various forms and methods of
energy production

LINKS:
L.1-construction of a mutual aid network for the
exchange of energy between the densely populated
areas of the city and other communities
L.2-potential areas for the construction of a network
of thermal users, becoming the new places of urban
energy which produce electricity and heat

DEPENDENCY:
D.1- construction of dependency relationships with
isolated neighboring communities for the exchange
of energy (for electricity and heat use)

Cluster energy

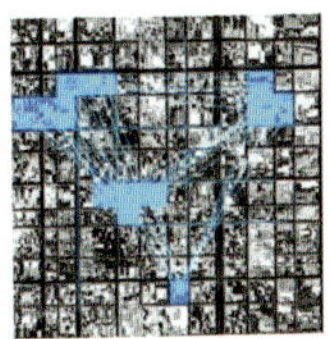

ACTIONS:
A3: **e-pull**

A3. 03. a: regeneration efficiency of closed areas -
urban enclaves

ORGANIZATION:
O.1 reactivation in terms of energy with purpose of
production in landlocked areas of the city (eg the
area of the prison);
O.2-renewable energy mix that can lead to a
continuous production through various forms and
methods

LINKS:
L.1-construction of a mutual aid network for the
exchange of energy between the industrial areas and
residential areas of the city
L.2 preparation of supra-local exchange networks to
enable processes of relationships, dependency and
energy exchange with / between others (including
remote communities);
L.3-potential area for the thermal network users (not
just electricity generation) becoming the new places
for urban energy

DEPENDENCY:
D.1- construction of dependency relationships with
isolated neighboring communities for the exchange
of energy (for electricity and heat use)

DISTRICT ENERGY

CLUSTER ENERGY

Energy infra SPACES

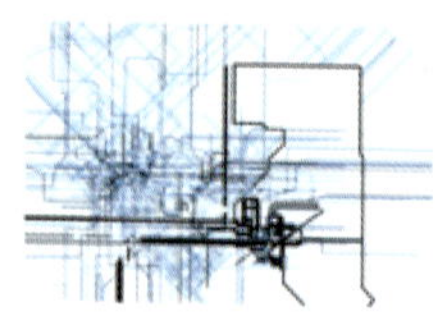

ACTIONS:
A2: **e-fill**

A2. 04. a:
activate virtuous processes in the spaces of relevance
and with relationships with the infrastructure for
linear/continuous energy production

ORGANIZATION:
O.1- identifying new areas for energy production;
O.2- introduction of different devices capable of
producing and supplying energy to areas crossed by
the same infrastructure;
O.3- revitalization of urban spaces between infrastructure and non-urban areas, seeking to define
new modes of production, transport and energy
consumption

LINKS:
L.1-typological and spatial hybridization of infrastructural space;
L.2-introduction of devices capable of capturing solar
energy and wind energy along the infrastructure

DEPENDENCY:
D1-establishment of links and dependencies with the
energy community determining a new continuous/
linear territorial energy wiring

E-plug

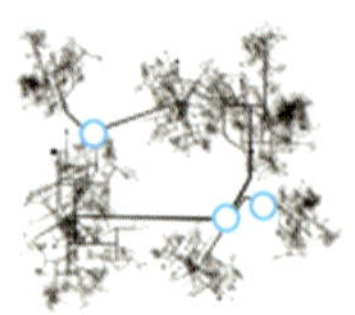

ACTIONS:
A2: **e-fill**

A2. 01. a:
integration of new devices capable of becoming new
urban energy machines
A2. 02. b:
Urban agriculture and integrated energy production

ORGANIZATION:
O.1-new spaces for urban cultivation for the integration between food and energy production systems;
O.2-establishing the mechanisms for food production
for short chain products (plants and animals),
O.3-integration with energy equipment and machinery for new diffuse production centres, integrating
territories, products and production (for a short chain
of energy)

LINKS:
L.1- typological and spatial hybridization of farms and
agriculture-related areas;
L.2-establishment of small centers of energy production, community composting facilities in order to
reduce CO_2 and close the cycle of wet waste ;

DEPENDENCY:
D.1- establishment of links and dependencies on the
surrounding energy communities (become structuring
elements for the territories)

INFRA-ENERGY

GREEN HOUSE ENERGY

Micro energy nodes

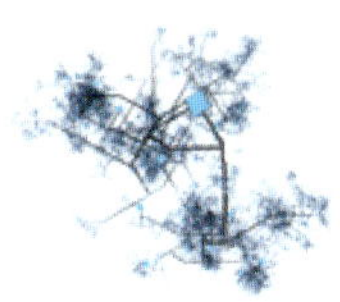

ACTIONS:
A1: **e-fit**
A3: **e-pull**

A1. 04. a:
energertic regeneration of housing areas
A3. 03. a:
energy grafts in areas of ordinary production

ORGANIZATION:
O.1-identification of areas available to accommodate
solar energy and/or solar-thermal production systems
O.2 identification of a production mix of renewable
energy systems able to determine a continuous
production through various forms and methods of
energy production

LINKS:
L.1-construction of a mutual aid network for the
exchange of energy between the densely populated
areas of the city and other communities
L.2-potential areas for the construction of a network
of thermal users, becoming the new places of urban
energy which produce electricity and heat

DEPENDENCY:
D.1- construction of dependency relationships with
isolated neighboring communities for the exchange
of energy (for electricity and heat use)

DISTRICT ENERGY

Cluster energy

ACTIONS:
A1: **e-fit**
A3: **e-pull**

A1. 01. b:
redevelopment of existing buildings
A1. 02. b:
 energy reactivation of the smaller hill towns - new
energy economy
A3. 01. a:
make urban energy grafts

ORGANIZATION:
O.1-deployment of photovoltaic and/or solar-thermal
energy production
O.2 inclusion of rain tanks to collect first rain water
closet for each unit;
O.3-introduction of microeolici systems in housing
open spaces

LINKS:
L.1-construction of a mutual aid network for the
exchange of energy between different units or
property;
L.2-introduction of small community composting
centers, in order to remove CO_2 and close the cycle
of wet waste;
L.3-provision of local exchange networks to favour
relationships, dependency and energy exchange with/
between other communities

DEPENDENCY:
D.1- construction of dependency relationships with
isolated neighboring communities without exchange
centers/energy storage

ENERGY ZONE

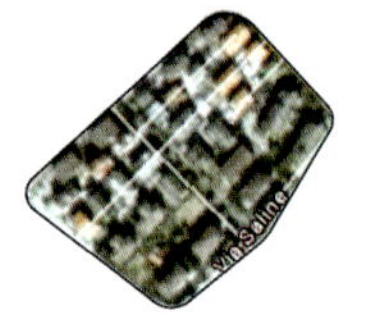

Micro energy nodes

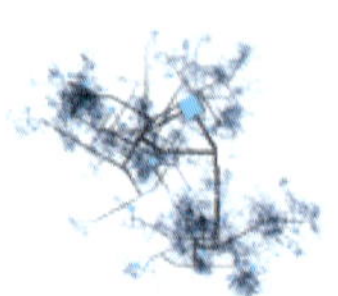

ACTIONS:
A1: **e-fit**
A3: **e-pull**

A1. 01. b:
redevelopment of existing buildings
A1. 02. b:
 energy reactivation of the smaller hill towns - new
energy economy
A3. 01. a:
make urban energy grafts

ORGANIZATION:
O.1-deployment of photovoltaic and/or solar-thermal
energy production
O.2 inclusion of rain tanks to collect first rain water
closet for each unit;
O.3-introduction of microeolici systems in housing
open spaces

LINKS:
L.1-construction of a mutual aid network for the
exchange of energy between different units or
property;
L.2-introduction of small community composting
centers, in order to remove CO_2 and close the cycle
of wet waste;
L.3-provision of local exchange networks to favour
relationships, dependency and energy exchange with/
between other communities

DEPENDENCY:
D.1- construction of dependency relationships with
isolated neighboring communities without exchange
centers/energy storage

ENERGY ZONE

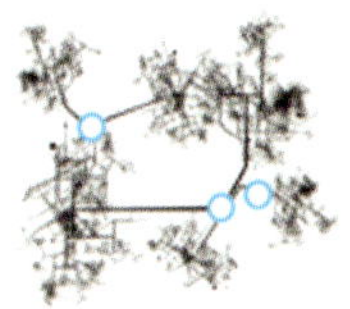

E-plug

ACTIONS:
A1: **e-fit**
A2: **e-fill**
A3: **e-pull**

A1. 04. c:
transformation of outcropping and underwater marine equipment
A2. 04. b:
energetic reactivation

ORGANIZATION:
O.1 energy-colonization of space at sea and floating islands;
O.2-entry devices that generate and produce solar, micro-wind and tidal energy;
O.3-rethinking barriers as opportunities for temporary summer structures, places for walks or a boulevard

LINKS:
L.1-construction of a mutual aid network for the exchange of energy for coastal equipment;
L.3-arrangement of supra-local exchange networks to enable relationships, dependency and energy exchange with the communities on the mainland

DEPENDENCY:
D1- Construction of dependency between isolated neighboring communities without an exchange centers/energy storage
D2-testing of new energy sites and new public space

E-border energy

ACTIONS:
A1: **e-fit**
A2: **e-fill**
A3: **e-pull**

A1. 04. c:
transformation of outcropping and underwater marine equipment
A2. 04. b:
off-shore Energy reactivation

ORGANIZATION:
O.1 energy colonization of space in the sea and sea platforms;
O.2-entry devices that generate and produce solar, micro-wind and tidal energy;
O.3-rethinking submerged marine barriers or offshore platforms as an opportunity for tourism revival in the Adriatic

LINKS:
L.1-construction of a mutual aid network for the exchange of energy for coastal equipment;
L.3-arrangement of supra-local exchange networks to enable relationships, dependency and energy exchange with the communities on the mainland

DEPENDENCY:
D1- Construction of dependent relationships with mainland communities for reactivation of energy sharing
D.2-experimentation of new energy sites and new receptive public spaces

WATER FARM

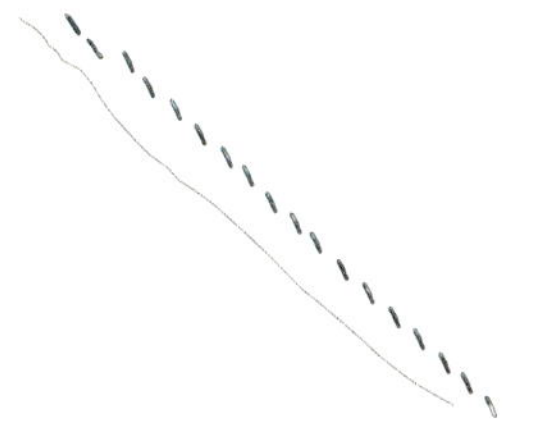

WATER FARM[3]

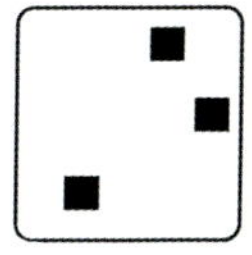

micro energy node

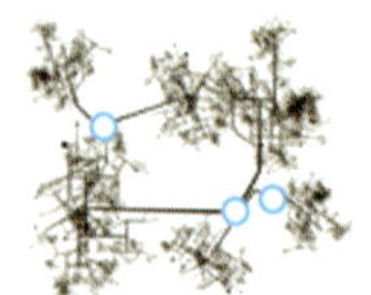

e-plug

micro energy node

energy park

COMMUNITY ENERGY

VERTICAL FARM

COMMUNITY ENERGY

ENERGY PARK

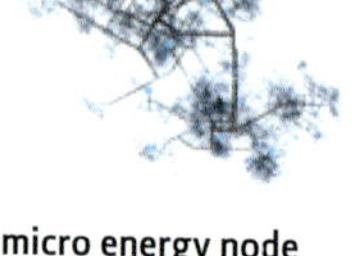

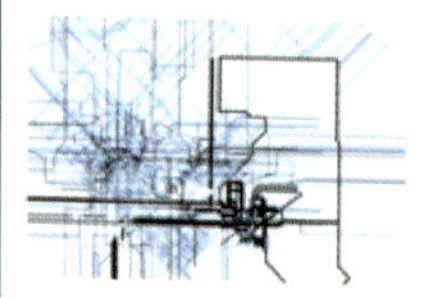

energy infra SPACES

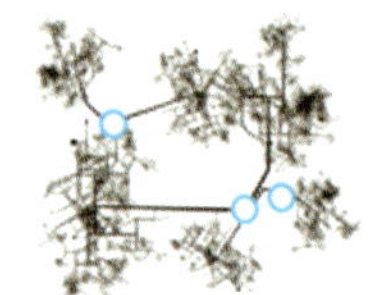

e-plug

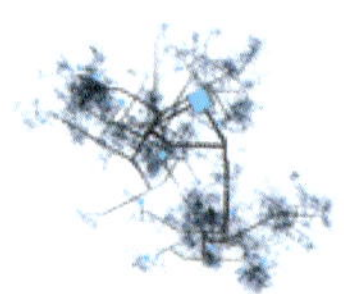

micro energy node

INFRA-ENERGY

GREEN HOUSE ENERGY

DISTRICT ENERGY

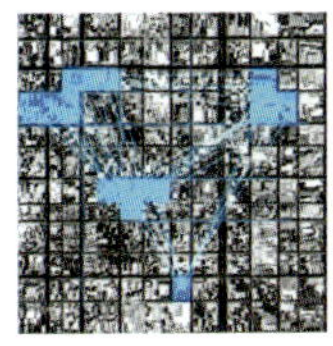

cluster energy

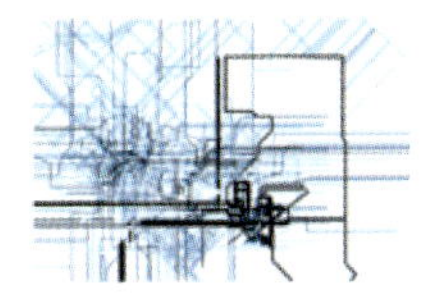

energy infra SPACES

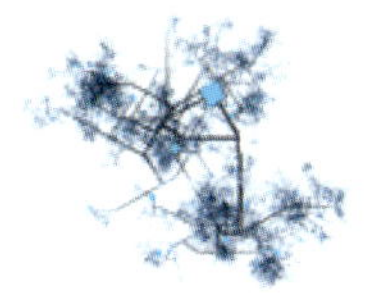

micro energy node

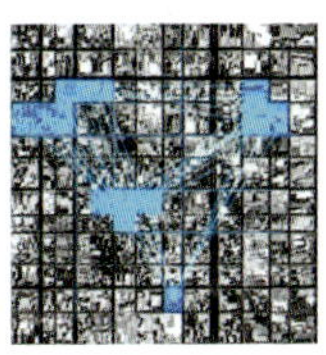

cluster energy

INDUSTRY ENERGY

KM²

DISTRICT ENERGY

CLUSTER ENERGY

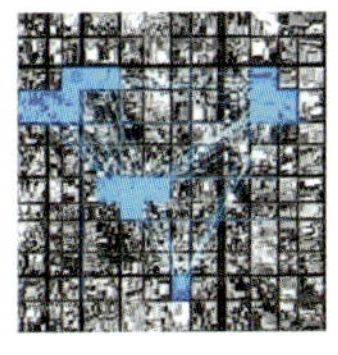

cluster energy

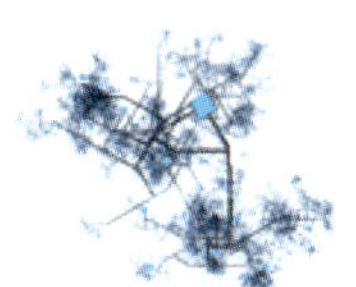

micro energy node

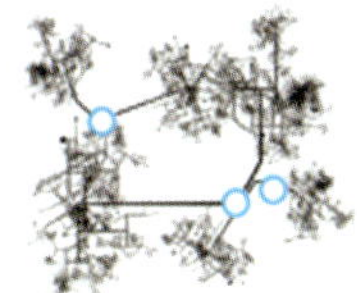

e-plug

e-plug

ENERGY ZONE

ENERGY ZONE

WATER FARM

WATER FARM³

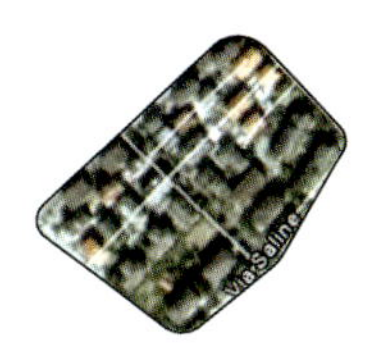

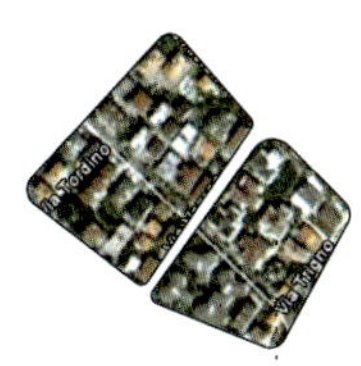

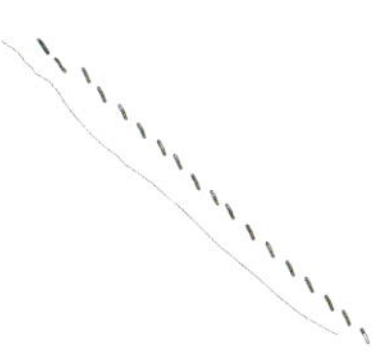

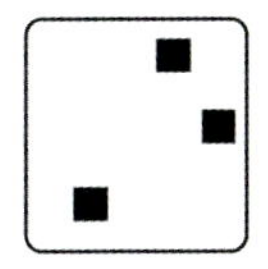

05
ENERGETIC RELATIONSHIP

In light of that previously defined, it is considered necessary to identify and define 3 scenarios (Centralized, Decentralized, distributed network) and the energy from each community, that determine the principles of energy associated with the development of a territorial system, to build the network. It is necessary to state that the electrification of urban areas is indifferent to the logic of development and urban planning. The urban electrification took place after the construction, development of the city.

The electricity infrastructure are the following urban disorder, networks are adaptive to different local contexts: The concept of energy supply of the territories and communities is not only linked to users of electricity but also thermal users (future development). This meaningful interpretation opens another very important aspect in the perspective of building a device based on a city's future energy mix (energy from different sources). In fact, the electric utilities have a different application and correspondence on the territory than, for example, to those stations. In fact, the electric utilities are characterized by the degree of capillary action inherent in the supply network (even at different voltages), in addition to networks that air can easily enliven, the existing overlap and juxtaposition; thermal ones, in contrast, never optimize the energy supply until they are "closed networks" (i.e. circular), resulting in the increase in "heat losses" during their journey. They are best when they have hubs (or points of attack / supply / socket / issue) very distant from each other, reducing and minimizing losses during the journey. Even the electricity networks are subject to losses, increased compensation by raising the voltage to reduce leakage along the network (constraint, defined by the experts, purely technological.)

The characteristic of heating networks is to facilitate orderly configurations, closed and short, contrary to the electricity grids, which should follow the urban sprawl, urban disorder, are often disordered in their geometry. The production of energy is almost always entrusted to a CHP plant that can produce both electricity and heat through thermodynamic processes. These installations have now been fed mainly by fossil fuels (natural gas, oil, coal, fuel oil), municipal solid waste, renewable (mainly using the geothermal potential of the territories and the ability to reuse waste heat from industrial processes). Usually the distribution of heat in the city always defines rigid configurational patterns, as are the rigid network topologies: ring (to optimize and close the system, resulting in devices within the process loop, because the pattern is considered more reliable, even in case of system failure), knitting (it's a pattern of multi-ring networks, one differing feature to be more adaptive than the rigid shapes of the blocks built on the city), tree (or branching, is the most simple pattern, as it is inefficient due to its characteristic of having branched trunks). These different types, in combination, define the patterns of the district heating network. With a view to decentralizing energy production processes, also the urban heating sector is witnessing a change versus a micro-distributed generation, redefining the relationship of physical and cultural proximity on which the urban settlement and the organizational logic of construction of our cities. A change in our territories is in place, which will soon be called (although some already are, but in an unconscious way) to build infrastructure through a re-plug process of the self-organized device (or eco-organized). This overlap of users is fully embedded in the logic of metropolitan and regional systems, capable of being served by a mix-energy production, where the whole is greater than the sum of the parts (as stated by Prigogine).

To define the 3 scenarios it is necessary to identify the parameters that affect the energy relations:
- "source" devices and "tank drain"
- reports of "autonomy" and / or "addiction"
- the processes of competition and trade (energy sharing).

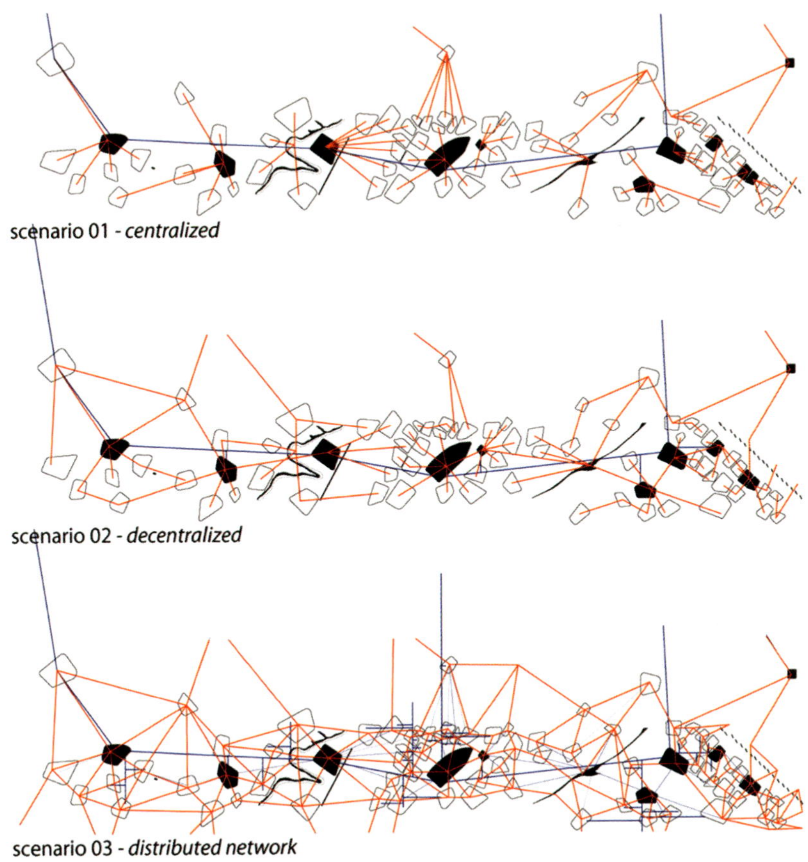

scenario 01 - *centralized*

scenario 02 - *decentralized*

scenario 03 - *distributed network*

SCENARIO 01 CENTRALIZED

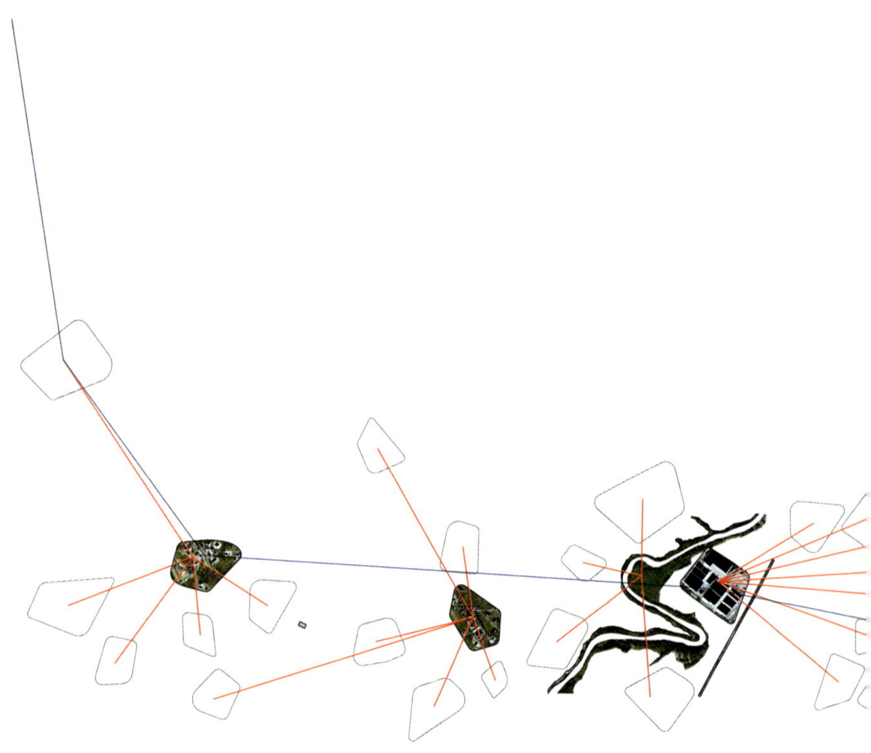

Identify "areas for" energy production as strategic areas within the territories
that constitute the first reports of energy dependency among the communities
and other parts of the city, through what we call the "energy carriers." The districts 'source', having achieved a first degree of its independence (the first stage
of saturation, where consumption is ensured by on-site production), begin to define the rules for trade with the territories 'reservoirs', such as tracing dependency
relationships that can ensure widespread autonomy in the territories of the city.
In this phase, the energy utilities are already beginning to differentiate, differentiate and electric (red) from the temperature (in blue) and considering that energy
conversions are secured at the contact points (exchangers or hub cities). In this
first scenario, it still recognizes a relationship of dependency related to the model
of centralized exchange, but calls for a first and important process of diffusion:
the specialization of the community as an energy hub of energy self-sufficient
urban areas, able to build the network by triggering a typical market mechanism,
through a process of competition between communities.

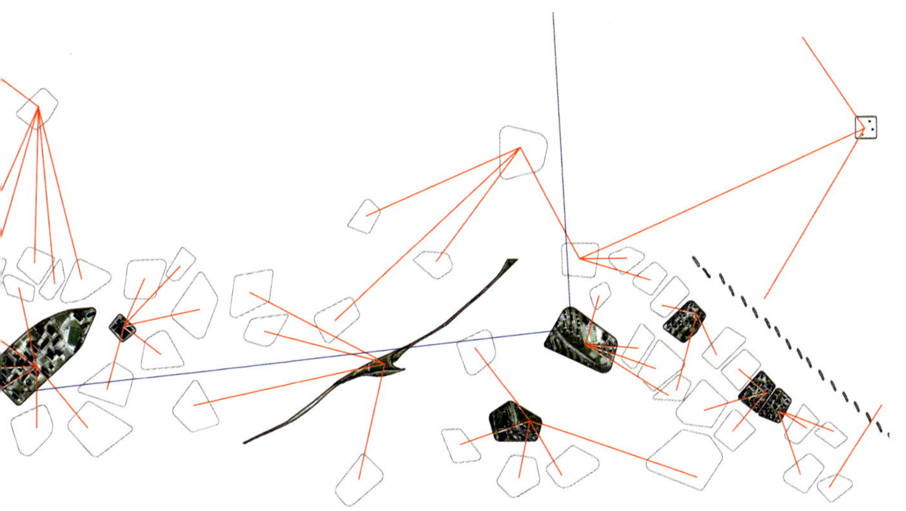

SCENARIO 02 DECENTRALIZED

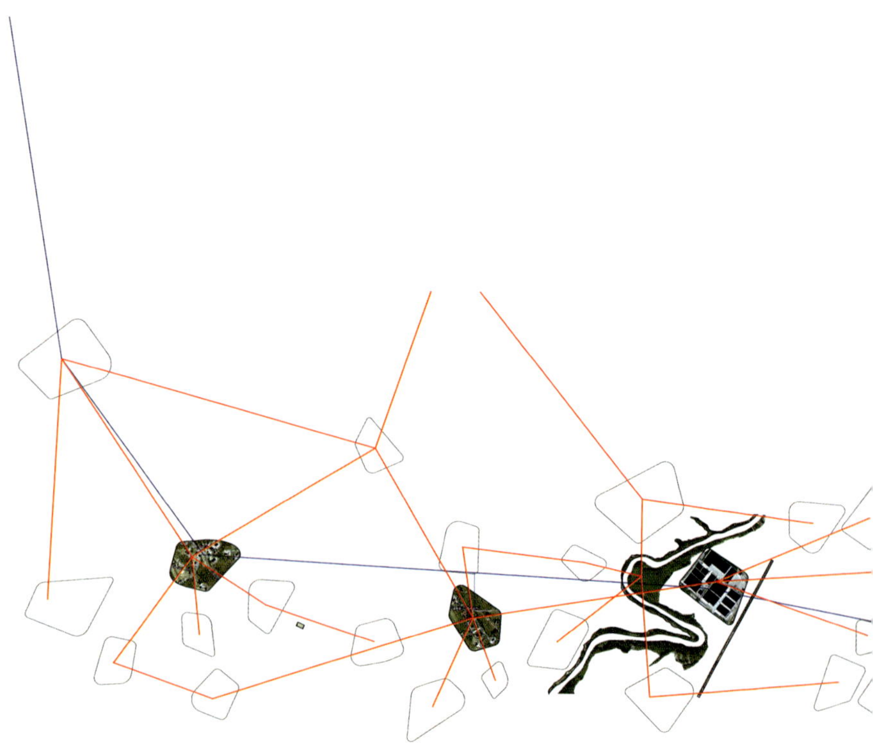

The evolution that occurs in the scenario 03 is concerned with setting up the network of energy relations between different communities, which become both sources and reservoirs. Communities grow again becoming places of production, accumulation and consumption, redefining those formulas localization, where [A P Đ Đ C], with ▲d = 0. (Đ: symbol of coincidence) The result is that it has built a network of relationships and opportunities for energy between the different communities and different local contexts. The new definition of [P A Đ Đ C], with ▲d = 0, is justified by the fact that the source device coincide with the tank. The relationship of autonomy and dependence is again becoming complementary concepts in a system in need of resources for self-organizing. The process of competitiveness becomes the driving force that enables the construction of a virtuous network. The exchange process provides an opportunity for territories in a self-generated economic autopoiesis-productive and not just energy.

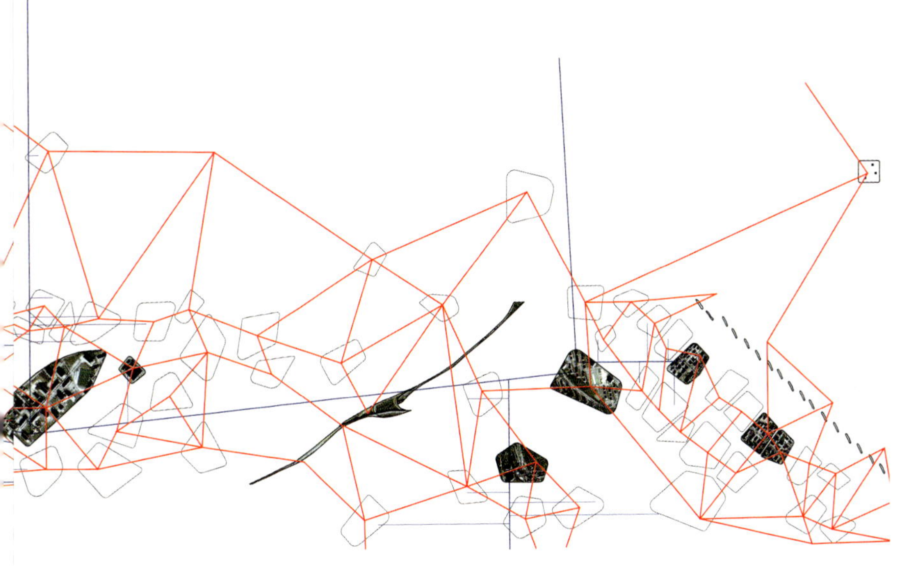

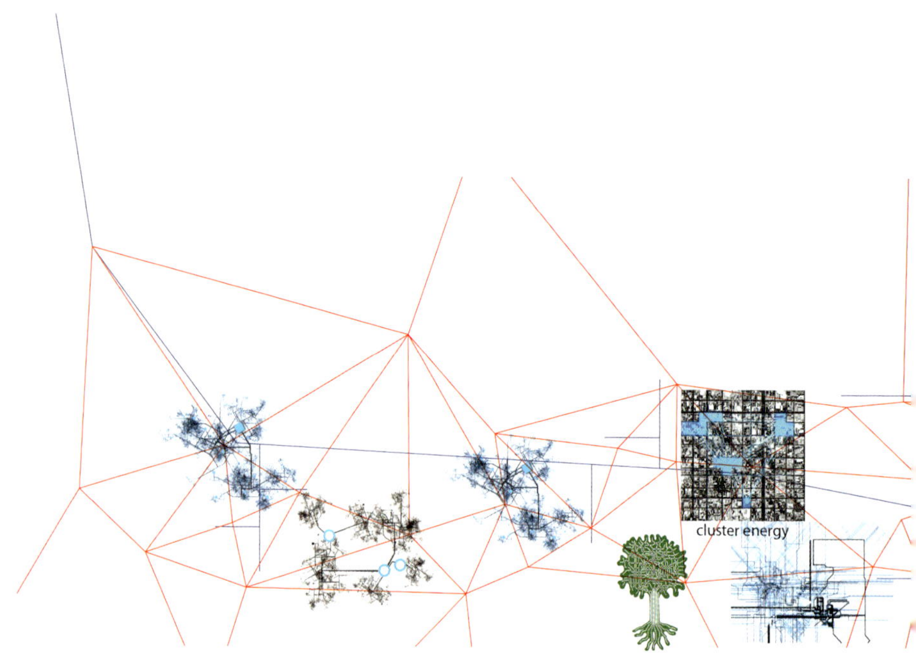

cluster energy

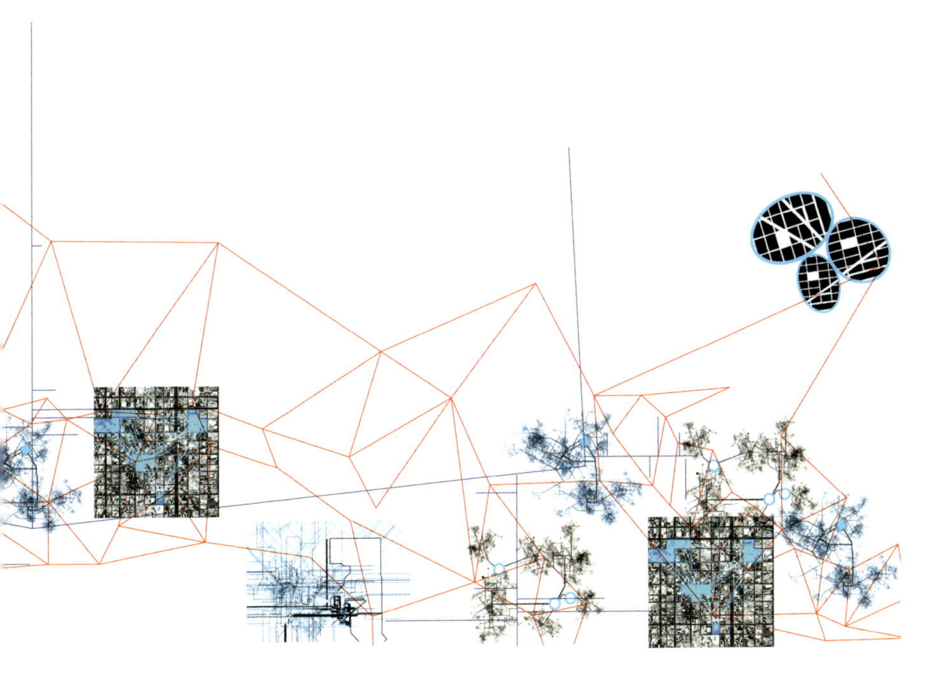

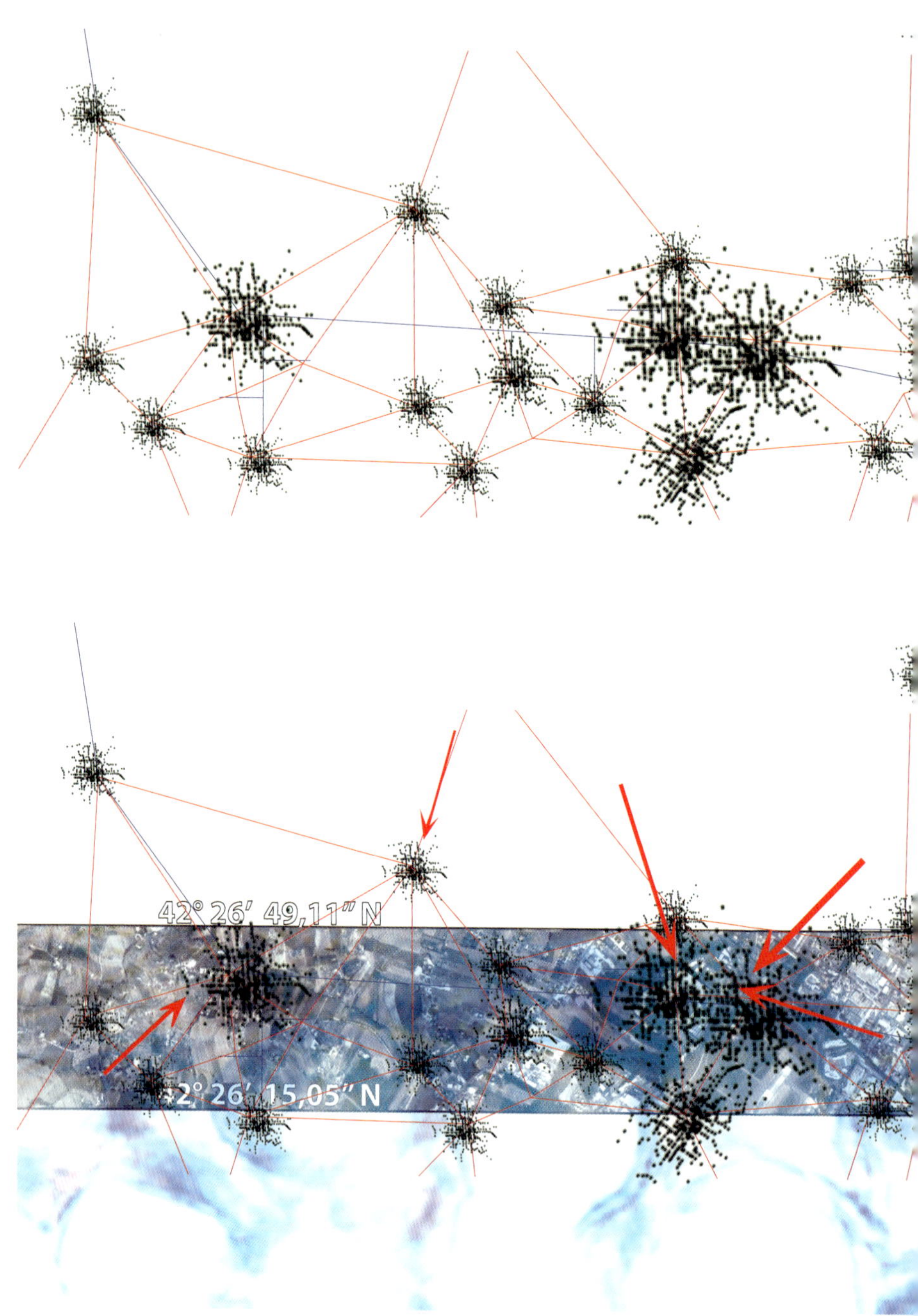

42° 26' 49,11" N
42° 26' 15,05" N

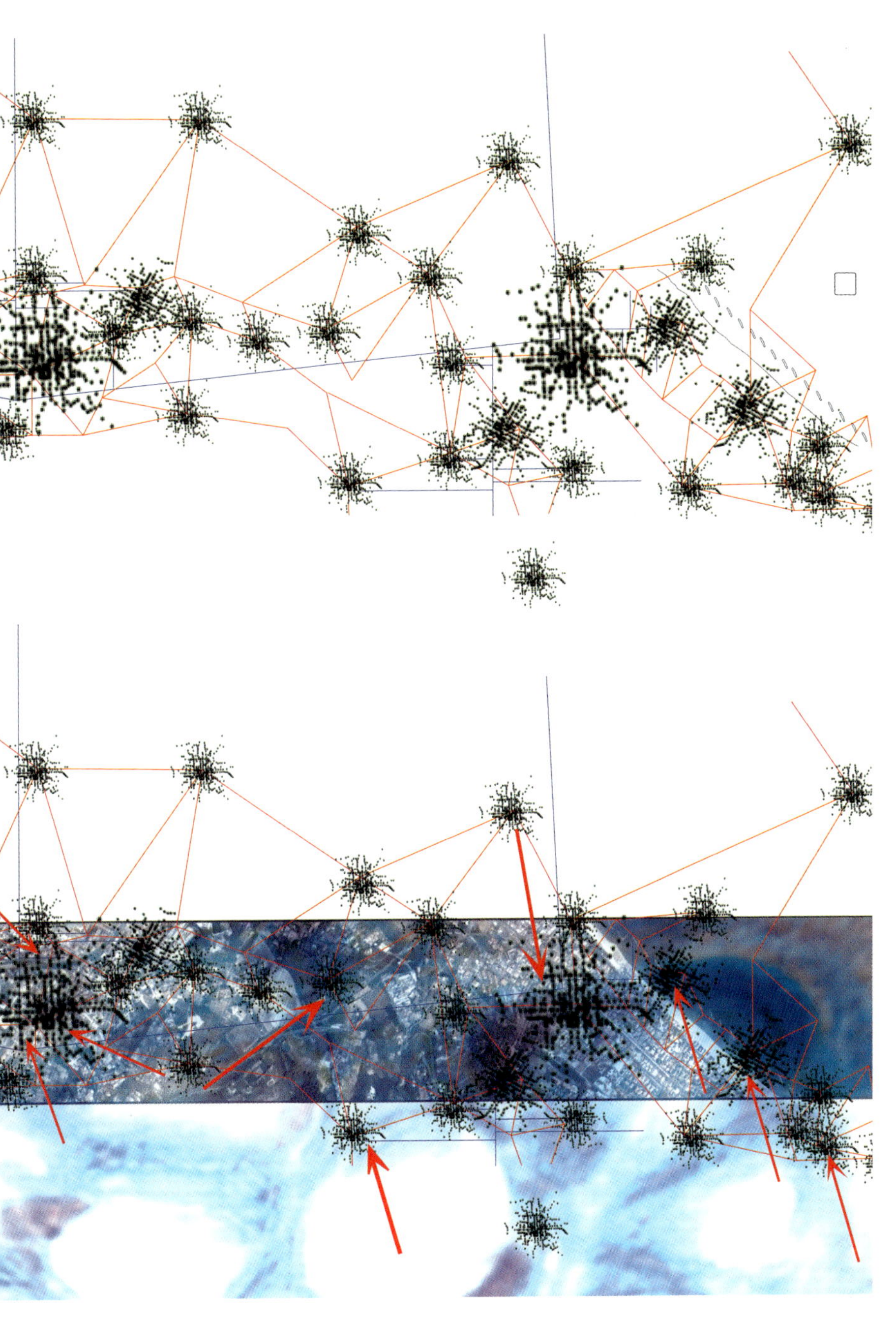

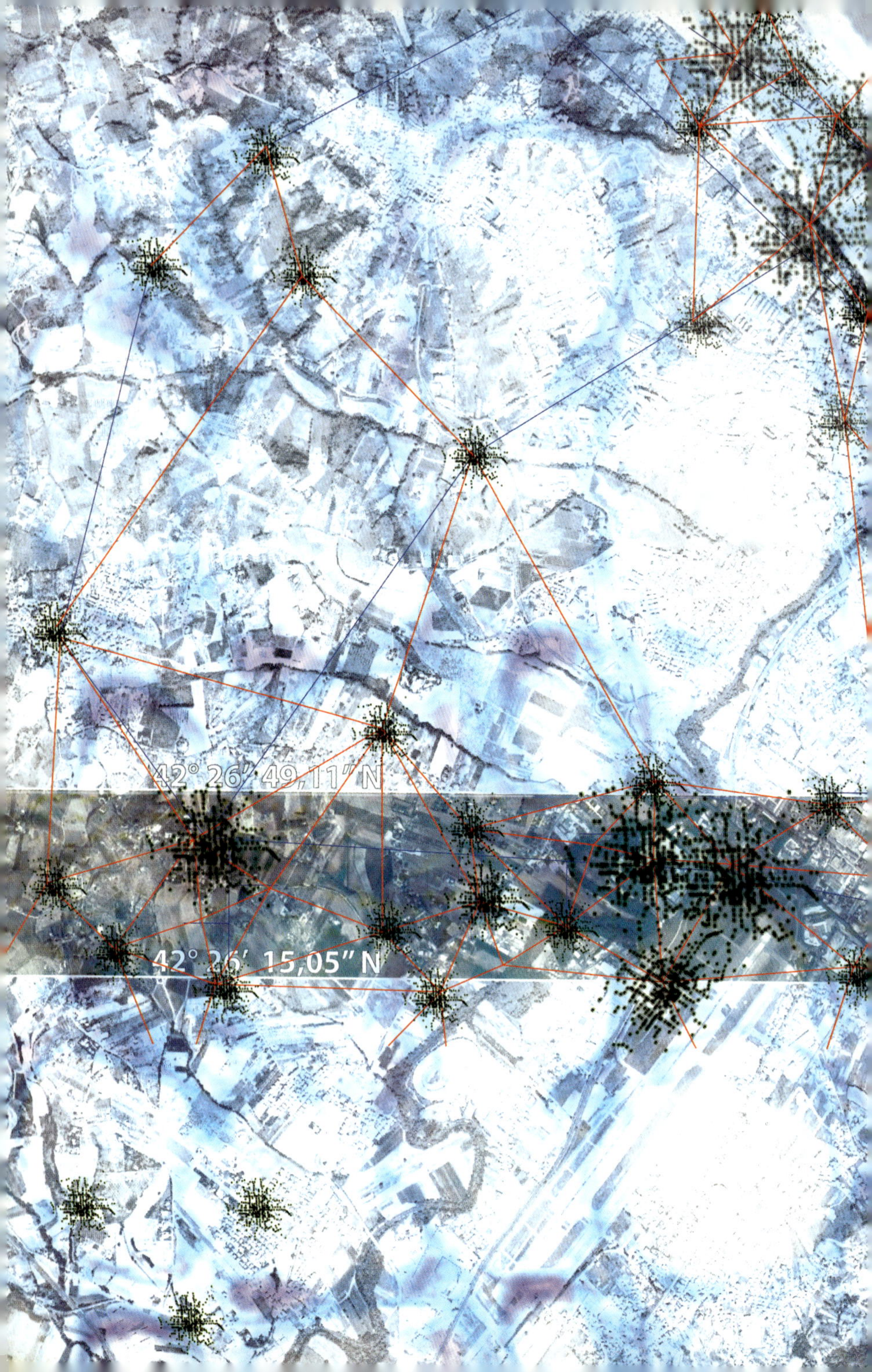

42° 26′ 49,11″ N
42° 26′ 15,05″ N

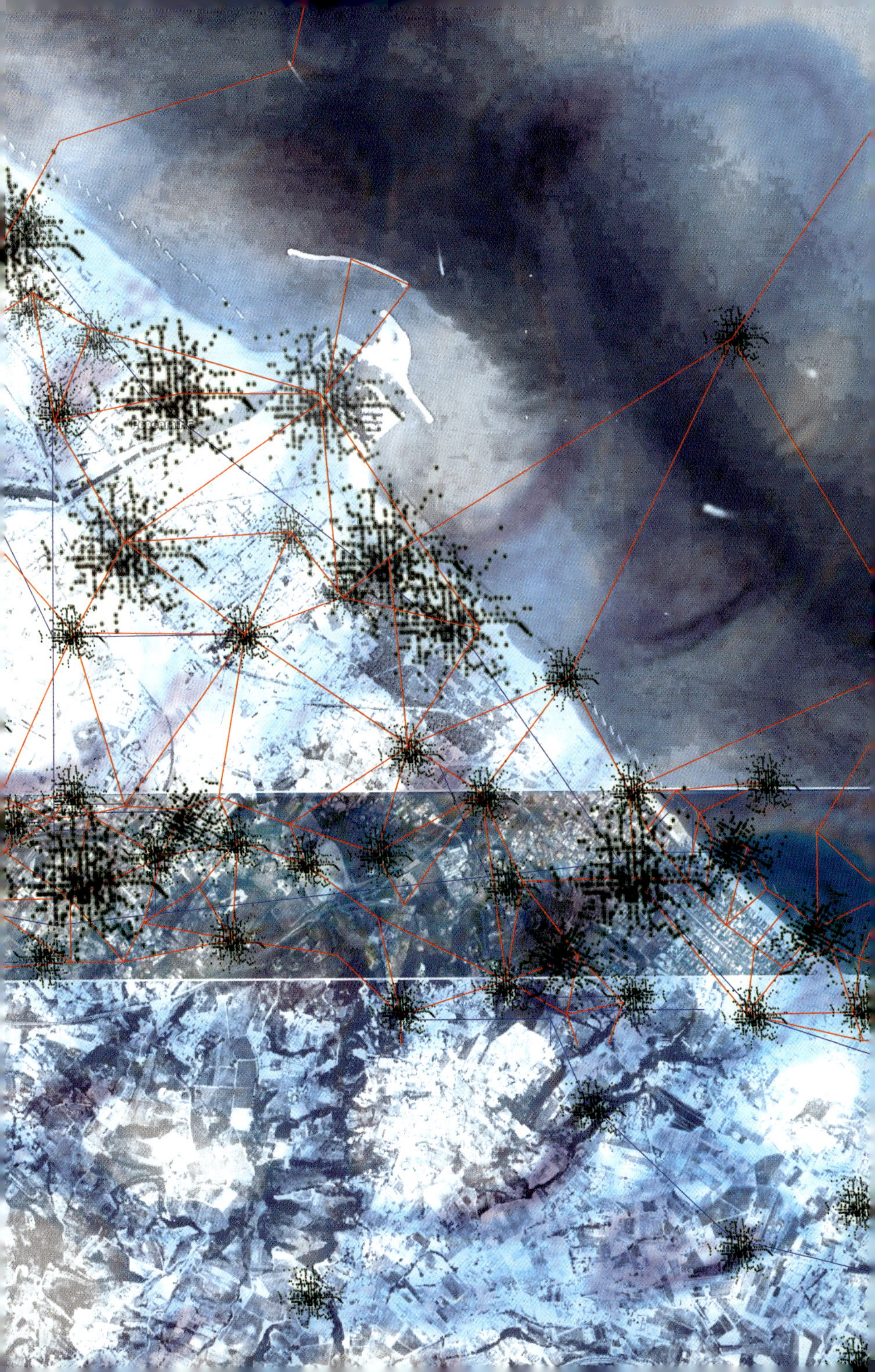

06
CONCLUSIVE
CONSIDERATIONS

Research Electropolis (which we propose to rename: e-lectropolis, and in the light of comments made previously about the power_city and by analogy to the research of e-topia in WJ Mitchell, P. Fusero and in-city) has as its main objective the development of a tool: the tool-kit (toolbox). The tool-kit is meant to be an instrument applied to a strategy of building, through what are known as operational tools, useful to the action of the architectural design for the operation more and more energy of the territories. The term tool-kit (in Italian is only used in computing) refers to a set of tools (software) used to facilitate and standardize the development of more complex derivatives. Transposed to new ways of looking and seeing (in filtered mode, the aim of energetics) the territories of living, the toolkit defines new paradigms related to energy issues, highlighting the possible configurations and applications of the principles of production, accumulation and consumption of renewable energy. The desire to "unify" the individual parts did not relate them to belonging to a range of objects, related to a method of using action as a probe design and synthesis, wanting to define ideographic devices (open processes of abstraction) and completed projects. The different parts are system, network building, form scenarios, always trying to repeat (device) in an adaptive way (in geocity Climates of the Zone). The toolkit is intended as an open array (in progress), in which you can always add, remove, swap (exchange) parts and tools, ensuring that they are networked together (net energy).

The idea of setting up the network of these devices is linked to two main characters:
-the first is the scenario will be defined as the construction of the Super Smart Grid (SSG) as a new pan-European corridor in the future for energy increasingly based on trade in services and goods (such as relationships between different parts of the Naked City),
-the second is the desire to build up image-sharing that leads to (re)configuring the city as energy agencies, defining new relationships between different parts of the city. It refers, in this sense, the metaphor of Cell-city as a city-building body, which defines energy islands connected to each other (for energy sharing), creating the conditions for new archipelago territories. The organismic view of the territories, cities, their mode of operation, report, construction, use, disuse (disposal) are attitudes of discussions and projects for the Mediterranean territories. A reading of the structure of the territory as "cavities" finds a common point (according to Franco Farinelli) between countries of the European coast and those of the African coast and the eastern Mediterranean. At a time when the modern territoriality is set (e.g. SSG) the problematic nature of the transition from a series of city-states to a single city-states will be expressed through a series of processes and common symptoms, by virtue of the uniqueness of impulse dictating the form of a different mediterraneanization. The analogy between urban systems and biological systems configures devices similar to a city-cell, defining new spacial "island" paradigms (for a city archipelago).

In research conducted by Enzo Tiezzi and Richard M. Pulselli, the city system is seen as a living organism, a system that breathes, eats, and shall assume its own identity, but at the same time belongs to the dynamic and variable condition, typical of natural evolution (in close collaboration with key concepts about the "complexity theory" of Ilya Prigogine, Nobel Laureate in Chemistry (1977), the father of natural evolution). The design vision for the Greater London Plan (1944), Sir Patrick Abercrombie, shows the London system configured as a set of membranes (cells) surrounded by a connective device cytoplasm. When Cacciari (in Archipelago) investigates the European landscape, he returns just as "Archipelago," that is characterized by plurality where the individual elements coexist as inevitably separate. In this plural vision of the area (due to presence of the territories) is associated with the definition of the Mediterranean by Fernand Braudel (one of the most knowledgeable in the modern history of the Mediterranean), which talks about the Mediterranean, expressed perfectly in a thousand things together. Not a landscape but innumerable landscapes. Not a sea but a succession of seas. Not one civilization, but a series stacked one on the other.Then he could develop these ideas in Leibniz's sense, each "island" would appear, then, as a "total individual", as that part which bears the whole from which he began (Cacciari). The devices are intended as a toolkit of applications-sample which bear the uniqueness of the context (characteristics of places and transformative potential of the district), through the construction of "maps" resulting from the overlap of the contexts and the information (geo data-measured). Their degree of ideogrammaticity, their abstraction (basic principle that is to define general actions) determines the possibility of recurrence of the processes and contexts in different parts of the Mediterranean that the city provides (the research on the Mediterranean / Mediterranean, L. Micara and E. Vadini). The process of defining the toolkit of devices does not have a linear definition, but they are children of a circular process that invades the mind of contemporary design. The definition of a toolkit highlights the willingness to go beyond the guidelines, with the ambition that the architect can regain shapes, forms and spaces within the development project of urban-contemporary energy. The vision behind the research is to imagine to superimpose with the territories inhabited the Mediterranean a weak energy system of components (elements and parts, of an energy-production that can be defined as a new array of weak urban re-write, taking them as reflections and weak theories of Branzi urbanism) able to relate to each other, build a system and network in order to anticipate new platforms and development of areas in relation to e-web and the possible application of the Super Smart Grid in Pan-European territory. These new codes, deliberately ideographic, express the virtuality of the possible configurations, applications, functions and actions within a meta-design process that keeps the background knowledge of ways-testing models of contemporary urban design (research fielded over the years by the group MVRDV, utopias and the reflections of urban Yona Friedman, Archigram, metabolites, theories and Andrea Branzi Archizoom members). To define the characters (logos) the

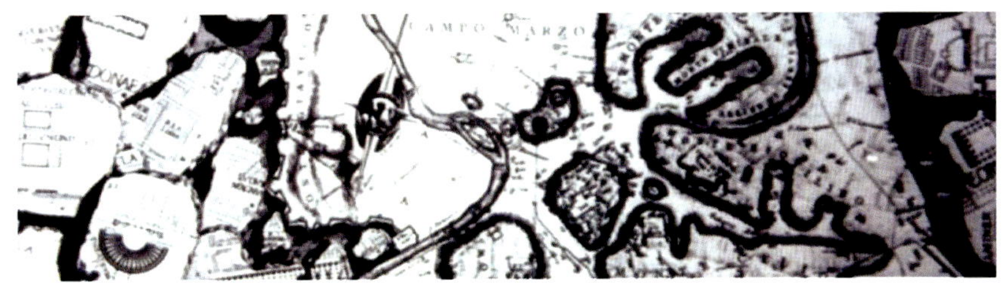

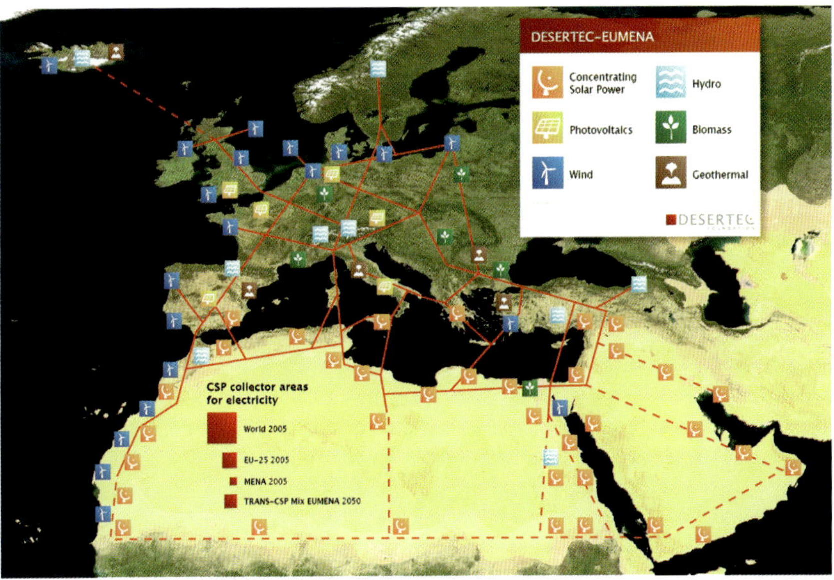
DESERTEC-EUMENA
Concentrating Solar Power
Hydro
Photovoltaics
Biomass
Wind
Geothermal
DESERTEC
CSP collector areas for electricity
World 2005
EU-25 2005
MENA 2005
TRANS-CSP Mix EUMENA 2050

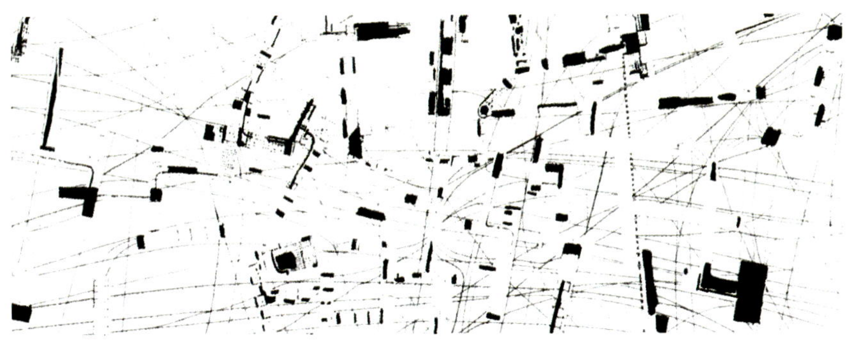

archipelago-city (logos) will give the specifics of the network nodes in the new venue (non-places or places) of the production of renewable energy: the energy cluster. Within the research, there are two foundational issues:

-the first in the intention of building materials / tools / processes to adaptive projects in the Mediterranean (through the definition of the toolkit), moving beyond sampling and over the definition of guidelines driving

-the second is to broaden our vision and look at the Mediterranean as a place for the future development of an economy tied to the Energy sharing. This last point highlights the problems and requires the use of new devices (or paradigms, this comes too late) for the definition of energy scenarios in the Mediterranean city of the XXI century. All this cannot be solved within a few pages of research, but arises from the combination and synthesis of several factors that make the complex system. Only through a "reading area" which reinforces the systemic vision of territories and networks of relationships, action, interconnection (flows of matter, energy and information) and production (especially energy). We must increasingly consider the different parts of the system as part (or parts) in isolation but as self-organizing systems and communities that are able to enable the construction of a mobile vision of the areas linked to self-organization and functioning of the reticular territories in metropolitan areas. As potential devices is it necessary to put in place, through the construction of different scenarios for the definition of energy relations (Distributed Network)? The traces, signs and movement between parts of the city are nothing more than the story of their relations returned by the reading process made visible and invisible, as in "Newspaper" by Jochem Hendricks. The German artist in 1994 was called to make an exhibition of contemporary art taking care of printing an edition of the "Allgemeine Frankfirter. In the edition, which has become a work of art, many titles, articles, photos, advertisements, banners, have not been printed and there is nothing left of the traditional structure of the newspaper. There is no longer the traditional page layout with text in columns, main titles and chapters that refer children to other pages. All pages have been deleted. And they are all scribbled. Traversed by a continuous thin black ink. Widespread. Messy. The novelty is that Hendricks leads to observe an everyday object from a different point of view. Or rather, the object of observation has changed. It is not the physical space with which we interact, but how we behave with respect to that space. In fact, the point is that the special edition of the "Allgemeine Frankfirter" was read. Eye movements were recorded that read, scanned and printed. Something of the reading process is otherwise invisible made visible, and a trace remained of the absorption of information, says Hendricks. In the context of urban studies is necessary to observe, monitor and anticipate the dynamic evolution of urban systems to reveal the overall operation. In this regard, Rem Koolhaas, Stefano Boeri (in Mutations) talk about the change and evolution taking place with respect to the "manifestations of the forces that shape the city, escaped from the sphere of the visible to the invisible, ... the city is no longer

Greater London Plan - di Sir Patrick Abercrombie (1944), in His Majesty's Stationery Office, London 1945.

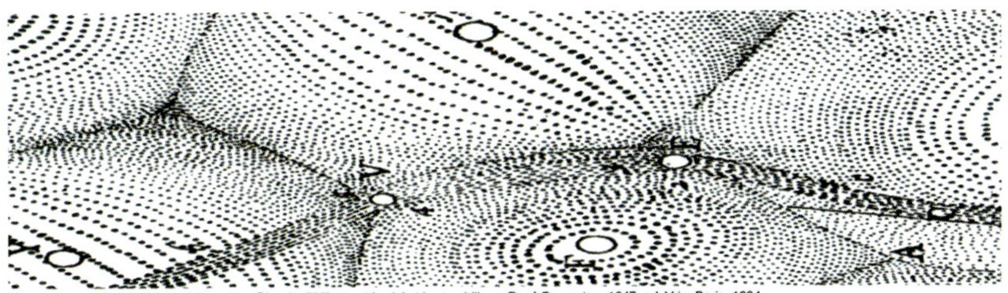

Les Principes de la philosophie - Planche III illustrant le ciel et les tourbillons, René Descartes, 1647, ed. Vrin, Paris, 1964

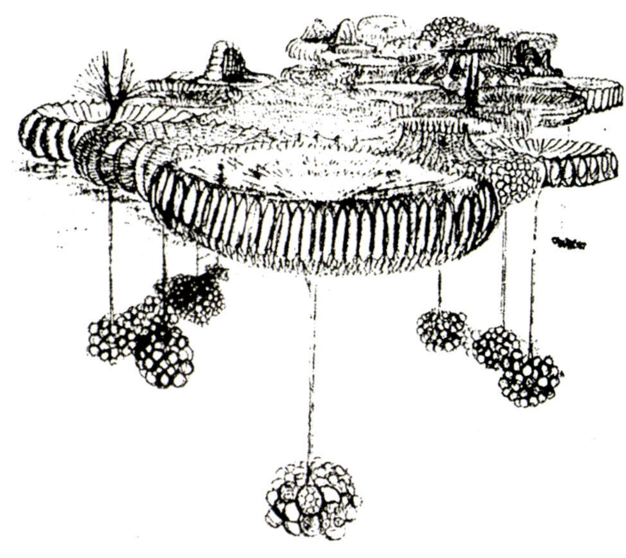

represented in terms of composition, gravity, or more material than it is through the investigation of demographic phenomena, social or economic." It is this phenomena that introduces a key to interpreting the organization of the city, a new perspective. The vision-guide within the case study: "City Vision: Pescara [42 ° 26'49, 11" N - 42 ° 26'15, 05 "N]" defines the characteristics and processes of a city increasingly linked by devices and the logic of energy production (locally). The key step is to be seized in the way of accessing the network (or networking) energy between the different communities in order to redistribute power, resources and opportunities in the territories. The development of new spatial configurations (Centralized, Decentralized, distributed network), creates new organizations, links and dependencies between parts of the city. Following the fragmentation of the sites of energy production (sprawl-energy) will perform three actions such as: e-fit, and fill-and-pull, capable of triggering through urban acupuncture, mutual aid processes energy (energy sharing) for the construction of a short chain of energy. Finally, it is to take into account that the resolution of energy issues is the result of a precise market, specific technological innovations in place, political choices (local and global), and assessments of energy development and policies of world peace. Once again, the Mediterranean is the square, the space of relationship, in relation to the Hall as a new reinforcement of the Mediterranean productive, commercial and creative capital flows, able to reshape new Mediterranean cultures that cooperate (Dicoter, 2007). In light of this, it is clear that one can not define a vision of the termination and closed-city area you are setting up in the era of the third industrial revolution, but what is happening is basically that of a large restructuring of the city (paraphrasing what is stated by William J. Mitchell, E-topia: "... the future of cities in the digital age .."). This change has the potential to create winners and losers. Trying to think more carefully about how we use energy infrastructure ("weak" in metropolitan areas or enclave-energy islands in so-called "remote areas") to increase the opportunity and social equity, rather than use it to increase the gap between rich and poor (William J. Mitchell). Electropolis research (fits into the research on the ongoing transformation: Transforming Electricity "from centralized to distributed network", Walt Patterson) wants to add a piece to the complex mosaic of global issues, offering a different point of view, selective for the construction of weak energy scenarios in the territory of the Mediterranean.

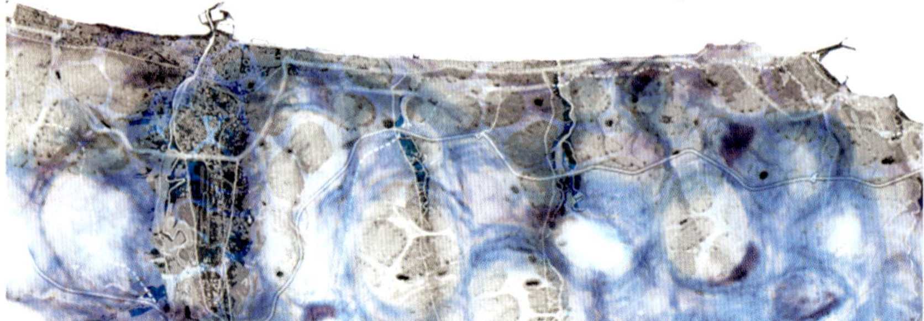

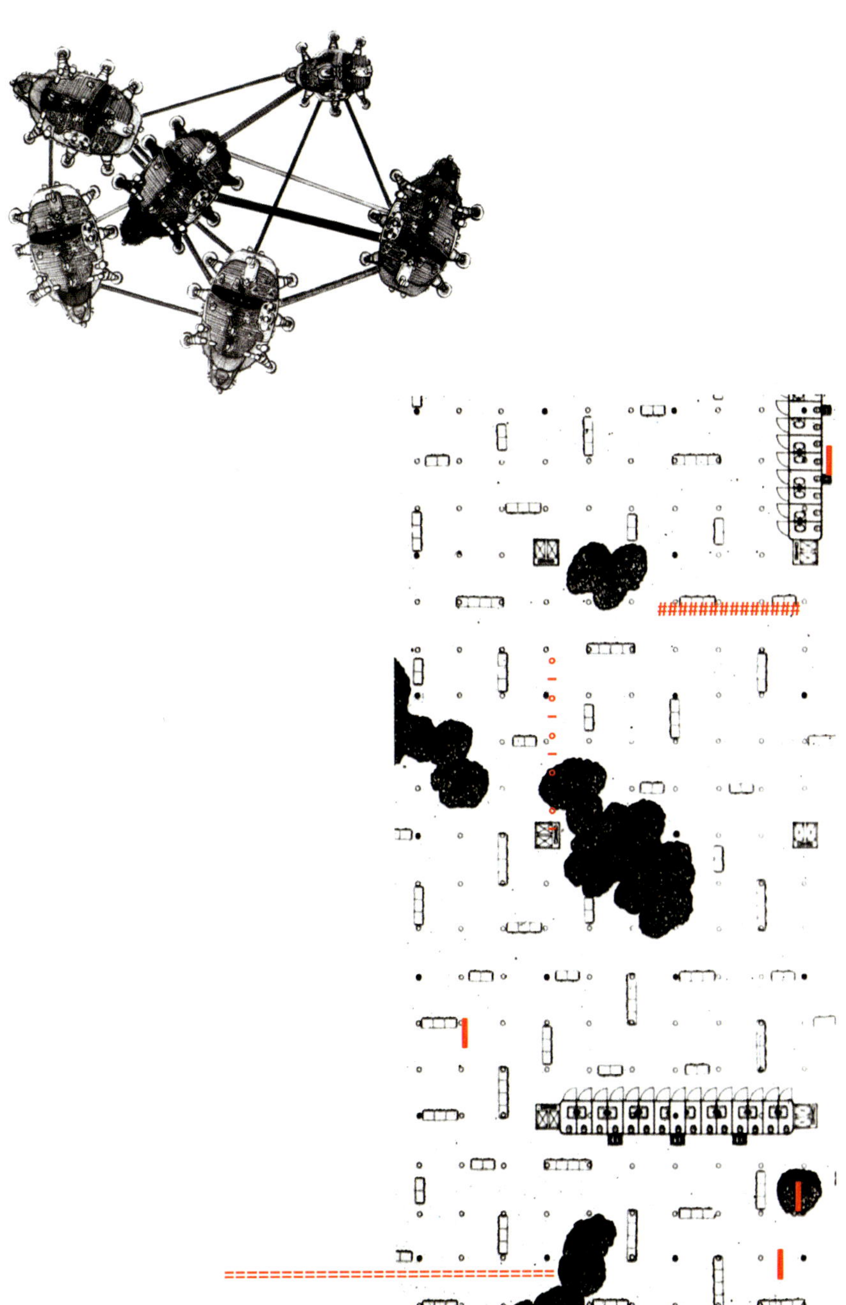

BIBLIOGRAPHY

AA.VV. (2003), hiCat – HiperCatalunya. Research teritories. Multilayered strategies, Iaac-metapolis, Actar, Barcellona.

AA.VV. (2004), Medesign_forme del Mediterraneo, Alinea, Firenze.

AA.VV. (2004), Rapporto sulle energie rinnovabili – 2004, Carsa editori, Milano 2004.

A A.VV. (2008), Storie del futuro. Gli scenari nella progettazione del territorio, Officina, Venezia.

Andriani Carmen (2010), Il patrimonio e l'abitare, Donzelli, Roma.

Angela P., Pinna L. (2006), La sfida del secolo, Mondadori, Milano.

Bauman Z. (2002), Modernità liquida, La terza, Roma-Bari.

Barbieri P., Metropoli piccole, Meltemi, Roma 2003.

Barbieri P. (2003), Infraspazi, Meltemi, Roma.

Barbieri P. (2008), OP_Adriatico1 – Opere pubbliche e città adriatica. Indirizzi per la qualificazione dei progetti urbani e territoriali, List-Actar, Barcellona.

Barbieri P. (2009), Hyperadriatica – Opere pubbliche e città adriatica. Indirizzi per la qualificazione dei progetti urbani e territoriali, List-Actar, Barcellona.

Branzi A. (2006), No-Stop City – Archizoom associati, HYX, Oleans.

Braudel F. (1985), Il Mediterraneo. Lo spazio, la storia, gli uomini, le tradizioni, Bompiani, Milano.

Cacciari M. (2004), La città, Pazzini, Rimini.

Cacciari M. (1997), L'Arcipelago, Adelphi, Milano.

Cacciari M. (1973), Metropolis, Officina, Roma.

Capra F. (1997), La rete della vita, Rizzoli. Milano.

De Santoli L. (2005), Energia e architettura, Kappa, Roma.

Droege P. (2008), La città rinnovabile, edizioni Ambiente, Milano.

Farinelli F. (2004), I Caratteri Originali del Paesaggio Pescarese, Menabò, Ortona.

Florida R. (2002), L'ascesa della nuova classe creativa. Stile di vita, lavori e professioni, Milano.

Friedman Y. (2003), Utopie realizzabili, Quodlibet, Macerata.

Fusero P. (2009), E-CITY. Digital networks and cities of the future, List-Actar, Barcellona.

Gore A. (2006), Una scomoda verità. Come salvare la terra dal riscaldamento globale, Rizzoli, Milano.

Gore A. (2006), film: Una scomoda verità, di Davis Guggenheim (100') - USA.

Gottman J. (1970), Megalopoli, Einaudi, Torino.

Gottman J. (1991), La città prossima futura, Laterza, Roma-Bari.

Griffa C. (2008), La città cibernetica, Meltemi, Roma.

Gregotti V. (2010), Tre forme di architettura mancata, Einaudi, Torino.

Herreros J. (2004), Isla ciudad, Arquitectura y energia en Mallorca, Actar-Pro, Barcellona.

Koolhaas R. (2001), Delirius New York, Electa, Milano.

Koolhaas R., Boeri S., Mutations, Actar, Barcellona

Mitchell W. J. (1995), City of Bits: Space, Place and the Infobahn, MIT Press.

Mitchell W. J. (1999), E-topia: Urban Life, Jim – But Not As We Know It, MIT Press.

MVRDV/DSD (2006), Space Fighter. The evolutionary City (game), Actar, Barcellona.

Patterson W. (1999), Transforming Electricity, Earthscan, London.

Pauli G. (1997), *Svolte epocali. Il business per un futuro migliore*, Baldini & Castoldi, Milano.
Pavia R. (1998), *Paesaggi elettrici. Territori, architetture, culture*, Enel, Roma.
Pulselli R. M., Tiezzi E. (2008), *Città fuori dal caos. La sostenibilità dei sistemi urbani*, Donzelli editore, Roma.
Pulselli R. M., Romano P. (2009), *Dinamiche dei sistemi urbani / Urban Systems Dynamics. Indagine di un'area metropolitana*, Alinea, Firenze.
Rifkin J. (2000), *L'era dell'accesso. La rivoluzione della new economy*, Mondadori, Milano.
Rifkin J. (2002), *Economia all'idrogeno*, Mondadori, Milano.
Rogers R. (1997), *Città per un piccolo pianeta*, Kappa, Roma.
Tozzi M. (2006), *L'Italia a secco. La fine del petrolio e la nuova era dell'energia naturale*, Rizzoli, Milano.
Ulisse A. (2008), *Spazio, tempo ed energie*, in Barbieri P., *OP_Adriatico1 – Opere pubbliche e città adriatica. Indirizzi per la qualificazione dei progetti urbani e territoriali*, List-Actar, Barcellona.
Ulisse A. (2009), *Chaleurs Urbaines*, Ed. Sala, Pescara.
Ulisse A. (2009), *Electropolis adriatica. 3 azioni / 5 indirizzi (+1) per territori sempre più energetici*, in Barbieri P., *Hyperadriatica – Opere pubbliche e città adriatica. Indirizzi per la qualificazione dei progetti urbani e territoriali*, List-Actar, Barcellona.
Véron J. (2008), *L'urbanizzazione del mondo*, il Mulino, Bologna.
Zardini M., Borasi G. (2008), *Désolé, plus d'essence. L'innovation architecturale en réponse ° la crise pétrolieère de 1973*, CCA, Montréal.

07

AFTERWORD

WHEN INFRA-ENERGY AND ENERGY PARK MEASURE THE SUSTAINABILITY OF MEDITERRANEAN SPACES.

by **Consuelo Nava**

university researcher, expert in sustainable design, is a professor of Sustainable Design at the Faculty of Architecture of Reggio Calabria and Environmental Design at the Faculty of Architecture of the Giulia Valle in Rome; was part of the evaluation commission of the doctoral thesis of Alberto Ulisse.

The written work of A. Ulisse and the traces of his research mark essential reading material in the contemporary debate concerning "forms of the project" in an interSCALAR sense able to entrust the management of between city networks/Energy zones and building/cluster Energy_industry Energy_green house energy, a report of relational networking with the absolute and indispensable role of spatial configurations and networks recognized by the names Infra - Energy and Energy Park. The speculative nature of the research that actually tries to define the new energy tools for the Mediterranean city, with the definition of e-tools, takes in trial any assumptions made to project the weight of reading about a new morphogenesis of these urban and suburban areas, which found their energy capacity, through the characteristics of places and the transformative potential of the district. With the contribution of this text in postscript, the lesson of A.Ulisse (AU), we wish to verify its exportabilty through some examples of teaching and applied research projects which will demonstrate in particular where the Infra-Energy and Energy-Park become privileged places of "exchange" and "conversion" can play a role in changing contexts, sustainable scenarios for the Mediterranean area. Referring to the project culture that sees such places as Junkspace (R. Koolhaas, 2006) or residual territories (G. Clément, 2005) as potential resources for ecological diversity, identifying the levels of social and environmental sustainability, with the aim of qualifying the nature of urban environments, their value in use and report their ability to reconstruct the landscape units and to solve soil permeability and morphology of linear tracks of land or space already dismantled, even before housing.The infra-energy, areas identified as areas of margin, often inactive and unused (AU), can play a role in the Mediterranean context of mitigation and filter core structures related to the environment and climate conditions.

1. Consider the green corridors and connections to the slow mobility (walking and cycling) which run along the infrastructure and mitigate the impacts, which improve comfort by lowering the noise and environmental noise pollution of dust and hydrocarbons , which control the sunny climate and resolve the relationship between permeable and impermeable surfaces, designing and flooring systems for the disposal of stormwater on a draft of the gradients which manages the run-off widespread accessibility at the same time. Such systems reclassified border territories and brought them back to the edge of usability, the sociality of the spaces between plant species and location of filter and natural barriers. The project is characterized as being particularly sensitive and that are located in areas of high natural character, eg. coastal zones (Figure 1 / Figure 2), both involving urban areas that face the sea and organize their mobility within the fabric of settlements (fig.3/fig.4).

01

02

VISIONE
NUOVO LUNGOMARE CON PISTA CICLABILE

03

VISIONE
DI NUOVE INFRASTRUTTURE, ACCESSO AEROPORTO
METRO

04

2. This refers to the reconnection of circuits in the urban areas of strategic polarity, which may be squares, streets and open spaces of buildings with high cultural value. These spaces "in.between" who bear the environmental burden of the use of their centrality, are also spaces that change their destination and their urban configuration, the nodes in which they relate. The level of social sustainability measures the environmental capacity of these new urban places "that serve to characterize the connection, but also stopping and sorting. The unifying character of various trims can increase the levels of maintenance of these areas and the organization of services, structures and substructures of the networks. Ecologically they often play the role of land clearing and restoration of environmental resources to be preserved (plants, water systems) in the urban consolidation. In their requalification project the objective is to define another level of use different from the one organized by providing areas for more frequent interaction, use and management savings. (Fig. 5 / fig.6)
The Energy Parks, which identify areas to be reclaimed as natural areas, or areas of natural/artificial high density cities, or areas to be retrained through the reuse of abandoned buildings and their relocation (AU), play a role in restoring the ecological equilibrium in and around urban settings, re-establishing the correct relationship between environmental systems and artificial systems, including ability to conserve natural resources and productive capacity of these.

3. The river courses, especially those of torrential character, typical of some areas of the Mediterranean areas, organize their course in urban and suburban sections connoting different units for each section and height of river bed. Along the course through natural still areas, where one can maintain their water system to serve the agricultural land and crops in typical weather conditions restoring the landscape and biodiversity typical of the foothills and valleys of the mild climate, where the flood areas ensure the territory and controlling the steepness of the materials through the artifacts and structures of fluvial terraces. These areas play their role for the stability of the slopes and the hydrogeological condition of normality of the permeability of water, washing out the higher ground. The project is interested in the restoration of natural and artificial systems, restoring areas of linear river park at auctions and suburban areas of the park with strong environmental concerns in urban areas, where the intended services to provide - recovering permeable and usable territory - can seek energy production, locating services and networks at the point of better insulation and wind (solar, wind, geothermal) or by providing storage areas and processing of various kinds of waste from the urban and suburban metabolism (biomass). It is these sparsely built energy parks that restore the relationship between urban systems and dense settlements scattered between areas of private and public spaces. Their balance is guaranteed by the maintenance of natural systems and compatible use of the context units (Fig. 7 / fig.8).

05

06

4. In remote areas, where the monofunctional use has seriously degraded the quality of the urban landscape, often undermining the functioning of any system-wide environmental networks and filter areas, recovery areas and the margin of their new functions in the park, to equipped areas, it becomes a necessary condition for restoring the relationship between open/protected space and confined/closed spaces conditions of social exclusion, privacy and urban insecurity. In such contexts the project of the terrain that characterizes the transformation in every sphere, is a condition of success if the building density is answered by defeat the island heat effect and reducing the albedo, by the resolution of permeable surfaces, (Green and gravel) and semi-permeable surfaces, but also by the different morphology of the plans and their status as productivity (green filter, green productive - vegetable gardens): in these conditions, the areas of controlled microclimate of open spaces to achieve a quality of living in common areas directly related to private buildings and structures in nature and receptive audience, through the correct sequence of shaded areas and areas exposed (bioclimatic outdoor spaces). (Fig. 9)

5. In abandoned areas, such as former industrial areas, the conditions of impact and damage affecting especially the quantitative aspects related materials are no longer viable in efficient energy cycles, spaces are no longer functional, from disrupted networks, to the no longer used structures: a existing environmental burden if it were to be decommissioned involves an important energy cycle for disposal. The reuse and redevelopment projects, create real energy parks, starting from the reuse of existing buildings, renovation of their construction quality and materials, the restoration of some network systems useful for new operations, capable of welcoming as integrated those levels of organization reported to apply the best use of resources. To allow the redeveloped area is not a functioning urban enclave, the more you work with measures for ecological restoration of natural systems to improve air quality and perception of the urban context of reference, the better the condition of urbanization the production site. It is to build and manage environmentally protected areas for consolidated urban areas (fig.10 / fig.11), but also for scenarios that can convert a sensitive area, characterized by the presence of protected nature sites, from single industrial products that are however part of a network, with a strong presence of a natural system and a climate favorable to ensure the best condition of adaptivity of any biological and plant community. In both cases, the maximum sustainable management shall be ensured by economic and ecological capacity of the site of latching and to produce extra energy, able to connect to "service efficiency" and "effective operation" with the production area and residential business or intended services in a continuous and sustainable urban metabolism.

53.4 m
50.0 m
47.6 m
43.2 m
40.2 m
39.0 m
Parco urbano
Skate park
Fiumara Sant'Agata

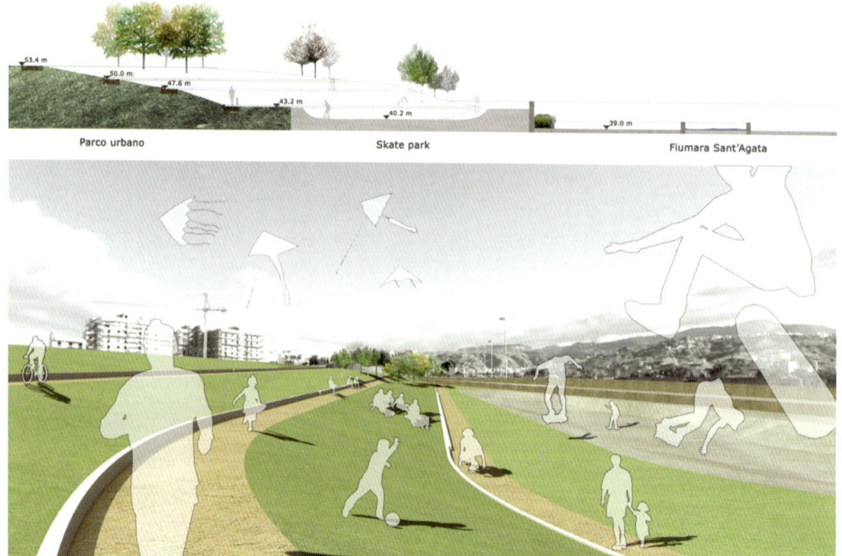

07

08

09

10

11

Sources of text

Project images *

Infra Energy
fig.1/ fig.2 _ project for the metropolitan city, Ionic coastal Reggio Calabria (A.Manti, S.Mercuri, D.Pata, M.R.Schiavello)
fig.3/ fig.4 _ project for the metropolitan city, outskirts south Reggio Calabria (G.Sanzo, G.Sorbara)
fig.5/ fig.6_ environmental project in high density urban areas, S. Giovanni port Rome (C. Borlan Ronchel, A. Reina Lopez, L.E.Salazar Bruque)

Energy Park
fig.7_ project for the metropolitan city, renovation of fiumara park S. Agata – Reggio Calabria (G.Bassetta, P.Rombolà)
fig.8_ project for the metropolitan city, renovation of fiumara park Valanidi – Reggio Calabria (A.Barresi, M.Scalzo, F.Silipo, F.Zupi)
fig.9_ project for the metropolitan city, renovation north periphery Arghillà Quarter – Reggio Calabria (F.Spanò, V.Polimeni)
fig.10_ environmental project in disused industrial areas, Tiberino zone / Aureliane wall in Rome (G.Poggi Madarena)
fig.11_ project for the metropolitan city, energy park in protected area of Saline J. – Reggio Calabria (A.Calabrò, C.Rodà)
(*) Environmental projects in disused industrial areas and in housing areas of high density, faculty of Architecture of Giulia valley, students of Environmental Design course 2009/2010, Rome
Sustainable Scenarios in changeable contexts _ Projects of metropolitan areas of Reggio Calabria, faculty of Architecture of Reggio Calabria, students of Sustainable Design course in Lab. Of Final Synthesis 2009/2010, Reggio Clabria

Text

De Pieri Filippo, (edited by), (2005), Gilles Clément – Manifesto del Terzo Paesaggio, Quodlibet ed., Macerata
Mastrigli Gabriele., (edited by), (2006), Rem Koolhaas – Junkspace, per un ripensamento radicale dello spazio urbano, Quodlibet ed., Macerata
Nava Consuelo, Saffioti Francesca, (2010), Visitatori di Città Generiche per piccole metropoli, In AAVV, Spazio e Società, CSAteneo, Reggio Calabria
Nava Consuelo, (2010) Efficacia ed Efficienza: il progetto sostenibile in area mediterranea, in G.Neri, Forme ed energia, ed.Kaleidone, Reggio Calabria

Acknowledgements

I would like to thank:

Pepe Barbieri
for his continuous encouragement, guidance and trust

Rosario Pavia
for having educated me about issues regarding Energy

Renato Ricci
for his precious advice, friendliness and patience

Nicolas Tixier
for the immense opportunities and hospitality

Consuelo Nava
for having encouraged me and helped me correctly see the "sense of things"

Marino la Torre
for having always been there and having shared unoauno_spazioArchitettura

Filippo Broggini
for having given me "opportunities" and for having shared visions and projects

Edoardo Zanchini, Federico Bilò and Paola Misino for the shared experiences

Luciano D'Alfonso
for his precious advice on the "creative city"

The DART department, and in particular he continuous help from Luciano, the consoling words of Francesco and Dr. Petrella's jokes!

A Hug:
to my parents and grandmother for having been over-present, also during this adventure

I Dedicate:
this work to Alessandro and Andrea, ...because in life I never give up on my dreams!

AU

Published and produced by
LIStLab
Laboratorio Internazionale Editoriale
Italy: Piazza Lodron, 9
38100, Trento
tel. +39 0461 282665
Spain: C/ Ferlandina, 53
08001, Barcelona
tel. +34 934422365
email: info@listlab.eu
website: www.listlab.eu

Author
Alberto Ulisse

Editorial coordination
Pino Scaglione

Art Direction
Massimiliano Scaglione

Graphic design
Simone Iovacchini

Translations
Violeta Toro-Freund

ISBN 9788895623405

Printed and bound in the European Union|
stampato e rilegato in Unione Europea,
december|dicembre 2010

Printed
Printer Trento

LIStLab is an editorial workshop, set in Barcelona, which works on contemporary issues. LIStLab not only publishes, but also research, proposes, endeavour, promotes, produces, creates networks.

Internationation Sales and Distribution
ActarD/ Birkhauser
Roca y Batlle, 2
08023 Barcelona (Spain)
BASEL, Viadukstrasse 42
NEW YORK, 151, Grand Street 5th Fl.
NY 1013, USA
office@actarbirkhauser.com
www.actarbirkhauser.com
+34934187759